Vance Randolph | **An Ozark Life**

Robert Cochran

Vance
Randolph

An Ozark
Life

University of Illinois Press

Urbana and Chicago

Publication of this work was supported in part
by a grant from the Andrew W. Mellon Foundation.

Library of Congress Cataloging in Publication Data

Cochran, Robert, 1943–
Vance Randolph, an Ozark life.

Bibliography: p.
Includes index.
1. Randolph, Vance, 1892–   2. Folklorists—
United States—Biography.   I. Title.
GR55.R33C625   1985   398'.092'4 [B]   84-8647
ISBN 0-252-01164-3 (alk. paper)

for my father and mother

Contents

PART ONE

Desired Country

Wherein is Discovered, the Manner of his
setting out, His Dangerous Journey; And
Safe Arrival at the Desired Country

—John Bunyan, *Pilgrim's Progress*

1

Introduction

He explained why dentistry was a purer science than
astronomy, biography a higher form than dance.

—God, in *The Living End,*
by Stanley Elkin

1

A biography was the last thing contemplated. And Vance Randolph—
he was first of all a very old man, bedridden in a pissoir of a nursing
home. Our first meeting, late in 1976, was sheer protocol, and the
first thing I liked was his distaste for it. "All I remember is your hair
was a mess," he said later.

"Professor," he joked another time, "I do believe you are come
among us under false pretences."[1] True enough, and a shrewd bit of
banter too, since in the pile of article reprints I'd brought him (my
credentials!) at his request, only two or three short stories were
mixed in. But they were the best things—no surprise from a writer
convinced no gallant courted Lady Truth like handsome Sir Fiction,
that next to him her other suitors were clods and bumpkins, Jug-
heads to dashing Reggie.

By 1978, many visits later, things were easy between us and we
were friends. Strange friends—I was, after all, a full fifty years his
junior. I brought him books, shopped for his pen refills and Brown
Mule chewing tobacco, and listened to his wonderful talk. The man
had seen Buffalo Bill, and Eugene V. Debs had called him by his
first name in Girard, Kansas.

First then, before the imposing, monumental work, was the lure
of the man himself, his fascinating adventure, blend of defeat and
achievement, virtue and shortcoming. It was this that appealed to
me, with my own idiosyncrasies, and captured my allegiance. My
friend Mike Luster and I put together a bibliography of his writings,
and were astounded to learn he'd appeared in print under some
twelve pseudonyms, often citing one in the work of another. Randolph encouraged the notion that a bibliography would suffice: "I

3

didn't do anything exciting," he said. "All I did was write books."[2]
But it was that work, along with the continuing conversations and
story sessions, which made clear the error of his words. The books,
after all, were an astonishing, truly motley collection, the magisterial side by side with the ephemeral, *Ozark Folksongs* in company with *The Modern Sex Book*.

Long gone, by this time, was the donnish vita imagined before we
met— the famed scholar is born, attends school, experiences magic
moment when youthful imagination fires to dinosaurs, to a haloed
photo of Saturn, to the stories of a Missouri river guide. He or she
submits to professional training, obtains Ph.D. and is paleontologist,
astronomer, folklorist, accomplishes research and publishes articles
and books, grades millions of examinations, feels fires smother and
fade, retires with *Festschrift*, and wonders now and again as the
curtain falls what became of the youngster in love with dinosaurs,
planets, yarnspinners.

All wrong, of course, wrong in any case. No life, however sheltered by institutional affiliations, could fall so simply, so unharrowed
by insight or dignified by struggle. But measured to Randolph the ill
fit was spectacular. He flirted, after all, with academic life on several
occasions, and rejected it at last consciously and emphatically. He
chose a different path, elected a life characterized first of all by its
urge to the edges. The grove of academe, the house with mortgage
of the rooted paterfamilias, the mainstream political attachments of
the citizen who wishes his representative to rule—Vance Randolph
repudiated all these, lit out for the margins, lived his life in the shoes
of that most native of American mythic figures: the loner, the iso-
lato, the man headed west, bound for the territory.

It was, then, as a maverick, as an outsider, that Vance Randolph
came to the Ozarks to chronicle the lifeways of "the most deliberately unprogressive people in the United States."[3] An outlaw himself, he would live among other outlaws, and would save their ways
from destruction. Had he arrived as a professor, the basic orienta-
tion would have altered.

Here, then, so close to the beginning, the biographer opens upon
the central insights of his enterprise. They seem to be two. The first,
put crudely, directs attention to the basically fictional nature of personality. In the accomplishment of his chosen labor, the collection of
his data, and the writing of his books, Vance Randolph managed
also the successful imposition of his persona. What matters is the
interdependence of the two—of character and accomplishment.
The abiding work is itself completed by a character, self-created and
sustained by a lifetime's labor. The character, in turn, is most truly

achieved in the work. Only there is it rendered visible, embodied, given permanence, made true.

One obvious index to the prominence of Randolph's persona in his work is the attention it attracted from reviewers. One notice of his first important book, *The Ozarks: An American Survival of Primitive Society,* goes on at considerable length about the author: "He has painted houses, managed an apiary, taught biology in a country high school, worked as an editorial writer on the *Appeal to Reason,* done a hitch in the Army, peddled tinware and insurance, written technical papers on biology and psychology, published books and pamphlets of popularized science and tramped over a large part of the United States."[4]

The work itself would soon eclipse these diverse employments, even as it materialized and substantiated the character behind them, but the important thing to insist upon is the consistency of that character, the one focus of many actions. The Randolph who peddled tinware and tramped through Florida and California had already chosen the lifestyles that would take him to Pineville, Missouri, in 1919 and encourage his interest in the dialect and songs of the mountain residents.

This first central insight thus grasped, one's subject understood in terms of a chosen character responsible for and most convincingly established by the tangible works of his life, the biographer is prepared to deploy the second. All true biography, as distinct from mere chronicle, requires of its maker some master image, clearly drawn, a figure by which the subject is succinctly shown, his paradoxes posed, his heart set to motion. It's metaphor one seeks, finally, in biography, by means of a procedure vaguely inductive.

Each fact is an isolate, particular thing, a note with no scale. A letter, for instance, written and mailed in 1923, offers Randolph appointment as assistant instructor in psychology at the University of Kansas for the 1923–24 academic year at a salary of $800. Across the acceptance form, in Randolph's hand, is scrawled a brief phrase: "I didn't take the job."[5] The biographer, commencing his work, appreciates all these dates and titles and dollars, and supposes his major task to be the assembly of as many such evidences as can be found. Only later does the true problem dawn, the obstinate inertia of the fact manifest itself. Like desert anchorites upon their perches, or high school boys at proms, the facts refuse to socialize. The band will play to an empty floor, and all the belles go home dismayed, unless the chaperones bestir themselves, encourage shy and sullen squires.

So too the biographer—he moves like a matchmaker amid his

facts, urges them to coherence, and thus it happens, after many months, that the fact of the Kansas letter is joined to another fact, equally isolate. A book published in 1957 briefly mentions Randolph's days in the early 1930s as a Metro-Goldwyn-Mayer screenwriter. Summoned to a supervisor's office to be told that the dialect in a script is inauthentic, Randolph reportedly tells his critic to "shove it!" In addition, "he spat a nice big splash of tobacco juice on the pretty green carpet, turned and walked out the door." His fellow writers give chase after hasty apologies to the supervisor, but they are too late: "Randolph had cleaned out his desk and gone. He was already headed for the Ozarks."[6]

The two facts, in spite of the decade's difference in their ages, dance nicely together. They were made for each other, and thanks to the helpful biographer they will live happily ever after. What unites them is character, the one man responsible for both acts— the Randolph most deeply comprehended in the costume of the man in motion, the man leaving the office, the man headed for the hills. The master image, then, the telling figure, is that ultimate elegance, Ptolemaic perfection, the circle, with center and circumference its poles. All he fled, urb and suburb, home and office, finds expression in the Parmenidean center, the middle's still point where the monist dreams. All he sought, the edge's action and the breeze of flux—that's the margin, the old Circumference Trail. By such a figure, abstracted clean to geometry, the biographer hopes to draw the man as he lived in his own eye. If his figure's well chosen, facts will find their home, fit like flesh to bone and seem to live.

By birth Randolph belonged to the center. His family was Episcopalian, Republican, town dwelling. Unlike a Jean Genet, foundling, born to the margin, "born without parents" and "preparing to die without descendants," Randolph's penchant for outsiders and outlaws was a matter of choice and temperament.[7] He chose to associate himself with Ozarkers and Jewish socialists, with bank robbers and freethinkers, to read everything he could find about gypsies, to drink too much, and gamble, to hobo around the country. Even his scholarship and writing were consciously tied to traditions beyond the pale of approved professional life—with Goliards, troubadours and Minnesanger, with Grub Street hacks and broadside ballad mongers, with wild Kit Marlowe and impoverished Robert Greene. His greatest hero and model was George Borrow, the British adventurer and writer once famous as the first Englishman to learn the gypsy language and now best remembered for his fictionalized autobiographies, *Lavengro* and *The Romany Rye*.

Randolph often described himself as a "hack writer"—he published an insider's account of the ghost-writing business in 1944
under the pseudonym of Peter Nemo in which he printed his own
name in a list of known ghost writers.[8] At first one is inclined to understand the phrase as deprecatory, a bit of modesty from the famous man. Wrong again, as I soon realized. He said "I'm a hack"
with matter-of-fact pride, in the same tones he used to say that Bill
Delladio was "a bootlegger, a good friend of mine," or that Leonard
Short was a bank robber.

All this encourages the comparison with Elizabethans like Greene,
folklore collectors before their time, who wrote with such attention
and such obvious admiration, perhaps sensing their own participa-
tion in the fraternity, of the cony-catchers, sturdy beggars, and low
strollers of their day. Randolph, for his part, wrote a number of short
biographies devoted to famous bandits, gunmen, and assorted male
and female desperados. In several of these his admiration is apparent. *Sam Bass, the Train Robber,* for example, written under the
pseudonym of Harvey N. Castleman, is subtitled *"The Life of Texas'
Most Popular Bandit,"* and opens with unabashed tribute: "To a boy
brought up in the Middle West 50 years ago, Jesse James was the
only top-flight bandit in the world. The story of the James boys, even
today, yields nothing to the legends of Robin Hood, Dick Turpin, or
Claude Duval. But to a boy of the same vintage who was reared in
Texas, even Jesse James was nothing in comparison to the splendid
figure of Sam Bass, who 'whupped the Texas Rangers' in the old
ballad. Hundreds of pilgrims still visit his grave at Round Rock
every year."[9]

Randolph was also quick to claim personal acquaintance with a
number of well-known outlaws. In *Belle Starr: The Bandit Queen,*
attributed to one William Yancey Shackleford, he informs readers
on the first page that "my father and my grandfather had both
known Belle personally, and I saw her daughter and other relatives
many times."[10] Cole Younger, Emmett Dalton, and "Pretty Boy"
Floyd are also described by Randolph from personal experience—
the latter impressed him as "a fine fellow" when the celebrated bad-
man entertained Randolph and other local men in his room at
Joplin's Connor Hotel.[11] But his one real friend on the wanted lists
was Leonard Short, a Missouri bootlegger and bank robber who was
gunned down in December, 1935, after shooting a Muskogee, Oklahoma, detective chief in a jailbreak. Randolph knew several Shorts
well—they were a prominent family in Stone County, Missouri,
where Randolph lived for a number of years in the 1930s and 1940s.

Leonard's brother Dewey Short was a U.S. congressman, and
Lillian Scott Short, Leonard's wife, is frequently cited as an informant in Randolph's collections. Randolph often compared the two
brothers, always to the congressman's disadvantage. "The bank robber was the better fella." In the last years of his life Randolph assembled a collection of articles and essays, to be titled *I Have Not
Forgotten*. He dedicated it "To the Memory of Leonard Short."[12]

In matters of religion, too, Randolph made clear his unorthodox
loyalties. As a young man he was inclined to a scoffing atheism calculated to shock and offend the faithful—in 1926, for example,
under his own name, he produced a virulent little screed entitled
"Do Scientists Believe in God?" which answered that question re-
soundingly in the negative. Recent statistical studies, Randolph reported, suggest that "the majority of American scientists are either
agnostics or atheists," and, in addition, that "belief in God is in-
versely proportional to ability in science." In conclusion, Randolph
asked who should speak for scientists, "the scientists themselves, or
a lot of gabbling preachers?"[13]

Americans Who Thought They Were Gods is another production
in this vein, published in 1943, again in Randolph's own name. It
gives thumbnail sketches of a great many healers and messiahs,
most of them in an openly comic tone, ranging from Jemima Wilker-
son, the self-styled "Publick Universal Friend" from Rhode Island,
to the better known Father Divine, who created quite a stir among
the faithful and the tax authorities in the 1930s and 1940s. By 1974,
in a letter to Herbert Halpert, his great friend among the academic
folklorists, the tone had mellowed a good bit. The stridency of former years is gone, but the old Randolph is yet recognizable in the
banter: "In recent year[s] my Shiksa wife and I have returned to the
faith of our fathers. We ain't exactly *religious* but you've no idea
how *moral* and *respectable* I feel walkin' out of Mass of a Sunday,
with my wife on me left arm and me fine new rattan walkin'-stick in
my right hand. Oh, them lyin', thievin' Yankees, as Booth Campbell
used to sing!"[14]

As late as 1977, confined to a nursing home in Fayetteville,
Arkansas, and virtually bedridden, Randolph could still enjoy twit-
ting the bumptious clerics who haunt such spots in droves, the
better to harangue an audience too desperate for company to be
choosy, too insensate to object, or too weak to walk away. Told by one
Baptist sky pilot not to fret about his health, that soon he'd go to live
with Jesus, Randolph replied, "Well, that'll be fine, I guess. I always
did like Jewish cooking."[15] He had no great interest in genealogy—I

didn't learn, for example, that his mother was a member of the DAR until I looked up her obituary—but he loved to tell one story about a personal relative. "My great uncle, in Virginia, was dying. He was an old man. They were all trying to get him to join the church—he never had. He wouldn't do it. He said, 'My name is Randolph. I don't need no God.'" [16]

II

So much for the old man assiduous in the nurture of his legend. So much, too, for the reluctant biographer, and the whole subjective, circumstantial matrix of their coming together. Enter at last the major books, the great collections, the works that forged their author's name. From *The Ozarks* in 1931 to *Pissing in the Snow* in 1976, the books are responsible, finally, for all the attention and bottles of Scotch. The books make all the difference. Very properly, too, they determine in considerable measure the direction of the biographer's concern. If Vance Randolph were Craig Claiborne, one might focus careful attention upon his diet. If he were Jack Nicklaus, one would be interested in his exercise. He was, instead, a writer, and it is appropriate that attention be concentrated upon his books. Among his writings, moreover, those addressed to topics of folkloristic interest have enjoyed the greatest renown, and thus attract to themselves a larger measure of critical interest.

There is, then, no observation here of that "division of labor" deplored by W. Jackson Bate in the first pages of his magnificent biography of Johnson whereby the biographer sticks to the "life" and the critic to the "works." "If we are to find our way into the inner life of a great writer," Bate suggests, "we must try to heal this split between 'biography' and 'criticism,' and remember that a very large part of the 'inner life' of a writer—what deeply preoccupied him, and made him a great writer—was his concern and effort, his hope and fear, in what he wrote." [17]

Biographical treatments of noted scholars are no longer rare and require no generic defense. In recent years, especially, a good number of such "history of the discipline" studies have appeared in the social sciences, and it may be that such attention to origins is a regular feature of the professionalization of an academic specialty. There is, for instance, a fine series issued by Columbia University Press devoted to "Leaders of Modern Anthropology," and folklorists themselves have joined in with book-length studies of Zora Neale Hurston, Jacob and Wilhelm Grimm, George Korson, and J. Mason

Brewer as well as recent monographs and articles about Stith Thompson, George Lyman Kittredge, Ruth Benedict, W. W. Newell, Lafcadio Hearn, and others.[18] Vance Randolph, loner and self-proclaimed "hack," belongs to this company, by virtue of his long lifetime's huge labor, by the books which make him "one of our earliest recorders of a complete folk tradition."[19]

I've kept in mind for several years now a remark made by Roger Abrahams in pinpointing his dissatisfaction with the work of a colleague: "I'll tell you what it is," he said at last, with the emphasis of one who has finally gotten to the core of the matter. "He fails to honor the fathers!"[20] It was a moral as much as an intellectual judgment, and it recurs now in connection with Vance Randolph. A discipline ready to chronicle its own emergence is involved in honoring its fathers and mothers, and Randolph's name should be put forward. He's a black sheep to be sure, a prodigal son who "took his journey into a far country and there wasted his substance with riotous living."[21] But it's in the nature of the discipline that such behavior can be turned to good account—that's why Randolph could be a folklorist even though he couldn't be a professor. Blessings upon such a discipline!

III

From subject and situation then, motives converge, and a biography takes shape. It's been the most challenging thing I've attempted. Vance Randolph as I groped to understand him proved complex almost beyond fathoming. He'd turned himself to saga long before I met him, and in our interviews he presided over the invention of a game we played until he died. He was a treasure that dispensed its own maps, all of them oblique. He often misled me, but he was usually delighted when I'd catch him out. "You know, Mary," he'd shout to his wife, "I'm coming to believe this fellow is dangerous! Nothing is sacred when he's about!"[22] Like George Borrow, far and away his greatest hero, he had a "fondness for anonymity and pseudonyms," a "passion for mystery and evasion in connection with his personal affairs."[23]

I've tried, of course, to run the facts to earth, to do my work responsibly and well. But I've always wanted, too, to play Knapp to his Borrow—to have it both ways, maintaining the "objectivity" of scholarship in balance with the bedrock admiration that motivated the enterprise in the first place. Randolph himself evidently believed such a thing possible, was convinced indeed that Borrow himself had been thus fortunate in his own chronicler: "The two-volume *Life of Borrow* by Professor William Ireland Knapp, published in London in 1899, is one of the most delightful biographies ever written in any language. Dr. Knapp was always an enthusiastic Borrovian, but he had no illusions about our hero's language studies."[24]

I've no illusions either, as regards a total separation of fact from fiction. There are times when all I can do is make plain my uncertainty. Randolph, for example, on several occasions dropped hints concerning a brief period of employment by the Mexican Army as some kind of drill sergeant. My repeated attempts to elicit details were parried with a cunning that now seems incredible. He'd catch my trying to lead him back to the subject—often after weeks had intervened since we'd last touched it—and he'd chortle with pleasure. "That's not important," he'd say. "You've got to remember you're writing about me as a folklorist!"[25] (This term too—"folklorist"—was loaded with humor, but more of that later.) "Give that round to Vance," I'd say to Mary, and on we'd go. That's how this book was made, out of our sparring. "Without contraries is no progression," said Blake.[26] It was a pleasure, and I still miss our visits. Randolph wrote in my copy of *Down in the Holler* that I was "a professor, but a fine fellow in spite of it." I hope he'd still feel the same way.

All of us have our familiars, folks in our heads who talk with us and give us counsel when we daydream or drive long trips at night. Mine tend to be codgers, corncob patriarchs, and kerchief-headed grannys. They speak to me in outlandish tongues, voices out of Synge or Dilsey, and give me sage advice. When the notion of biography was raised, they gave me their thoughts on the genre. "You come to write down the life of a man or a woman it is requisite you got your largest mind and Sunday heart plugged in and all your bills paid up." "It is an occasion calls for rising."

2

People of His Own Kind

> But now, the sun and the bossman were gone,
> so the skins felt powerful and human. They
> became lords of sounds and lesser things. They
> passed nations through their mouths. They sat
> in judgment.
>
> —Zora Neale Hurston
> *Their Eyes Were Watching God*

I

Vance Randolph's reputation is sustained primarily by two groups of admirers. The first, a diverse band, is comprised of celebrators of the Ozark region, people who for reasons of residence, family connection, patriotic ardor, huckster greed, or some mix thereof have made it their business to publicize the virtues of the area. For folks of this allegiance, especially as they tend to focus their veneration upon the past—the pioneer hardihood of the old-time "residenters," the sturdy independence of their culture—Randolph has long been a virtual demigod, a name to conjure with. His name affixed in praise to a book addressed to this audience—one of the myriad volumes in the *They Were the Last, These Were My Mountains, Grandpa Did It This Way* vein—confers instantaneous cachet. Even today, at local heritage festivals, old-time music fairs, and historical society meetings all over northern Arkansas and southern Missouri, Randolph is frequently honored with one or another form of "salute." Like the oldest grad at homecoming, he provides depth, roots, a vatic dimension. For these proud regionalists and their less savory cousins busy peddling heritage to newly arrived retired Chicagoans, Randolph is the mythologus, the singer of their tale. He's Mr. Ozark.

The second group of Randolph fans is more homogeneous, composed of scholars—folklorists, cultural geographers, Americanists, historians, students of regional dialect, anthropologists. Many of these academics are professionally interested in the Ozarks, but others have appreciated Randolph for his methodological innovations or the perspicacity with which his work has anticipated the concerns of more recent investigators.

Within this group, however, the attitude toward Randolph is decidedly more ambivalent. He was in their world—publishing articles in their journals and, later, books with their presses—but not of it. He wasn't a professor, never held a full-scale faculty position, and got his only Ph.D. as an honor from the University of Arkansas in 1951. He never graduated from high school. His first important books, *The Ozarks* (1931) and *Ozark Mountain Folks* (1932) were published by a press associated with socialism, lacked the standard bibliographic apparatus, and were ignored by the academic journals. Except for Herbert Halpert, his great friend and champion inside the academy, he had no close friends in the ivory tower. The American Folklore Society didn't get around to making him a Fellow until 1978.

With the scholars, moreover, Randolph's nearly exclusive attention to Ozark subjects—the very thing that has motivated his canonization by the Ozark heritage enthusiasts—has been a matter for suspicion and criticism, the central charge brought against him when he is designated a "collector" instead of a "folklorist." Richard M. Dorson, for example, for many years the director (at the University of Indiana) of one of the nation's most prestigious academic folklore programs and perhaps the fiercest defender of academic orthodoxy among contemporary folklorists, classified Randolph among the "Regional Collectors," in the company of figures like Texas's J. Frank Dobie and Pennsylvanian George Korson. "Randolph admits," says Dorson, stacking the deck with the verb, that "his concern begins and ends with the Ozarks." Now the genuine article, the true folklorist, as envisioned by Dorson, will reject such "parochial" limitations. "But our potential American folklorist does not intend to be an Ozarkologist or a Texologist. He is concerned with the whole civilization, and with all its regions and occupations."[1] He is, as Randolph used to say, quite a fellow.

It is true, however, that Randolph did a good bit to promote this almost chthonic rootedness, the nearly seamless identification of man and region. Introducing a booklet entitled *Wild Stories from the Ozarks,* for example, he waxes eloquent: "There is only one place in the world that really seems like home to me, and that is the Ozark region of southern Missouri and northern Arkansas. I was born in Kansas and never saw the Ozarks until 1899, when my parents brought me down for a week's stay at the O-Joe Club near Noel,

Missouri. I was only seven years old at the time, but I perceived at once that a guide named Price Payne was the greatest man in the world, and that the Ozark country was the garden spot of all creation."[2] Hindsight, with its zeal for telos, its penchant for symmetry, has prompted other rememberings in this vein. "All the value of my life is after 1920," Randolph once told an interviewer. "Before, I led a wandering life."[3]

There's truth, of course, in all of this. The overwhelming bulk of Vance Randolph's important labor was accomplished in the Ozarks and was devoted to Ozark subjects. It's true, too, that Randolph lived for many years in isolated Ozark towns, and that some sense of directed purpose, however inchoate, must have urged the original move to Pineville, Missouri, in 1919. But it is true, too, that this same man went to Worcester, Massachusetts, to study psychoanalysis with G. Stanley Hall, and then proposed doctoral work in anthropology to Franz Boas at Columbia. His travels ranged from Florida to California and he met or corresponded with such nationally known figures as Theodore Dreiser, Emma Goldman, H. L. Mencken, Thomas Hart Benton, Eugene Debs, Carl Sandburg, and Pretty Boy Floyd. His work was in the Ozarks, but he lived an American life.

Something important, then, is lost in exclusive focus on the Ozark-centered achievements of Randolph's career. Hindsight's clarity, foregrounding the early manifestations of Ozark themes, sacrifices both life's complexity and the basic thematic romanticisms that rendered the young Kansan susceptible to the call of the mountains. Young Kansan indeed—Vance Randolph's first twenty years were lived in southeastern Kansas, in the coal-mining region of Crawford County, just west of the Ozarks. He was born there, in Pittsburg, in 1892, and he was in his twenties before he ever left. Kansas was the home country, the origin in fact and spirit, for Vance Randolph, and it's to Kansas the researcher must turn to appreciate the sources of that singularly advantaged combination of attitudes and abilities he brought to his chosen tasks.

II

Crawford County was a striking place in the 1890s. Everything was new—the county itself was in its twenty-fifth year when Vance Randolph was born in 1892, and the town of Pittsburg was even younger, having been platted in 1876 by a lawyer and three zinc mine promoters from Joplin, Missouri, thirty miles to the southeast.

The county was named for the then governor of the state, Samuel J. Crawford, but the promoters hinted at their ambitions by naming the town after Pennsylvania's coal-mining and railroad metropolis.

Their new Pittsburg never rivaled the old, but it did flourish in its early years, as the Pittsburg Coal Company met its need for skilled deep-shaft miners by importing laborers from a dozen European countries. Twenty years after its establishment, in 1895, the town boasted a population of nearly 9,000. The resulting ethnic diversity became an identifying characteristic of the region—the area is still known locally as the "Little Balkans." When Kansas governor Arthur Capper visited the town in 1916 for a political rally, a "Tower of Babel Banquet" took place in which some thirty naturalized citizens welcomed him with short speeches in as many native tongues.[4]

Southeastern Kansas was also, partly as a consequence of this ethnic diversity, a hotbed of political activity throughout the years of Randolph's youth. The Populists especially, inheriting the issues, platforms, adherents, and often the leaders of the Grangers, Greenbackers, Farmers' Alliancemen, and other agrarian movements of the 1870s and 1880s, had enjoyed great success in the region. Kansas sent a Populist senator to Washington in 1890 and gave 48 percent of its popular vote to Populist candidate James B. Weaver of Iowa in the presidential election of 1892. Mary Elizabeth Lease and "Sockless" Jerry Simpson, two of populism's best-known oratorical firebrands, both hailed from Kansas. "I met Jerry Simpson," Randolph remembered. "I heard him speak in either Topeka or Pittsburg. It was after my father died, I think—I know my parents weren't there because my father hated Populists. He thought they were a menace."[5]

The "menace" subsided rapidly after the 1896 elections, which left the Populists deeply divided over the party's support of Bryan, the unsuccessful Democratic candidate. But at its height the mood it raised was exhilarating: "It was a religious revival, a crusade, a pentecost of politics in which a tongue of flame sat upon every man, and each spake as the spirit gave him utterance. . . . The farmers, the country merchants, the cattle-herders, they of the long chin-whiskers, and they of the broad-brimmed hats and heavy boots, had also heard the word and could preach the gospel of Populism."[6]

As the People's party divided and declined after 1896, the crusade was sustained among the faithful by the newly emerging Socialist party, especially by the nation's most important socialist newspaper, the weekly *Appeal to Reason.* "Clear continuities existed between populism and socialism in the Southwest during the early 1900s.

Radical Populists in the Oklahoma Territory formed Socialist clubs several years before the Socialist party was founded in 1901."[7] Probably the most significant figure in this transition was Julius A. Wayland, founder of the *Appeal to Reason*—in his varied and improbable career the ferment of the time and place may be sensed at the level of personal experience. Besides, he ended up with his newspaper in Girard, Kansas, right next door to Pittsburg.

Wayland came west from Indiana in 1877 as a young man rising fast in the best Alger mode. By 1882, he was in Pueblo, Colorado, doing very well in the printing business and speculating in real estate on the side. But in 1890 everything changed. Supplied with reading matter out of Ruskin, Bellamy, and Fabian tracts by an English cobbler named William Bradfield, the young businessman embraced socialism, supported Populist candidate Davis Waite in his successful gubernatorial campaign in 1892, and began to consider "the idea of founding a paper of his own for the purpose of preaching the socialist gospel to the man in the street."[8]

By 1893, with the nation troubled by a major depression, Wayland was back in Indiana—he'd seen the crash coming and sold off all his Colorado and Missouri properties—where the idea was made flesh with the first issue of the *Coming Nation* on August 19. Within one year it was making money, and eventually achieved a circulation of more than 60,000. The *Coming Nation* may have been weak on recondite matters of revolutionary theory—the scholarly Daniel DeLeon, leader of the Socialist Labor party, called Wayland a "Salvation Army sentimentalist"—but it obviously gave its readers something they wanted. It "Americanized" socialism.[9]

But Wayland was just getting started. Ever since he'd read Bellamy's *Looking Backward,* he'd been intrigued by the notion of a cooperative community, and now the time seemed ripe. By the middle of 1894, accordingly, the publisher and a group of co-workers were preparing to move their presses to a 1,000-acre tract of land in west-central Tennessee. They called their community Ruskin, they started with some 125 enthusiastic utopians, and they planned to use the income from the *Coming Nation* to help them get established.

But paradise was soon troubled. Like countless similar communities, Ruskin was first sapped and then destroyed by internal disputes. After just one year Wayland threw in the towel and left, leaving the *Coming Nation* and its presses behind. Embittered and disappointed, he headed for Missouri, to Kansas City. His biggest success was just ahead. On August 31, 1895, the first issue of the *Appeal to Reason* appeared, with a press run of 50,000 copies.

The *Appeal,* unlike the *Coming Nation,* took a while to find its audience, and it was a move in the name of lower publication costs that brought him to Girard after a few months in Kansas City. Once he got going, however, Wayland's new paper succeeded like no paper of its kind had ever succeeded before. By the end of 1900 it had a regular subscription list of more than 140,000. Debs himself would serve as a contributing editor. In 1902 Wayland began turning the direction of the *Appeal* over to Fred D. Warren, "The Fighting Editor," whose sobriquet pays tribute to his pugnacity without noting his shrewdness. The founder himself ended his adventurous life unhappily and by his own hand in 1912, but his paper went on to even greater heights under Warren's editorship. In 1913 the *Appeal* boasted a circulation of over 750,000—not even the *Saturday Evening Post* could match it.[10]

Which brings things back to Randolph, since it was Warren's successor as editor, Louis Kopelin, who hired him as an *Appeal* staff writer in 1917. "It seems to me I knew Kopelin before. I'd been over in Erie and Parsons selling insurance for two or three months— Church got me the job—and I may have come over to Girard doing that. Anyway, I knew people there—my parents had lived there once. There was an inter-urban line between Pittsburg and Girard."[11] It was this job that introduced Randolph to Emanuel Haldeman-Julius, a young socialist newspaperman from Philadelphia who would soon make his name as the originator of the famous "Little Blue Book" series. Down the road, in the 1920s, 1930s, and 1940s, Haldeman-Julius would help Randolph through some very lean times by publishing, and paying promptly for, scores of his booklets and articles. The role of these leftist political connections in Randolph's "career" choices is clearly significant, and the Kansas roots of this involvement will offer important clues to an understanding of the attitudes that informed and motivated his work.

Added to the ethnic diversity and political radicalism of the region was a vestige, residual but still strong, of the frontier culture of the recent past. The Oklahoma "Indian Territory," famed as a refuge for outlaws, was just a few miles to the south, and the great Kansas "cowtowns" had enjoyed their brief, notorious moments of glory as the railheads for Chisholm Trail cattle drives only twenty years earlier. Wyatt Earp was serving as assistant city marshal in Dodge City as late as 1879, and "Wild Bill" Hickok was city marshal of Abilene in 1871. Closer to home was Coffeyville, Kansas, site of the famous bank robbery attempt, two banks in one raid, that marked the end of the trail for the Dalton gang. The Daltons got theirs on October 5, 1892, when Vance Randolph, fifty miles east, was eight months old.[12]

This aspect of his Kansas background also made its mark on Randolph:

> My father and grandfather, in Pittsburg, always wore pistols. My grandfather had very strong views on the subject of pistol wearing. He was very disturbed at the prospect of men going about unarmed, thought the whole idea was deplorable. He went clear back to the Civil War—fought in the battle at Pea Ridge with the Illinois Cavalry. He was pretty tough, but even he was impressed by the folks down in Oklahoma Territory. He went down there after the Civil War, came back to Kansas and talked ever after about how rough it was down in the Territory.
>
> Late in his life he went so far as to trace what he saw as a decline in public manners in particular and human behavior in general to the disappearance of an armed citizenry. "Folks were more inclined to be polite," he used to say, "when the man they were talking to was wearing a pistol in plain view. Figured they might be held *responsible* for what they said!"[13]

Randolph also liked to tell a story in which guns were involved in providing him with a sense of his own worth. It seems that sometime around 1910, in Frontenac, Kansas, a mining town just north of Pittsburg, the teenaged Randolph was brought under fire for the first and last time in his life. "Some scoundrel," he'd begin, relishing the melodramatic phrasing, "fired at me with a six-shooter, from a distance of about forty paces. He was drunk, I guess—he was a local tough guy, drunk most all the time. Hell, I was drunk too." "Argument?" he continued, in response to a question. "There wasn't any argument. We never even spoke. I was standing with some friends, and he shot at me from down in a little valley by an automobile garage. Made me mad as hell. I walked straight at him—I never thought about the danger at the time. He shot once more, then throwed down the gun and run off. The whole thing was over in a few seconds."

Randolph, as he told it, did not immediately appreciate the significance of the incident, and only the circulation of the story by his friends back in Pittsburg alerted him to the singularity of his bravery. "After awhile, with my friends speaking respectfully of my conduct under fire, I got to thinking that, by God, it *was* a hell of a thing! Hadn't I tackled this terrible desperado bare-handed, and run him plumb out of town? Faced him down unarmed, and him shooting at me with a big pistol? The more I thought about it the more it seemed I had performed quite a deed after all, and I swaggered around something fierce inside of me for quite a while."[14] The importance of this incident can be found in an autobiographical account written some forty years later. "For a long time afterward," he wrote, "I strutted about with an incredible new assurance, an inward vanity which seems idiotic today. But even now . . . I feel myself in possession of a physiological indifference to calamity, a kind of irrational fortitude that sets me apart from my neighbors."

Once he got going in this vein, Randolph was capable of a thumping braggadocio otherwise conspicuously absent from his work. In his most saber-rattling moods, he could rise (or sink) to celebration of hand-to-hand combats: "Do you think that our ancestors," he wrote, "who risked death in duels over trifles were all fools? Do you believe that generations of German students, fighting with sharp sabers for no apparent reason, gained nothing from their experience? A Prussian scientist of international renown, with many decorations and degrees to his credit, said that he valued a saber cut on his cheek above any honor that the Emperor could confer. Was he talking nonsense? I don't think so."[15]

This tone is most prominent in the hunting and fishing articles Randolph wrote in the 1920s for *Field and Stream* and other outdoor sportsman's magazines. In "The Pistol as a Hunting Arm" he opens with a little psychology: "For some strange reason, which even the Freudian psychologists have not yet satisfactorily explained, the average red-blooded American has always found a peculiar satisfaction in the appearance, the feel, and the possession of a pistol." A little later the note of assertive pride is sounded: "the American has always held the pistol in high esteem, and his singular proficiency in its use has been remarked by every alien people with which he has ever come in contact."[16]

"Small Game with Big Pistols" gives Randolph a forum for brief political comments. The prospect of legislation controlling the sale of guns or ammunition provokes a reference to "a certain little group of fanatics" out to deprive "Doc and Bill and I" of the "wholesome pleasure" provided by their pistols. "Proficiency with the one-hand gun has been of inestimable benefit to the American people in the past, and it may serve us again some day—perhaps sooner than some of our optimistic statesmen suspect."[17]

On rare occasions, such bellicosity spills over into other works.

Writing about Lafcadio Hearn, for example, under the pseudonym of Arthur S. Tolliver, Randolph says of a passage from *Exotics and Retrospectives* that it's "good reporting, but I don't care for it. As I write these lines, some of my kinsmen are fighting the Japs in the South Pacific, and I am tired of hearing about the Rising Sun."[18]

But Randolph did turn the western and frontier culture of his Kansas background to more substantial account. In *Gun-Fighters of the Old West,* published in 1943 under the Shackleford pseudonym, he ends his survey with nostalgic reminiscence. "When I last visited Coffeyville, in 1914, one could still see here and there the marks of bullets fired at the Daltons in 1892." There's pride, too, in the same book. Noting that he "met and talked with Emmett Dalton several times in the 1920s," Randolph closes on a "we shall not see their like again" note: "The era of the old-time gun-fightin' outlaw really ended with the downfall of the Daltons that bloody day in Coffeyville. Times have changed in crime as in everything else, and not always for the better."[19]

III

This place, then, this Kansas, with its rich ethnic mix, its political tumult, and its flavors of the old western frontier, was home to Randolph for the first twenty years of his life. There's a sense, too, in spite of the long Ozark residence, in which he never left. In 1946, for example, with twenty-five years of residence in Pineville and Galena, Missouri, behind him, he writes to his closest Pittsburg friend, Ralph Church: "There comes a time when a man needs to be with people of his own kind. I like these Ozarkers better than any people I ever knew, but after all they are not my people. Despite the twenty-five years I have spent here, I am still an alien."[20]

This is overstated, of course, though in line with Randolph's basic attraction to the role of outsider. It needs remembering, too, that in 1946 the great era of publication by university presses and recognition from the academy was just beginning. What his work had mostly attracted, in 1946, was indifference or outright hostility. Still, one finds similar comments dotted through the letters of the 1940s, so that if the sense of estrangement from the Ozarks may be doubted, the sense of attachment to Kansas gains emphasis. In 1945, in a letter to Frances Church, Ralph's wife, Randolph complains about the monotonous diet in Galena and longs for the more varied menu available in Pittsburg: "We live mostly on chicken here now, and no meat except a few homecured bacon and sometimes ham. What I want is veal with seasoning in it, or some goulash like Mrs. Joe Premk, or maybe Katrina, used to make. And some good smoked sausage too, maybe."[21] A more general comment, again addressed to Ralph Church, makes clear the continuing importance of Randolph's Kansas roots: "I figger on coming to Pittsburg a little oftener from now on. I can drive over, stay a couple of days, and come back full of vittles and good spirits, with corny stories in my head and garlic on my breath."[22]

Following these roots to their immediate cause, the father and mother responsible, the researcher encounters not cowboys, socialists, or eastern Europeans but solid citizens of Episcopalian persuasion. "My parents were respectable people," said the son in summary. "My father was in politics, and my mother taught school and ran the library."[23]

The Randolphs came to Kansas in the person of Dr. W. J. Randolph, Vance's paternal grandfather, a physician who served as a surgeon with the 1st South Carolina Volunteers during the Civil War. Dr. Randolph came to Kansas in the early 1870s, after previous residences in Pennsylvania and South Carolina, and settled in Riley County. Vance remembered little about him, except for one visit. "We went out there once, stayed maybe two weeks. He lived on a big place, quite pretentious. He practiced medicine for a long time. He'd remarried, too; I'm not sure if it was after he'd come to Kansas or before. I remember we had a hired girl who went with us—my mother wanted help with the children while traveling—but my father had her stay at a hotel while we went out to the farm. He was concerned about the reaction of his father to a wife who needed help with her children."[24]

John Randolph, Vance's father, was born in Lawrence County in western Pennsylvania on September 9, 1857, and came to Kansas with his father in 1870. He was thirteen, and he would stay the rest of his life. After completing his schooling in the district schools of Riley County, John Randolph was employed first as a fireman on the Union Pacific railroad out of Ellis, Kansas, in the western part of the state, and later as a schoolteacher in his home county. In 1878 he undertook further schooling himself in a "normal academy" operated in Paola, Kansas, by a Professor Werrel, and in 1881 secured appointment as principal of the public school in Girard. There he was credited with establishing a high school curriculum in 1882 and with founding the Crawford County Oratorical Association in 1883.

In 1886 new opportunities called, and the young educator resigned his position to read law with a Girard attorney, James Brown.

On October 1, 1887, he "drove to Columbus and took an examination before Judge Chandler and was admitted to the bar." Moving then to Pittsburg, he practiced law for some fourteen years with various partners, was "always ready with time and talent, to uphold the cause of the Republican Party," and helped lead a drive to establish a municipal library.[25] He married in 1890 and fathered three sons—Vance the eldest—before his death on December 8, 1901, at the age of forty-four. He served one term as city attorney of Pittsburg, an appointive office, in 1888, ran unsuccessfully for county attorney in 1890, and was a delegate to the national GOP convention in St. Louis in 1896, where he cast his vote for McKinley. His obituary notices make clear that he was, in southeastern Kansas, a well-known and respected figure. The *Girard Press,* for example, reprinted a notice of his death from the neighboring *Chanute Tribune:* "Mr. Randolph was one of the brainiest men in Southern Kansas, and has frequently been mentioned in connection with the third district congressional nomination. As a political orator and a camp fire speaker he had few, if any, equals in the state."[26]

John Randolph also comes in for extensive treatment in a turn-of-the-century history of Crawford County. No mean purple proser himself, the unnamed chronicler treats Randolph sympathetically under the heading of "Republican Leaders," even though he identifies himself as "of a different political faith":

> Within the knowledge of the present writer one of the most talented leaders was John Randolph, who, but for one failing, might be a shining light in the political firmament, even though he had to appear in a galaxy of brilliant orbs. Rising from a humble place as a country school teacher he ascended by slow but steady degrees to an eminence in his profession which secured to him the county superintendency, and gave him prominent standing as an educator. . . . At first his aspirations seemed to lead entirely in an educational direction, but after entering the legal profession, it was not long til he entered also the political arena, where he soon rose in the estimation of his fellows, till but for the one fault he would have occupied a seat in Congress. . . . But such is the baleful effects [*sic*] of man's deadliest foe and the devil's most active and successful agent. It first blotches, then blights and withers consciences, and utterly destroys the fairest and best of earth's sons and daughters, and leaves nothing to compensate for their loss save broken vows, broken hearts, disappointed hopes and sad memories. Will men ever be wise enough to let it alone, except to drive it from the earth?[27]

Nearly fifty years later, recounting the story of his own struggles with "man's deadliest foe" under the cover of yet another pseudonym,

Felix V. Rinehart, Randolph alludes briefly to his father's drinking habits. "Father drank enough whiskey to float a battleship, but insisted all his life that he was a moderate drinker. . . . Mother persuaded him to try the Keeley Cure once, but it didn't do any good."[28]

"Mother" was Theresa Gould Randolph, and her respectability was if anything more formidable than her husband's. Born in Illinois in 1868, she came to Kansas with her family "as a child." Her father, Farwell Gould, had come originally from Maine, from a family of "sailors and lumbermen," according to the grandson's remembrance. "They were fanatical, meetin'-house Puritans. Grandfather Gould told me he never heard of Christmas until he was twelve, and then his mother said, 'It's just a Catholic holiday.'" Farwell Gould's wife, Susan Sayre Gould, was English, and her grandson remembered several of her pronunciations as "striking." "She said the word 'quite' so that it rhymed with 'wait.'" The Goulds lived in Girard until the death of Vance's grandmother, at which time Farwell Gould came to live with his daughter and son-in-law in Pittsburg. "Farwell Gould lived with us for many years. I knew him much better than my other grandparents."[29]

In fact, Vance Randolph's relationship with his maternal grandfather served him directly in his work, since Farwell Gould is cited as an informant for several songs in the second and third volumes of *Ozark Folksongs,* and is the source for some eleven stories in the folktale collections issued by Columbia University Press in the 1950s. At no point does Randolph identify his informant as his grandfather. In *Kate Bender, the Kansas Murderess,* a Haldeman-Julius booklet published in 1944, he hides his own identity under yet one more pseudonym, Allison Hardy, and casually cites his mother's parents as an "elderly couple named Gould, who lived at Girard, Kansas, in the 90's."[30]

Theresa Gould taught school in Girard before she married John Randolph—she'd been a high school student there while he was principal—and after his early death she served as head librarian of the Pittsburg Public Library for nearly thirty years. For several years she wrote weekly book reviews for the local newspaper. She was a member of the DAR and, according to her son's report, the Browning Society. Photographs of Mrs. Randolph reveal an imposing, severe figure. One published account describes her as "a woman of rare friendliness beneath an exterior of dignity and reserve," and there can be no doubt that her eldest son established with her the pattern which characterized his relationships with women for the rest of his life.[31] From the days when she provided room and board at home so long as he was enrolled in classes at the local college, until her death on February 9, 1938, Mrs. Randolph played the role of admiring and dependable caretaker for her accomplished but improvident son. She was impressed and proud; he accepted her care as his due. No doubt he was grateful, much as he behaved with elaborate gallantry toward the other women who cared for him. But always, with mother, wives, lovers, and friends, he presented himself as the "brilliant scholar" at the door, in need of a meal, a nurse, a place to work. In one early magazine portrait, written by a Pittsburg woman and published in 1936, the essentials of this pattern are clear:

> For years I had wanted to meet Pittsburg's own brilliant scholar and facile writer, the aloof, unapproachable Vance Randolph. There seemed to be little chance, however, for he was living in some mythical place in the Ozarks. He returned now and then, unheralded, for a day's visit with his mother, but was gone again before anyone knew that he had come. Sometimes this elusive young man spent a month here writing, leaving home early in the morning for a retreat in another part of the city, there to work undisturbed. Sometimes, too, he sat on the porch with his mother in the summer evening.[32]

These are, on both sides, mainstream connections. Even in spiritual matters the Randolphs moved in the best circles. "When I was a boy in Kansas I was confirmed by the Bishop," Vance Randolph remembered, "a regular High Church bishop with a golden mitre two feet high."[33] He also remembered dancing classes at which his parents required his attendance: "As a child in Pittsburg they made me go to a dancing class every week. They'd let me stay home from school, but they would never let me miss a dancing class." There were also family vacations: "Every summer my parents would go to New York or Washington or someplace—lawyers in those days had [railroad] passes. I went as a boy to New York several times with my parents . . . before I was old enough to know anything very much about it." Vance Randolph's remembered childhood presents, in sum, a pleasant, sheltered scene. "We were well off," he said.[34]

The contrast with the rude life of the surrounding mining camps could hardly be more striking. They were outlandish places, home to exotic people, and the socialists in Girard and the labor radicals from the strong United Mine Workers local in Pittsburg would offer political perspectives markedly different from the staunch Republicanism of the home he was born to.

As early as 1900, the eldest son of these community pillars was branching out, exploring the world around him with something of the careful, piercing attention that would later characterize his work as a recorder of Ozark folkways. "When I was eight or nine," he recalled, "I had a job delivering 'special delivery' letters on my bicycle. I got eight cents for each one. Most of them were addressed to the whorehouses—huge, rambling mansions with ornate bathrooms. One of them was the biggest frame house I ever saw, I think, down in the southeast part of town. It had elaborate grounds, with gravel walks and carefully tended lawns. I met all the girls—they used to invite me in for soda pop and a piece of pie. They had names like Shirley, Donna, and Karen. My parents knew about the job, of course, but they didn't know about the whorehouses."[35]

Actually, considerable credit for Randolph's painstaking observational habits must go to his youthful involvement with science and the devotion to "scientific method," which gradually came to mean anything systematic and which stayed with him in this sense all his life. This note sounds with particular prominence in the earliest booklets written for Emanuel Haldeman-Julius in the 1920s. *Ancient Philosophers,* for example, a speedy tour of Greek and Roman thinkers issued in 1924, is notable for its comparison of Aristotle and Plato: Aristotle "did not write as well as Plato, but his works are infinitely more valuable, because he attempted, at least, to collect facts and interpret them scientifically."[36] In *New Experiments in Animal Psychology,* published in 1925, the older "method of anecdote" is discredited by contrast with the modern "method of experiment," which has "brought comparative psychology out of the wilderness and into the laboratory."[37]

John Randolph, despite the fact that he died before his son's tenth birthday, was likely a major encourager of this interest in things scientific. Noting that Vance was four and a half years older than his brother John, with the third son, Gould, coming close enough behind to make natural playmates of the two younger brothers, thus isolating the eldest, one interviewer goes on to describe Vance's father as his "intimate companion": "Often the two would sit in the swing on a summer evening: the father would point out the constellations and teach him their names. Then there were long tramps in the woods and happy adventures with all sorts of bugs, butterflies, moths, toads, and snakes."[38]

An especially cherished boyhood memory—this one also connected with his father—centered on the visits to Pittsburg of the famous Buffalo Bill Cody, with his touring Wild West Show. "As a boy in Kansas I saw him several times," Randolph (as Shackleford) later wrote in a Haldeman-Julius booklet devoted to Cody. "He was always dressed in buckskin, with polished jackboots reaching far above his knees. We marveled at his fabulous moustache and goatee, and his long gray hair flying in the wind."

The booklet goes on to detail the experience of this extravaganza as it seemed to the youngster in Kansas. The first order of business when the troupe appeared in town was the erection of the giant tent. Then, on the morning of the show, there would be a great parade, led by Cody in person. "Following him came a great cavalcade of mounted Indians, scouts, trappers, soldiers, cowboys and other frontier characters in costume." The performance itself was held in the afternoon and evening (a typical show ran to three or more hours) and featured war dances, skirmishes between Indians and U.S. cavalrymen, a buffalo hunt, Pony Express riders, and other thrills. A special attraction was "the famous Deadwood Stage Coach—an ancient vehicle drawn by six horses, with passengers inside and armed guards riding on top. Suddenly the stage was attacked by Indians, who rode close up and discharged arrows—one could actually see the feathered shafts sticking in the sides of the coach! The passengers defended themselves with revolvers, while the guards fought to the death with great booming buffalo-guns. Just in the nick of time came a troop of cavalry, led by Buffalo Bill himself, and drove the redskins off with heavy losses."

"Shackleford" goes on to emphasize the "odd sort of authenticity" involved in the show, noting that "mere description makes it appear that the Great Wild West Show was mostly hokum, but somehow it was not." The booklet ends with a straightforward assertion of Cody's stature: "To American boys of my generation, Buffalo Bill Cody was a very great man. He became a sort of legendary hero in his own lifetime, and he will be remembered after many a famous General and President has been forgotten."[39]

To one boy in particular, Cody's visits brought a great enhancement of local prestige. "My father," Randolph recalled, "always claimed that he had been out west in the 1870s [perhaps when he was based in Ellis, Kansas], and that he knew Buffalo Bill. And when Bill came to Pittsburg he did come out to my house. He remembered all of my father's tales and swore they were true. He was the most handsome man I had ever seen in my life, with long white hair. All of the kids in the block looked up to me for a year afterwards because Buffalo Bill was in my house."

In other moods Randolph was more inclined to skepticism: "After all, my father was the city attorney and a prominent lawyer, and Buffalo Bill's show had to get a license. This might have jogged his memory. Of course, there's no way of knowing. . . ."[40] True enough, but it is encouraging to know that the story is at least plausible, that Buffalo Bill did, for example, visit Pittsburg in the years between Vance's birth and the death of his father. One possible date would be October 4, 1900, although it seems clear from the newspaper accounts of this visit that Cody came to Pittsburg often, with a show that varied widely. The 1900 version, for example, was billed as Buffalo Bill's Wild West Show and Congress of the Rough Riders of the World. It featured a number of attractions—Hawaiians, Annie Oakley, Cossacks, Bedouins—not mentioned in "Shackleford's" account.[41]

Another famous visitor was Carry Nation, the hatchet-wielding enemy of alcohol and self-styled "Home Defender." She, too, according to Randolph's account, was a visitor in the Randolph home. "I was just a little boy when Carrie Nation came to Petersburg [read Pittsburg], but I got a good look at her through a crack in the kitchen door. It was a hot day, and Carrie was a very ugly woman. She kept waving her arms, and yelling at the top of her voice. Nothing like that had ever happened in our house before. We were all shocked and embarrassed."[42]

Carry's ire was centered on the "joints," all twenty-seven of them according to Randolph's count, which were operating on "Main Street" in defiance of Kansas law. "Father was the City Attorney in those days, and Carrie wanted him to put the saloon-keepers in jail. But father did not believe in bothering saloon-keepers, so long as they kicked in regularly."[43] Carry's visit, if it failed to galvanize the father, nonetheless made quite an impression on his son: "I was only ten years [old] at the time, but I remember exactly how Carry looked. To my eyes she was exactly like the political cartoons of Mark Hanna. She was the ugliest woman I have ever seen."[44]

In spite of such occasional attractions and excitements, however, the Pittsburg he was born to was often a stultifying place. It was taken for granted that the sons of such respectable parents would follow closely in their footsteps, and would themselves eventually grow up to occupy responsible positions in the community. But for Vance Randolph, when such a future seemed bleak and uninviting, there was another world, exotic and exciting, immediately to hand. He'd visited it first, in fact, in the company of his father, when he tagged along on campaign forays into the surrounding mining camps. "My father was always running for something," Randolph told an interviewer. "He wasn't much of a lawyer, but he was a spellbinder. He knew a little bit of French and Italian, and a smattering of German. Enough to ask the miners how their families were com-

ing along. He made the damndest political speeches and jury ora-
tions. The juries would weep and carry on. In his speeches to
miners he would use all three languages. Very ornate, flowing
speeches." [45]

Several examples of John Randolph's oratory have survived, including one address to the Kansas Day Club in 1899, on the occasion of its eighth annual banquet. The speech opens with a denun-
ciation of populism that certainly bears out Randolph's memory of
his father's hostility, and closes with an equally spirited paean in celebration of Republicanism. Brief excerpts:

> And speaking of fools leads by natural and easy descent to a mention
> of the late Populist party, and thereupon I advise you that the decease
> of that party was the very least of its offending; and furthermore, that
> its most grievous smell is yet to reach you. As thus: Let a cat be vio-
> lently slain and the carcass jerked from public notice and cast into a
> byway. If you go at once, you may come near the body and find it giv-
> ing forth no offense; but tarry not long, for the deceased, like the body
> of Populism, is at work—at work decomposing, and in a very short
> fulness of time the moment of its greatest stench is come, at which
> time go not near, for it is an abomination. From this time on the degree
> of offense lessens, until the time comes when you may stand in com-
> fort, without obstructing your nostrils, above the fragments, and ob-
> serve the bleached bones, with here and there a tuft of hair.

So much for "the loyal opposition," though several pages of like
matter follows. Near the close of his address Mr. Randolph turns to
a consideration of Republicanism: "You are further advised, that
when any man lifts up his voice in a Republican assembly or where
the name of Republicanism is not taken in vain, that such man
should speak as one just emerging from the holy of holies of American patriotism, and that upon his robe there should be no stain of
personal desire, and no symbol except those which our fathers
meant the flag to bear—the stars of equality and the stripes of human liberty." [46]

No wonder his audiences wept and carried on! But the important
thing, to the son who accompanied the orator, was the world he entered on these forays. In such experiences a striking and fundamental polarization presented itself. At home, at the center, there
was Pittsburg itself, the Republican party, the Episcopal church, the
parents active in establishing the public library. Surrounding this,
circumference to the center, were the mining camps—Frontenac,
Chicopee, and the others—exotic places, alive with many languages,

different foods, different politics. It was a universe drawn close. The ordinary and the alien, for Vance Randolph, were side by side, as close as the camps or the whorehouse "in the southeast part of town." The proximity was extraordinary, and very early on Vance Randolph, his isolation by age from his younger brothers perhaps exacerbated by his father's early death, would feel himself attracted.

IV

Randolph's initial experiences in the public schools were troublesome. He recalled even as an old man that he was "painfully shy" and soon developed "a bad stammer" which made things more difficult. He remembered also that he thought his teachers "stupid and ignorant": "When I was six years old my people made me go to the old Washington School on Locust Street. I didn't like it very much. I could read pretty well, before I ever went to school at all. . . . The only teacher for whom I felt any respect was Blanche Howard, who had been to Hawaii. She taught us to sing several songs in the Hawaiian language, and I remember some of them to this day."

Randolph remembered one particular incident that encouraged his low regard for the educational achievements of his teachers. "Later on I went to the new Lakeside School, where the principal was Martha Sandford. She read aloud to us out of a book called *The Five Little Peppers and How They Grew*. When Miss Sandford came to the word 'camera' she accented the second syllable, and it was evident she had no idea what the word meant."

Despite these drawbacks, the young scholar managed to struggle through the years of elementary school. "I cannot recall why," he said in the 1950s, "but the idea of high school terrified me. I was much more afraid of high school at thirteen than I am of death now. After a week or two—I remember that the high school was at Eighth and Broadway, clear at the other end of town—I got over it, but I never liked high school very much. Finally I quit, against my mother's wishes, and got a job in the Roberts Pool Hall on East Seventh Street."

Other short-term jobs followed, including one in a local garage. Having a dropout for a son was likely a severe trial for Mrs. Randolph, and it is easy to appreciate her relief when, after approximately three years of truancy, the pool-hall denizen "suddenly felt a yen for more schooling."[47] She was quick to encourage this impulse with an offer of free board and lodging—contingent only upon continued enrollment and good academic standing—and in the fall of 1911 Vance Randolph began his studies at Pittsburg's State Manual Training Normal School (now Pittsburg State University).

This institution, like everything else in southeastern Kansas in those days, was new; established by the state legislature in 1903, the school opened its doors with an enrollment of forty-three and a faculty of five. By 1910, the year before Randolph enrolled, things had improved, and thirty-two teachers greeted a student body of 723. The suspicions of professorial inadequacy continued unallayed— the teachers at the college presumably knew what a camera was by then, but other crucial flaws soon revealed themselves. "I really wanted to be a writer and went to college to major in English," Randolph told an interviewer in 1936, "but I was unlucky in my teacher. Miss X prided herself on her reading of Shakespeare, but she didn't know how to teach. Besides, she never read current literature and she discouraged creative work. I never dared ask her a question. And then when I discovered that she hadn't even heard of George Borrow, the English author and gypsy scholar, of whom I was rather fond, I lost all confidence in her." [48]

All in all, however, college seems to have suited Randolph much better than his brief encounter with high school. He graduated in 1914, with most of his course work centered in the natural sciences, with a good bit of sociology and psychology, some literature, and a sprinkling of what today would be called education courses ("School Methods and Management" and "Practical Teaching"). There was a brief misunderstanding over the matter of which degree would be awarded—instead of "the coveted A.B.," Randolph was surprised to find himself the less-than-proud holder of a B.S. in education, but he "cornered Mr. E.W. Hoch, a member of the Board of Administration, and made such a disturbance that he promised to get me an A.B., which he did several months later." [49]

Looking back twenty years later, he had good things to say about several of his teachers. The best courses, he reported, were given in the biology department by O. P. Dellinger, who held a "bona fide Ph.D.," had established an "international" reputation for work on "locomotion in the amoeba," and was "easily the strongest man in the college at that time." But Randolph's highest accolades are reserved for C. F. Lee, who taught psychology, and it seems reasonable to credit him substantially for his student's decision to undertake graduate study in that field. Lee was a "very poor lecturer" and had "very little knowledge of psychology," but in spite of these shortcomings he influenced Randolph, by Randolph's own accounting, more than any of the eminent teachers he was to encounter at other universities. "He taught me what little I know of literature, and introduced me to what were then regarded as very advanced conceptions in politics, and ethics, and sociology. . . . I thought that he was a very great man, and I still think so."[50]

The 1914 edition of the college's yearbook, *The Kanza,* pictures an unsmiling, clean-shaven Randolph, and describes him as receiving the A.B. in biology with memberships listed in the agriculture, industrial, and biology clubs as well as the Porterian Literary Society. A short apothegm, after the manner of yearbooks everywhere, is appended to this record: "I don't care what happens, just so it doesn't happen to me." There is also, in the same yearbook, a strange photo of thirteen figures robed in sheets, seated in a semicircle around a grinning skeleton, also seated. The photo is labeled "Corrigenda," Latin for "corrections to be made."[51] "It was a secret society," said Randolph. "I was a member. The name meant we were interested in improving the quality of things in the town and the school. All the members were men, but I think we had some members who weren't in school. I'm in the picture—my friends Allison and Church were members too."[52]

Ralph Church would become Randolph's closest friend and steadiest correspondent. The two men met in 1913, while Randolph was a student and Church, who was seven years older, was living in nearby Erie, Kansas, selling insurance. Church stayed in the insurance business and did well. There were times in the 1930s especially when Church assisted Randolph through some difficult times. He accompanied Randolph to the West Coast for his brief stint as a screenwriter in 1933, and the two men also traveled to Illinois together several years later to undergo the then famous cure for alcoholism at the Keeley Institute in Dwight. Randolph stayed off the booze completely for at least eight years, but Church's cure was less successful. "He could have been president of the insurance company," Randolph claimed. "He made a good deal of money—got so high up they couldn't put him out. He was a hopeless drunk all the time for years."[53] Much later, at the end of the 1940s, Randolph lived for several years in Church's home in Eureka Springs, Arkansas—"I was living in the basement when he died," he said. "They lived upstairs and used the third floor for guests. I lived there for several years before Church died. Frances' mother, an old lady, was there some of the time, too."[54]

Vernon Allison was another college friend—they were about the same age, graduated from college the same year, and went off to

Clark University in Worcester, Massachusetts, for graduate study together. "He lived in Pittsburg when I met him," Randolph recalled, "but he'd gone to high school in western Kansas—around Great Bend, I think. We both liked to shoot, both studied sciences. He published some papers on dragonflies; I did butterflies. Allison made himself a huge net to catch them—couldn't get it in a car. We had a hell of a time all one summer—hiked all over the area."[55]

Allison stayed in science, majoring in chemistry at Clark. "Clark gave us both tuition scholarships," Randolph remembered. "Dellinger recommended us. Allison got his degree in chemistry, and went on to become a specialist in explosives. Even back in Pittsburg he was always playing around with chemistry tricks. He'd paint some liquid mixture he'd concocted on logs and benches—when the stuff would dry it would blow up. He loved things like that. I remember he used to carry dynamite around in his pockets—scared me to death."[56]

Allison and Randolph kept in touch after their days at Clark, with the chemist going to the other Pittsburgh, in Pennsylvania, and Randolph, after a brief stay in New York, returning to Kansas. In the 1920s their paths crossed again when Randolph, living then in Pineville, Missouri, became involved in an archeological controversy over the so-called "Pineville Mastodon," the leg bone of a deer engraved with what some investigators took for a mastodon. If genuine, the find was important, since man and mastodon had not been convincingly associated in the New World. Various experts from the American Museum of Natural History journeyed to Pineville, and several excavations were mounted. Randolph recounted the whole story in a short piece, "The Pineville Mastodon," published some fifty years after the events described, and much earlier, in 1926, Allison and Randolph collaborated on a piece for the *New York Times Magazine* entitled "Ancient Man Is Traced in the Ozarks."

The amusing thing in all of this is the studied formality Randolph maintains in his reference to his old friend from the dragonfly hunting and trick explosions days. It's always "Dr. Vernon C. Allison" in print, much as his grandparents are "an elderly couple named Gould." The boys in Corrigenda continued in their liking for disguise! And the citation game worked both ways, since there is a short note by one Vernon C. Allison of Linden, New Jersey, in a 1929 issue of *American Speech*, correcting a point of pronunciation in an earlier Randolph article in the same journal. Allison, too, adopts a formal tone, refers repeatedly to "Dr. Randolph," and mentions "meticulously scientific papers in his own field, which is, or used to be, experimental psychology."[57] Wrapping up the continued association of the college friends and fellow members of Corrigenda, there is Randolph's recollection that "Allison visited me once in the Veteran's Administration Hospital in Fayetteville, and he came to Eureka Springs once too, while I was living there."[58] There is, too, a Haldeman-Julius booklet entitled *The Essence of Catholicism* issued in 1924 under the name of Ralph W. Church. Randolph first described it as a pseudonymous work but later listed it as a "collaboration."

All in all, Randolph's undergraduate years seem to have been pleasant ones. In 1955 he told an interviewer that college students had become "a solemn lot." "We were more lighthearted in college," he said.[59] When he revisited the Pittsburg campus in 1935, to write one in a series of articles about Kansas colleges, he was taken to a party where the festivities provoked a reminiscent mood: "The blonde with whom I danced was easily the prettiest girl in the room, but I was thinking a little wistfully of Lucille Richey, and Eula English, and Nell Clark, and that DeYoe girl who married Si Burton and went to Texas. The young men were pleasant enough, too, but I was remembering such outstanding individuals as Rex Tanner, and Pat Crowell, and Vernon Allison, and Ben Fuller, and Ed Dudley."[60] (Even here Randolph has his tongue in his cheek at times. Rex Tanner, for example, is an official hero at the college. There's a plaque on the wall even now, in the administration building, noting that Tanner died in a fire that destroyed the college's major building, Russ Hall, in 1914. The official version has it that Tanner was there attempting to put out the fire and save the building. Randolph, however, was on the scene too, and his memories were markedly different: "We'd been drinking beer all day at Church's house across the street. When the fire broke out we ran over—we thought we could steal some microscopes. There were some wires down, and he electrocuted himself somehow. He wasn't no hero at all.")[61]

The young man who headed off to Massachusetts in the fall of 1914, then, was clearly headed for a career as a "scientist." He'd do his work at Clark University in psychology—and by this, it is crucial to remember, he meant "experimental psychology," the psychology that has come "out of the wilderness and into the laboratory." But what about folklore? What about the Ozarks? Given hindsight's advantages, what hints of Randolph's future can be discerned? The answer is in the reading, and the most significant figure, again, is George Borrow. "I knew about him even in high school," Randolph remembered. "I was impressed by any kind of little known stuff—esoteric, underworld stuff. I read travel books—Burton and Charles Doughty's Arabian books. I'd read everything on gypsies I could find before I finished college. Charles Godfrey Leland wrote some books about gypsies. I saw gypsies in Kansas many times, but I never did know them well. They were all over the middle west."[62]

In addition to Borrow and the other books about gypsies, Randolph was reading the great ballad collections. He remembered reading Child "very early," and "learned about Percy and Scott." He read Sharp, too, "as soon as it came out," and remembered doing most of this reading in the Pittsburg library. "I read Aubrey like a Borrow. *Brief Lives, Remaines of Gentilisme,* one other. I was in college." Another early enthusiasm was Olive Schreiner—"I read *The Story of an African Farm* when I was a boy, probably in high school."[63] A more important influence was Clifton Johnson, the prolific New Englander whose children's stories and travel books were great successes in his own day and whose local history and folkways studies have enjoyed a more lasting renown. "I knew about him before I graduated from college—he wrote a lot of highways and byways books. He was a very good writer."[64]

But most important, now and forever, was George Borrow. In 1980, in the hospital and fixing to die, he asked to be read to out of *Lavengro* and *The Romany Rye.* He loved especially the passages where Jasper Petulengro speaks of Gypsy life and its pleasures: "There's night and day, brother, both sweet things; sun, moon, and stars, brother, all sweet things; there's likewise a wind on the heath." Asked of death, Jasper is brief: "When a man dies, he is cast into the earth, and his wife and child sorrow over him. If he has neither wife nor child, then his father and mother, I suppose; and if he is quite alone in the world, why, then, he is cast into the earth, and there is an end of the matter."[65] From first to last, and through all the trouble between, it was George Borrow who provided Vance Randolph with his brightest image of life at its best, who showed him a path he could walk as his own.

George Henry Borrow is succinctly described as a writer, traveler, and shade-tree linguist. He was born in 1803, the second son of Thomas Borrow, a professional soldier. The family was Cornish, royalist in politics and Church of England in religion. His father's regiment moved about in England, Scotland, and Ireland during the years of George Borrow's youth. In 1813, for example, the family was in Edinburgh, where the schoolboy became acquainted with a

drummer boy named David Haggert, who later became a notorious
pickpocket, highwayman, and murderer, famous all over Scotland,
Ireland, and northern England. Haggert was hanged in 1821 at the
ripe age of twenty, but not before he dictated an autobiography to
the prison chaplain that was, Borrow wrote later, "the crowning
stone to thy strange deeds."[66] Randolph mentions Haggert, too, in
his "Arthur S. Tolliver" booklet on Borrow: "It may well be that this
early contact with Haggert was the beginning of George Borrow's
life-long interest in thieves, highwaymen, murderers and low characters generally."[67]

In 1815 Thomas Borrow's regiment was sent to Ireland, where
his son soon fell in with one Murtagh, who gave him lessons in Irish
in return for a pack of playing cards. The experience in Ireland
marked him forever: "On a wild road in Ireland I had heard Irish
spoken for the first time; and I was seized with a desire to learn
Irish, the acquisition of which, in my case, became the stepping-
stone to other languages." Even more significant than the choice of
Irish are the reasons given for its attractiveness:

> First of all, and principally, I believe, the strangeness and singularity
> of its tones; then there was something mysterious and uncommon as-
> sociated with its use. It was not a school language, to acquire which
> was considered an imperative duty; no, no; nor was it a drawing-room
> language, drawled out occasionally, in shreds and patches, by the
> ladies of generals and other great dignitaries, to the ineffable dismay of
> poor officers' wives. Nothing of the kind; but a speech spoken in out-
> of-the-way desolate places, and in cut-throat kens, where thirty
> ruffians, at the sight of the king's minions, would spring up with bran-
> dished sticks and an "ubbuboo, like the blowing up of a powder maga-
> zine." Such were the points connected with the Irish, which first
> awakened in my mind the desire of acquiring it; and by acquiring it I
> became, as I have already said, enamoured of languages.[68]

Associations and desires of such a kind could bring little but
worry to the mind of a loyal soldier like Thomas Borrow. His first son
was a delight, a soldier like his father. But George was different and
his father knew it, as Borrow himself reports his conversation: "'I
sent him to school to learn Greek, and he picked up Irish!'"[69] This
predilection seems to have troubled Thomas Borrow recurrently, for
he was himself no friend of the Irish, since the same matter crops
up in another conversation, where the subject is the young man's
future. "He particularly dwelt on the unheard-of manner in which I
had picked up the Irish language, and drew from thence the con-

clusion that I was not fitted by nature to cut a respectable figure at an English university." The church was also considered but rejected for similar reasons.

Indeed, Borrow seems almost to have agreed with his father and to have sympathized with his perplexity:

> And I have no doubt that my excellent father was right, both in his premises and the conclusion at which he arrived. I had undoubtedly, at one period in my life, forsaken Greek for Irish, and the instructions of a learned Protestant divine for those of a Papist gassoon, the card-fancying Murtagh; and of late, though I kept it a strict secret, I had abandoned in a great measure the study of the beautiful Italian, and the recitation of the sonorous terzets of the Divine Comedy, in which at one time I took the greatest delight, in order to become acquainted with the broken speech, and yet more broken songs, of certain house-less wanderers whom I had met at a horse fair.[70]

The father at last decided upon the law as a possible career for his son, and George Borrow was articled in 1819 to a Norwich law firm. He did the work, but he continued to seek the company of the "houseless wanderers," the Gypsies he'd first encountered as a boy. He also studied Welsh—"Blackstone kept company with Ab Gwilym" is the way Borrow describes his days at the law office—and Danish, undertaking to produce translations of verse in both languages.[71] These manuscripts he took to London in 1824, following his father's death, hoping to publish them and gain "both profit and reputation."[72] He got neither, though he did bring out *Romantic Ballads from the Danish* at his own expense in 1826, and was forced to literary hackwork in order to eke out a living. During this period he traveled frequently with Gypsies, in whose company he had many adventures later recounted in *Lavengro,* including one in which he nearly lost his life when he was poisoned by an old woman he calls Mrs. Herne. She's Jasper Pegulengro's mother-in-law, and she resents the *gorgio* Borrow's inquisitiveness into Romany words and ways. When Jasper and his wife accept his company, Mrs. Herne leaves them. "'You say you like him: in that we differs: I hates the gorgio, and would like, speaking Romanly, to mix a little poison with his waters. . . . In all kinds of weather have we lived together; but now we are parted. I goes broken-hearted—I can't keep you company; ye are no longer Rommany. To gain a bad brother, ye have lost a good mother.'"[73]

In 1833, after several years of wandering, Borrow managed to land a job with, of all things, the Bible Society—he'd spent six months studying Manchu with the understanding that a job editing a Chinese translation of the New Testament in St. Petersburg depended only upon a demonstration of his proficiency in that language. He spent two years in Russia, completed his work, and then persuaded the society to send him to Portugal and Spain, where he associated with Spanish Gypsies and translated the Gospel of Luke into their dialect. He called it Calo-Romano, and the small edition of this translation was the first book ever printed in the Gypsy language. Two other works on Spain and Spanish Gypsies followed— *The Zincali, or An Account of the Gypsies in Spain* in 1841 and *The Bible in Spain* in 1843. The first sold well enough, but *The Bible in Spain* was a bestseller that made Borrow financially secure and allowed him to work at leisure on the autobiographical volumes which are the basis of his reputation today. *Lavengro* was published in 1851, to mixed reviews, which disappointed and infuriated the author, and *The Romany Rye*, his last important book, followed in 1857. Borrow died in 1874.

The impact of this swashbuckling career on the fatherless adolescent already given to rambling about the Kansas countryside cannot be overestimated. Even the superficial correspondences are striking. The lengthy subtitle of "Tolliver's" life of Borrow—"Vagabond, Scholar, Horse-witch, Tinker, Blacksmith, Author, Linguist, Boxer, Adventurer, Jail-bird, Peddler of Bibles—There was Never Another Like Him in the World"—is more than a little like the list of occupations applied to Randolph himself by the reviewer of his first book on the Ozarks. They also shared a fondness for "mystery and evasion" concerning their private lives—Randolph's many pseudonyms are matched by Borrow's assumption of a different name for every country he visited. In Russia, for example, he followed the custom of the country, used his father's name as a patronymic, and called himself Yegor Phomitch Borrou. In Spain he called himself Don Jorge, among Gypsies he was Lavengro, or "word-master," and there are apparently pieces of writing published under the name of Olaus Borrow, for reasons that have never been explained.

Both men were good haters too. Borrow was so incensed about the tepid reception accorded *Lavengro* that he ended *The Romany Rye* with a long "appendix" devoted largely to impressive invective. Of "pseudo-critics," for example, Borrow begins by noting that many "meritorious writers" have permitted themselves to be injured by "malignant criticism." Borrow quickly distinguishes himself from this group, however, by recording his own intentions: "he will rather hold them up by their tails, and show the creatures wriggling, blood and foam streaming from their broken jaws." And even this, enough to give any critic pause, is not all. Borrow's abuse climaxes with a sneer at the manliness of his attackers: "Does any one imagine that the writer was not well aware, before he published his book, that, whenever he gave it to the world, he should be attacked by every literary coxcomb in England who had influence enough to procure the insertion of a scurrilous article in a magazine or newspaper! He has been in Spain, and had seen how invariably the mule attacks the horse; now why does the mule attack the horse? Why, because the latter carries about with him that which the envious hermaphrodite does not possess."[74]

Randolph's rancors fall far short of this staggering level, but they are reserved for precisely the same sort of folk, the scoffers who ridiculed his work in the long years when his collecting had no immediate prospect of publication. Writing to Church in 1945, he mentions the upcoming publication of "my folksong book" and adds that its appearance will "burn up that *#! so-and-so used to talk about my 'crack-brained industry' when I was collecting them songs, and it will be bigger & better as them silly little books he wrote, and I will still be setting in libraries in good company when there won't be a single son-of-a-bitch on earth will even remember what his name was."[75]

Even in their relationships with women the two men exhibit a startling similarity. Neither had children, and both were married late to women with assets in addition to their personal charms. Here is "Tolliver" on the subject of Borrow's marriage:

> Mrs. Clarke was an estimable women, but she had been 22 years a widow, and was considerably older than Borrow. She had lately inherited an estate, with an income of nearly 600 pounds a year, and had quarreled with some of her relatives about the inheritance. She needed a formidable husband to protect her interests and manage her affairs. Besides, she and Borrow were old friends. Her influence had helped him to a position with the Bible Society in 1832, and they had corresponded ever since. Borrow was not a family man, and had often repeated a Spanish proverb to the effect that "the halter is easier than the yoke." However, he was nearing 40, he had worked hard, and he had no money. His job with the Society was gone. And he liked Mrs. Clarke well enough. . . . [76]

While "Tolliver" may or may not assess Borrow's motives accurately, he surely reveals a great deal about himself. Randolph, too, married when he was "nearing 40," in 1930, and again in 1962, at seventy, some twenty-five years after the death of his first wife. In between, he proposed marriage to several other women, some of them "considerably older" than he. All owned cars or houses and were well-educated women impressed by intellectual and artistic achievement. Most were also gainfully employed.

Most important, in this array of traits shared by Borrow and Randolph, is the general rejection of the "respectable figure at an English university" envisioned by the parent, the basic romantic predilection for "thieves, highwaymen, murderers, and low characters generally." *Lavengro,* wrote Borrow in defense of his book, "is the history up to a certain period of one of rather a peculiar mind and system of nerves." It chronicles the youth and young manhood of an individual possessed of "much curiosity, especially with regard to what is wild and extraordinary." By the book's end the young man is "about to quit his native land on a grand philological expedition."[77]

Randolph was ready to leave too, in 1914. Like Borrow's autobiographical hero, he will face compromises, but he will keep his vision in sight: "if he is a hack author, he is likewise a scholar." Certain doors have already closed—"it is hardly to be expected that he will become a very precise and straightlaced person; it is probable that he will retain, with his scholarship, something of his gypsyism."[78] Randolph would return to Kansas often, of course, would even live in Pittsburg again for brief periods. He'd continue to flirt with the mainstream world now and again, as when he enrolled at the University of Kansas in 1921 as a Ph.D. candidate in psychology. He'd quit though, short of the degree, and head back to the hills, his "gypsyism" ascendant again. It was an old move by then, second nature to the man who as a kid quit high school for the pool halls, and preferred the company of Germans and Italians in Frontenac to the solid citizens of Pittsburg.

"Yeah, I liked the miners and the radicals," he recalled.

I still think about them sometimes—Alec Howat, the local UMW leader. I used to see him every day. I knew him as well as Brewer. He didn't speak as much—more of a working man. I used to go see him, talk about "affairs of Egypt" a little—party matters. He was primarily a labor man. I always admired him.

Caroline Lowe, and the Callery boys . . . Debs—I'll never forget how pleased I was when he called me by my first name one day over in Girard. Every now and then I'll still remember one of those fellas—like Lewis Lewis, a Welshman from Frontenac, or Bill Delladio and his wife. They were bootleggers, good friends of mine. They were fine people—seems like they had a lot of fun, enjoyed themselves more than the folks back in Pittsburg."[79]

Vance Randolph, it's clear from all this, came to his labors in the Ozarks prepared to listen, to respect, even to identify with the mountain people he would describe many times as "deliberately unprogressive." A shared marginality, a romantic liking for stubborn eccentricities of character not really appropriate in a devotee of science's deterministic gods—these traits, born and bred in Kansas and nourished on the swaggering prose of George Borrow, served him well in the Ozarks, in the accomplishment of his chosen tasks. The mountain folks, Randolph's own disclaimer notwithstanding, were in fundamental ways similar to the miners of Frontenac, the Gypsies of Borrow, and the socialists of Girard. They were, all of them, people of his own kind.

3

East & West: 1914–1920

Honey, you don't know my mind.
I'm lonesome all the time.
Born to lose, a drifter that's me.

I been a hobo and a tramp.
My soul has done been stamped.
The things I know I learned the hard, hard way.

I've heard the music of the rails,
Slept in every dirty jail.
Gal, you don't know my mind today.

—Harmonica Frank Floyd
"You Don't Know My Mind"

I

Vance Randolph and Vernon Allison left Kansas together in the fall of 1914 to enter Clark University in Worcester, Massachusetts. Allison was enrolling as a chemistry student, while Randolph planned to specialize in psychology. Their destination was one of the nation's most innovative institutions, founded upon principles then generally known as "the Hopkins idea" after the example of the Johns Hopkins University in Baltimore. Clark itself was established in 1887 (but actually opened its first session in the fall of 1889) as the only university in the country offering courses exclusively at the graduate level. The original endowment was the gift of Jonas Gilman Clark, a native of the Worcester area who went to California as a "forty-niner" and made his fortune in the mining equipment business.

Johns Hopkins had been founded some fifteen years earlier, in the middle 1870s, and led in its early years by Daniel Coit Gilman on the principle that the best teachers were those able to undertake "original researches," that a university was a place dedicated first of all to the "advancement of knowledge."[1] Impressive as Hopkins was in its own right, its example to other universities was equally significant. "By the time Hopkins opened, various other colleges had inaugu-

41

rated nominal graduate work, but none had given the sheer advancement of knowledge so prominent and serious a place in their programs. A bright beacon for cultivated Americans everywhere, the Hopkins idea was the capstone of the movement for educational reform."[2]

The first president of Clark University was G. Stanley Hall, himself a Hopkins man—he'd been professor of psychology and pedagogy there since 1882, and had established the nation's first laboratory for experimental psychology. He also founded the first English-language psychology journal, *The American Journal of Psychology,* in 1889, and while at Hopkins had supervised the graduate study of John Dewey. At Clark, Hall would play a direct role in Vance Randolph's career, serving as his thesis supervisor. In 1947, some twenty years after Hall's death, Randolph would dedicate *Ozark Superstitions,* his first book with a university press imprint, "to the memory of G. Stanley Hall." In a letter written in 1955 Randolph paid tribute to Hall's influence: "I majored with G. Stanley Hall at Clark, and Hall was a psychologist of the old school, steeped in the *Volkpsychologie* of the German universities. Hall was an expert in summarizing or epitomizing the works of others—boiling down a long treatise into two or three paragraphs. I learned a lot from Hall; he showed me how to take a lot of brief items on cards and string them together into a logical or pseudo-logical order so as to make a book."[3]

As Clark University's new head, Hall first undertook a strenuous and ambitious "pedagogic tour" of European universities, visiting more than fifty institutions in nine months of travel, in order to conduct a survey of educational practices "without precedent in the history of education." Returning to Worcester in April, 1889, "with my head full of the loftiest academic ideals," Hall promptly assembled for his five original departments of chemistry, physics, mathematics, biology and psychology a faculty "then nowhere equaled in the country."[4] Albert A. Michelson, who in 1907 won the first Nobel Prize in physics awarded to an American, was appointed head of the physics department, and Franz Boas, then a young scholar of thirty, was hired as docent in anthropology.

The new university's early years had their rocky periods—most especially in 1892 when fiscal worries left Hall's prized faculty vulnerable to shameless raiding by the newly established "Standard-Oil institution" in Chicago. William Rainey Harper, the energetic president at Chicago, hearing of the troubles at Clark, journeyed to Worcester, met with the people he wanted at the home of biology head C. O. Whitman, and "engaged one morning the majority of our staff, his intentions and even his presence being unknown to me." Harper's method, according to Hall's report, was the essence of simplicity. Backed up by $800,000 from John D. Rockefeller's ample coffers, he made offers difficult to refuse. "Those whom we paid $4,000, he gave $7,000; to those we paid $2,000, he offered $4,000, etc., taking even instructors, docents, and fellows." Presented with this *fait accompli* (and indeed asked to join the "hegira" himself), Hall could only threaten appeals to the public and to Rockefeller himself in order to hammer out a compromise by which Clark was able to retain "one or two of the younger men I particularly wanted."[5] The University of Chicago itself, of course, went on to an illustrious future as perhaps the best known of the "Hopkins idea" universities, dedicated to making "the work of investigation primary, the work of giving instruction secondary."[6] But it was Clark University, and the faculty assembled by Hall, that served, in Hall's words, "as a nursery, for most of our faculty were simply transplanted to a richer financial soil."[7]

But there were triumphs, too, in Clark's first years. Perhaps the most spectacular was the twentieth anniversary celebration in 1909 which brought the world's best known psychologists and psychoanalysts to Worcester. Among the notables was Sigmund Freud himself, who made his only trip to the United States to attend the conference and give a series of lectures. Freud himself saw the conference as the "introduction of psychoanalysis into North America," and discussed the event at some length in his "History of the Psychoanalytic Movement."

> In the autumn of 1909, Jung and myself were invited by President Stanley Hall, of Clark University, to take part in the celebration of the twentieth anniversary of the opening of Clark University, by giving some lectures in German. We found, to our great astonishment, that the unprejudiced men of the small but respected pedagogic-philosophical university knew all the psychoanalytic writings and had honored them in their lectures to their students. Thus, even in prudish America one could, at least in academic circles, discuss freely and treat scientifically all those things that are regarded as offensive in life.[8]

The lectures given by Freud at Clark were subsequently expanded and published in English in Hall's *American Journal of Psychology*, and have since served several generations of readers as a highly regarded introduction to the founder's work. In 1971, for example, one general survey of Freud suggests that the "best introduction to Freud's work is provided by Freud himself in the brilliant *Five Lec-*

tures on Psychoanalysis, based on lectures he gave at Clark University, Worcester, Massachesetts."[9]

Hall was himself aware, by the time he wrote his autobiography in 1921, of the importance of the 1909 conference. "Freudian views," he wrote, "from this date developed rapidly, so that in a sense this unique and significant culture movement owed most of its initial momentum in this country to this meeting."[10] By now, of course, Hall's own reputation is based primarily upon this association with Freud, but in his day he was a considerable figure in his own right, one of the country's leading university administrators and pedagogical theoreticians as well as a well-known psychologist. His appreciation for Freud, in fact, was that of an independent investigator, rather than that of a mere disciple or proselytizer. "Hall ended as a very respectful critic [of Freud], but a critic nonetheless."[11] Moreover, for all his mainstream attachments and interest in the professionalization of academic life, he was, like his student from Kansas who would end in the Ozarks, something of a maverick: "Hall began as a theological student, meandered through philosophy and a chain of interests (pursued along the circuit of German universities in the same decade, the seventies, that Freud spent as a student in Vienna) before gravitating into teaching and clinical work in psychiatry. The first generation of psychoanalysts was drawn heavily from among just such maverick intellectuals; they are a type which invariably fills the ranks of a new discipline until it becomes economically respectable.[12]

Randolph's course work at Clark was centered in psychology, of course, but he did take one sociology course and another in philosophy. His record also lists a one-hour course in neurology. "Once a week I was in a class that visited Massachusetts General Hospital [in Boston]. I think it was called Abnormal Psychology—it was taught by Dr. [Edward] Cowles, a Harvard professor."[13] Most of his work was done with Hall, from whom he took courses in psychoanalysis and psychology of Christianity, in addition to a seminar and a one-hour course in education. His thesis, entitled "Some Notes of a Preliminary Study of Dreams," was also completed under Hall's supervision, and was submitted with his recommendation for the M.A. in June, 1915. The thesis consists of five chapters plus a bibliography, and runs to ninety-one typewritten pages. The heart of the work, comprising nearly half of its length, is the fourth chapter, "Sexual Symbolism," in which the young scientist refers several times to his "collections of the complete dream records of several individuals." (Randolph kept records of his own dreams too, following the example of Freud himself, and mentions elsewhere in the thesis the "records of temperature changes during the period covered by my dream records.")[14] The bibliography cites the standard figures from the pioneer era of the psychoanalytic movement—Freud himself, of course, and Jung, Ferenczi, Brill, Abraham, etc.

The thesis is characterized throughout by a tone of common-sense assurance. In the second chapter, "Naive Psychoanalysis," Randolph notes that the "salesman, the poker player, the base-ball pitcher, must be in a greater or lesser degree psychoanalysts," and goes on to conclude that psychoanalysis is "simply accurate and systematic observation." There's a bit of the wise-acre flippancy, too, that would later be so prominent in the Haldeman-Julius booklets on philosophical and religious topics. "Even the selection of one woman from among the many, or of one god from the many, is only fetishism after all; it is the concentration and centralization of affection. But monotheism and monogamy are the criteria of civilization, we are told."[15] Ten years later, in 1925, one Anton S. Booker would publish with Haldeman-Julius a booklet entitled *Freud on Sleep and Sexual Dreams* that consists almost entirely of material from this thesis. Several of the dreams reported by "Booker" are acknowledged as his own in Randolph's thesis.

Randolph also engaged in a bit of "naive psychoanalysis" himself while he was at Clark—he did his first ghost writing there in the form of term papers for undergraduate students (Clark had added undergraduate work in 1902). Randolph would turn these experiences to good account, just as he did with his master's thesis and his trip to Illinois to undergo the Keeley cure for alcoholism in the late 1930s—he wrote about them for money from Haldeman-Julius, and in the process provided a bit of thinly disguised autobiography. According to "Peter Nemo" in *Confessions of a Ghost-Writer,* the success of his first ghost-written term paper was a "turning-point of my life," and it is certainly true that Randolph went on to do a good bit of work in this vein. At Clark he limited himself to term papers and tutoring, but by 1922, at the University of Kansas, he had moved up to ghosting M.A. theses. "Nemo" omits the move to Kansas, keeping himself at the "one-horse college in New England" where he began. The "old newspaper man named MacDougal in a nearby city" who buys features from "Nemo" and prints them over his own name was in fact named A. B. MacDonald, of the *Kansas City Star,* and the "nearby city" was Kansas City, Missouri, close to Lawrence.[16]

Randolph's ghost writing wasn't limited to academic papers. In the middle 1920s, after his last fling with an academic career at the

University of Kansas, he published his first booklets for Haldeman-Julius on scientific topics, and in 1926 returned briefly to New York where he did a number of similar books for Vanguard. During this period, too, he undertook his most ambitious ghost-writing projects. One of these is reported by "Nemo" as the revision of an autobiographical manuscript produced by a writer nicknamed Too-Frantic:

> Too-Frantic's book dealt with the Americanization of an immigrant—all about the difficulties and problems of a "greenhorn" in New York. The book was packed with anecdotes and personal experiences, sincere and vivid. Too-Frantic had written it in his native language and then painstakingly translated it into English. The manuscript ran more than 100,000 words, and Mottke's cousin [an editor] wanted it reduced to about 80,000. Most of all he wanted to put into more readable American English, but in such a way as to preserve the charm of the author's heroic struggle with an alien tongue.[17]

Randolph did the work for $250, according to "Nemo's" account, but "Too-Frantic" was not pleased. "'Oh Lord God Jesus!' he cried in anguish. 'These Yankee have ruined all.'" When the need for a more vernacular style is explained, "Too-Frantic" will not be mollified. "'You make me, who am the artist, talk like I am the barber, the policemen, the base-baller, the loafer, the boom!'" Only when chapters from the book, heretofore returned by magazine editors, begin to find acceptance in their revised form, does "Too-Frantic" begin to see the light. Later, however, he becomes "a very successful writer," and "pretends nowadays that he does not remember me at all."[18]

Another ghost-writing experience is even more bizarre, presenting Randolph, though not his name, as an expert on etiquette. "Nemo" reports this as an editorial assignment that sent Randolph to see a fat woman in "a ramshackle cottage down on Long Island." The lady could not write, and she was "not at all the sort of society woman one reads about," but she was a distant relative of such a woman and did have the same name. She sold the name to the publisher, and the publisher hired Randolph to write the book. It was no easy task, for etiquette was not a subject to which he had applied his best attentions—"I doubt if there was a single literate American in all New York who knew less about etiquette than I." Still, there was $75 a week to be made, and Randolph applied himself gamely to the job:

> It took me nearly two months to grind out the required 60,000 words about etiquette, and it was the most exasperating job I ever tackled. But finally I got it all typed out on legal-size paper with very wide margins, expecting that the "society lady" would need plenty of space for

her corrections and addenda. She kept the manuscript about a week, but made no changes at all, so far as I could see when I read the proof. She told the publisher that it was very good indeed, and even came uptown to autograph books for the customers in one of the big bookstores. I still have the copy she sent me, with a patronizing inscription on the flyleaf.

The story has the obvious ending—the book sold very well, the lady with the famous name made thousands, and Randolph himself, "the poor chump who really wrote the book," got $650.[19]

Randolph's own later recollections stressed the drudgery of ghost writing. "It seemed to me I was getting short-changed," he said, "since I'd done so many books, and such a lot of work, and so many newspaper and magazine stories that my name wasn't connected with at all." Remembering the ghosted newspaper articles for the Kansas City feature writer, he stressed the difficulty of the job. "You got to study the man's work, so there's no sudden break in the style. I had to not only write the damn stories, but I had to imitate old MacDonald, and he had peculiarities of paragraphing and one thing and another." All in all, it was generally unrewarding labor. "It was a lot of work. It sounds easy enough, but it ain't when you get down to it. . . . I hope you don't have to do anything like that to make a living."[20]

The only ethical dimension to the whole enterprise, in Randolph's opinion, was the obligation he felt to keep quiet. In 1975, explaining why ghosted works are omitted from a manuscript bibliography, he noted that "people paid cash for my silence, and I must keep my part of the bargain."[21] Speaking of the ghosted term papers and theses, "Nemo" is equally succinct: "As for the ethical aspect of the thing, I never gave it a thought."[22] And Randolph himself, remembering some speechwriting done for a Republican candidate, stressed that "I didn't let my own convictions about it interfere with my job. I was making a living out of it."[23]

But ghost writing wasn't the only thing that occupied Randolph in New York. He'd come in the first place to see Franz Boas, at Columbia, about doing doctoral work in anthropology. He wanted to do his "field work" in the Ozarks. "I wanted to be an anthropologist, to write popular books on anthropology. But old Boas didn't have no patience with me."[24] "Old Boas" was, of course, the leading figure in the establishment of anthropology as a professional academic discipline in the United States. He'd come to Columbia in 1895, charged with developing a program of anthropological study, and he would stay there as "Papa Franz" to a whole generation of Boas-trained anthropologists and folklorists, until his retirement in 1937. Born in Germany in 1858, Boas's academic training was centered in the natural sciences—he received a doctorate in physics, with a minor in geography, from the University of Kiel in 1881—and his later approach to anthropology "was definitely shaped by a desire to approach culture with the rigor of the physical scientist."[25] He came to the United States in the middle 1880s, and in 1889 was one of G. Stanley Hall's recruits for Clark University's faculty. In 1909 he came to Clark's twentieth anniversary celebration and had his picture taken with Freud and Jung and the other assembled notables, and in 1910 his article, "Psychological Problems in Anthropology," appeared in Hall's *American Journal of Psychology.*

All of this—the basic allegiance to "scientific" rigor, the connection with Clark, the interest in psychological matters—would seem to augur a warm reception for Randolph at Columbia. Boas was interested in folklore too, throughout his career. He corresponded with William Wells Newell, who published the researches of Boas and his students in the *Journal of American Folklore,* as the two men worked together along similar lines in their emergent disciplines. "Newell hoped that anthropological materials would strengthen the scholarly output of the *Journal.* Moreover, his alliance with Boas, and anthropology more generally, placed the weight of Boasian insistence on professional science along German academic lines behind Newell's own efforts to professionalize his fellow folklorists. The relationship of Newell and Boas proved mutually beneficial over a number of years.[26]

Boas himself served as president of the American Folklore Society in 1900, and was succeeded in that office by a long procession of his students. From 1909 through 1924, for example, the only non-Boasian officeholders were H. M. Belden in 1910–11, and John Lomax in 1912. Ruth Benedict, yet another Boas student, edited the *Journal of American Folklore* from 1925 until 1939.

But in spite of such connections, Randolph's proposed study, in the summer of 1915, failed to gain Boas's approval. "He was interested in Indians and Eskimos, and blacks, but I don't care anything about blacks or Indians, and I sure as hell could never go up to study Eskimos. It seemed to me ridiculous. I was interested in white mountain people."[27] Columbia's would-be anthropologist declined the opportunity to apply himself to the then acceptable "primitive" groups, and left for thirty years. In 1947 he'd return with a manuscript, *Ozark Superstitions,* for publication by Columbia University Press. In the 1950s there would be five others.

But in 1915 the doors of academic anthropology were not open to the aspiring ethnographer of "white mountain people." There was little to do but head back to Kansas, where a job peddling insurance could be had, courtesy of Church's connections. But now he had connections in New York, and soon after his return to Kansas he managed to place a poem in the *Masses* that has importance only as his first known publication. It was published without the author's name in the August, 1915, issue, and is surely more significant for its indication of the company Randolph was keeping than for any intrinsic merit:

> "Seek . . ."
>
> "Seek; ye shall find."
> Great God in Heaven! We've sought
> Ten thousand years!
> What have we found? Water and dust,
> And Blood and Tears
>
> "Ask, and receive."
> Almighty God, we've prayed
> Ten thousand years!
> And what received? Water and dust,
> And Blood and Tears.
>
> "Knock; it shall open."
> My God! But we have knocked
> Ten thousand years!
> No answer. Only Water and Dust,
> And Blood and Tears.[28]

The *Masses* began publication in 1911, the brainstorm of a restaurant operator named Piet Vlag, but it didn't achieve its memorable shape until a year later, in 1912, when Max Eastman, freshly fired from Columbia, took over the editorship. From then until the end of 1917, when the magazine ceased publication under pressure of prosecution for its antiwar stands, the *Masses* attracted contributions from the leading radical and reformist writers and artists of the day. "It thrived because of the self-sacrificing devotion of its editors and most immediate contributors centering in Greenwich Village. No one received a single dollar for poems, drawings, articles, or stories. The entire editorial expenses were the twenty-five dollars paid weekly to Eastman, the editor, and twenty dollars to Floyd Dell, the managing editor. John Sloan, the art editor, and his wife, Dolly, the business manager, received nothing, and gave freely from their outside earnings."[29]

Floyd Dell himself, in *Love in Greenwich Village,* provides a good portrait of the whole ambience of the Village in the *Masses* era: "Up on Greenwich Avenue was the office of the *Masses*. It declared itself in its editorial manifesto to be 'a Revolutionary and Not a Reform Magazine; a Magazine with a Sense of Humor and no Respect for the Respectable; Frank; Arrogant; Impertinent; a Magazine whose Final Policy is to Do What It Pleases, and Conciliate Nobody, Not Even Its Readers.' It did not pay for contributions, because it had no money; but it was felt to be a privilege to appear in its pages."[30]

The *Masses* was especially active in support of labor causes, with John Reed and Arturo Giovanitti providing on-the-spot reportage of strikes from Paterson to Colorado, while Art Young and Robert Minor supplied effective cartoons and drawings. Art and politics were drawn close in the heyday of the *Masses,* and Greenwich Village became a crossroads of sorts—"as the *Masses* people went into the labor halls of New Jersey and Colorado, so Bill Haywood, the IWW one-eyed giant, came to Greenwich Village and its studio gatherings."[31] The presence of such notables made the Village a magnet for a diverse collection of writers, artists, revolutionaries, and hangers-on:

> Lesser figures, half-radicals, half-hoboes, drifted into the Village. A new colorful word, Hobohemia, was the result. Floyd Dell wrote a story devoted to the new type in the Village, exclaiming in the title: "Hallelujah, I'm a Bum!" He said of his tramp-hero: "He had discovered in Greenwich Village a kind of tramp he had never known before—the artist kind. These painters, poets, story-writers, were old friends in a new guise. He and they understood one another perfectly." The bum took to modeling in clay and to free love with artist-girls; also to studio parties where he taught the Villagers to sing the Wobbly songs.[32]

Vance Randolph, briefly in 1915 and again in 1926, when he was writing his *ABC* guides on scientific topics for Vanguard Press, was a member of this motley company. He remembered meeting Theodore Dreiser at a party—the great man was "objectionable to everybody, nobody liked him." There was also the famous Joseph Ferdinand Gould, immortalized by Cummings as "little joe gould," mentioned by Pound in the *Cantos,* and remembered by Randolph as "the seagull man" who "flapped his arms and ran around the room crowing like a seagull."[33] Gould was ostensibly at work all his life, compiling his *Oral History of Our Time,* a massive project that was reportedly eleven million words long and stood seven feet high in manuscript form. The *Oral History* remains unpublished, but

Gould is credited with one masterful witticism: "I have delusions of grandeur," he said, with an offhanded irreverence that typifies the whole Village metier at its best. "I believe myself to be Joe Gould."[34]

As "Nemo," Randolph recalled staying at "the old Union Square hotel, on 14th Street," which was "a sort of headquarters for political radicals of one kind and another—Socialists, Syndicalists, Communists, Anarchists, and members of the Industrial Workers of the World, this latter group being popularly known as Wobblies." These folks proved far more interesting than the denizens of Greenwich Village, who more often than not were mere poseurs, writers "who had never published anything at all," and "'poets' who had written nothing but miserable little pamphlets of *vers libre* which they had printed themselves."

> Since the Villagers that I was able to meet did not appeal to me, I began to cultivate the Union Square radicals and found them vastly more interesting. Some of these fellows seemed to be genuine revolutionists, very different from the so-called "radicals" of the Village, and very different also from the "pinks" that I had known at college. Many of the Union Square boys were of foreign descent, and this interested me, because most of my associates up to this time had been old-stock Americans. At the meetings I attended on 14th Street it was not unusual to hear four or five different languages spoken in one evening, to say nothing of half-a-dozen different brands of broken English.[35]

The basic figure—circle, with center poised to circumference—complicates itself in these reflections. There are entities betwixt and between, folks who are not what they seem. The "writers" who did not write, the "so-called 'radicals'"—it was necessary to distinguish these from "genuine revolutionists" and working writers. The man in Borrow's footsteps had encountered phony gypsies, and he was quick to assert his distance. "Some of the Village radicals seemed to think it was very daring to live openly with women to whom they were not legally married. But plenty of people in my home town were satisfied with common-law marriages—even those who raised big families and sent their children to the college. I couldn't see anything startling or romantic about it."[36] If, as an undergraduate back in Pittsburg, he'd scorned the local *Appeal to Reason* in favor of the more "sophisticated" *Masses,* he was ready by the end of 1915 to appreciate Kansas. The Villagers might show off Big Bill Haywood at their studio parties, but back in Kansas Randolph's friend Ralph Church, already a rising insurance mogul who was "infatuated with anarchism" on the side, was on a first-name basis with the IWW leader. "I knew Haywood myself—met him many times—but not intimately. Church knew him well."[37] All in all, the "little up-country college" and "my home town" had come out smelling like a rose in comparison with the Big Apple. Not even Boas could interest him in British Columbia. He was ready to return.

II

Back in Kansas, the life of an insurance salesman soon paled. "The first month I did pretty well, I made about $600," he remembered. "But I found out the next month I couldn't hardly make anything. . . . I realized that I'd sold all my friends, close associates, and I used 'em all up in the first month. Then I had to go out and really sell the damn stuff. . . . I couldn't make a living at it, so I quit that in a few months."[38] By the fall of 1916 the ex-salesman had landed a job teaching biology in the Pittsburg high school, focal point of his childhood fears. The local *Daily Headlight* for September 15 of that year includes his name in a list of teachers assigned to the high school. He'd come full circle, from dropout to youthful scholar. There are people still living in Pittsburg and Frontenac today who were Randolph's students in high school—their reports picture him as a witty, innovative teacher, embarrassed a little by his stutter but interested in his work and his students.

The school board, however, was not impressed. His "irregular" lifestyle was offensive to important people. The last straw, in the spring of 1917, was an "immoral proposition" reportedly offered to a waitress. "She told her father; he told the superintendent," recalled Randolph. "They were mostly Christians and Baptists. I was a Socialist. I gambled too, and I drank too much. They didn't like the way I taught either—I took the students on field trips. We collected a great deal of stuff. I dissected cats, too—another bad thing, according to the school board."[39]

Things quickly went from bad to worse. "They told me the school board was going to investigate my conduct—hold a hearing about me. I didn't much like the idea of this investigation, so I resigned, and went to work for the *Appeal*. I knew I had to go into the Army pretty soon anyway."[40] Randolph's own manuscript bibliography lists his work for the *Appeal to Reason* as "Many signed and unsigned articles and editorials, and practically all the paragraphs [by which Randolph explained that he meant "filler" paragraphs] . . . between July 14, 1917 and October 1, 1917."[41]

The move to the *Appeal* was no sudden immersion in socialist politics. His friend Church knew, in addition to Haywood, "all the socialist big shots in the region. . . . Church was a literary fellow—

he never threw any bombs or anything like that."[42] As a college undergraduate Randolph had, of course, seen copies of the *Appeal* in Pittsburg—the paper in those days had experienced dramatic growth under Fred Warren's direction, doubling its circulation in the years from 1908 to 1912. But Randolph and his friends were not impressed. "We didn't think much of it then," he recalled. "We were young midwesterners, and like most others we tended to look down on the local product. We thought it was lowbrow, and we were more impressed with the New York crowd—with the *Masses*. We thought they were more intellectual and sophisticated."[43]

Randolph's real flirtation with socialism, however, seems to have begun while he was at Clark. "I heard John Reed speak at Harvard. He was a fine fellow."[44] His writing in New York was done for the then socialistic Vanguard Press, which would later issue several of his "crambooks" for students as well as his first two major works in folklore. It was appropriate, then, that his first acknowledged work should be written in Kansas and appear in the *Masses*. "Seek . . .," as Randolph recalled it in 1978, was in fact inspired by the plight of Kansas miners:

> I got pretty worked up when I was a child about the wrongs of the miners. They—the working conditions were something terrible in those days, they really were. They didn't have any union or anything, not a goddamn thing. The operators were—bunch of sons of bitches— men worked ten hours a day for three or four dollars, besides being dangerous as hell, no workmen's compensation or nothing. If a man got killed in the mines his wife would take his old hat and go around the bars collecting money enough to bury him. . . . It was pretty bad. . . .
>
> I spent a great deal of my time out in the camps—I liked the for- eigners better than the 100% Americans that lived in Pittsburg.[45]

In a later reminiscence, this one from 1979, he returned to the same theme more briefly: "I rated higher in Frontenac than I did in Pittsburg."[46]

Back in Pittsburg, Randolph's socialist leanings soon became known and added fuel to the school board's case against him. "I car- ried a Party card in those days," he remembered. "I never did carry a Wobbly card, even though I sympathized with the IWW—most so- cialists did. While I was teaching in the high school some damn fools put me up for the school board on the Socialist ticket. One of the radical papers even listed me, but I told them I wasn't running. There was a little story in the *Headlight*—'Randolph Won't Run' was the head."[47]

Randolph worked for the *Appeal* less than three months, from the

middle of July through the end of September, 1917, but he obviously enjoyed the work and liked to talk about it sixty years later. It
was during this period that Eugene Debs himself called him by his
first name. Sixty years later, speaking from his bed in the nursing
home, Randolph could breathe fire on the subject of Debs. "Oh, he
was awful good, the best of them all, a genial popular fella." Mention
of Debs would stimulate the telling of memorable anecdotes—Debs
running for president of the United States from his Atlanta penitentiary cell in 1920, Debs and Haywood being branded as "undesirable citizens" by Teddy Roosevelt and workers all over the country
responding by wearing badges reading "I Am an Undesirable Citizen." Once off and running in this vein, Randolph could sing old
IWW songs in a boisterous quaver—Archie Green reports that his
interview with Randolph in 1963 was enlivened by a rendition of
"Conditions They Are Bad"—and deliver close paraphrases from
Debs's most famous speeches and writings. "Debs was a violent
fella when he got to talkin', pretty goddamn direct." [48]

Randolph was proud, as long as he lived, of his radical connections. In 1938 he published a piece in *Esquire* about Commonwealth College, a radical labor school located in the rural Ouachita
Mountains near Mena, Arkansas. During his visit to the "campus"
he was invited to speak to a class interested in "proletarian literature." His talk "dealt largely with the practical mechanics of hack
writing," but he did attempt to impress the students by presenting
his own radical credentials. He told them he'd worked for the *Appeal,* "that I knew Gene Debs and Bill Haywood personally, and that
I had met Emma Goldman and John Reed." [49]

In June, 1980, he was still proud, still fond of telling stories about
Ben Reitman and Emma Goldman and Alec Howat and "Jack"
Reed. "I still am pretty radical when I think about it," he said. But
Debs was always the first figure in his remembrances—for Randolph as for a whole generation of workers and radicals, immigrant
and native, Debs was the major man, the leader who ran for president and went to jail, who told them in stirring tones that their
cause was progressive, humane, and just, that he was with them
and of them. "While there is a lower class, I am in it; while there is a
criminal element, I am of it; while there is a soul in prison, I am not
free." When President Wilson denied a recommendation commut-
ing Debs's prison sentence in 1921, the old firebrand was quick to
respond, "It is he, not I, who needs a pardon." [50]

Randolph loved to tell these stories, and it was his brief tenure on
the *Appeal* that gave him his most concentrated acquaintance with

Debs and his fellow socialists. "He was there for weeks at a time. I made a photo of him—Warren was in it too, and one of the Wayland boys."[51] Only two pieces of Randolph's *Appeal* work are signed. One is titled "Proverbs and Poverty" and the other is "The Motives of Men." The former offers a brief glimmer of folkloristic interest, although Randolph's list of aphorisms and epigrams is subordinated to their analysis as instruments of capitalist oppression. "The literature of capitalism portrays poverty in one of two ways: it is either a virtue or a chastisement, either a commendable quality or a merited punishment. . . . The purpose of both is to quiet the worker and make him content with his humble lot, that he may not complain or revolt against the established order."[52]

"The Motives of Men" is more abstract. It contrasts "two great philosophies" on the issue of human motivation. One, "the scientific, practical, rational view of life," is contrasted, greatly to its advantage, with the other, described as "the poetic, abstract and metaphysical view of life." The "scientific" view holds that "man's actions are determined by his physical surroundings," while the "poetic" philosophy would have it that "man's acts are free and independent of his physical surroundings."

Randolph goes on to a speedy dismissal of the "poetic" view, which is characteristic of "ancient thinkers" and "which, of course, lifts the study of sociology from the realm of law into the realm of caprice and chaos." The remainder of the column is devoted to the "scientific" views of "modern" thinkers, especially to two great modern schools, the Freudian and the Marxist. Of these, the latter is said to have a greater number of adherents, and indeed Marx is hailed as "the founder of modern Socialism." In conclusion the reader is urged to consider the "individual capitalist" objectively. "It is of no use to thunder forth scathing denunciations," since the capitalist, like the worker, is "a product of his environment and training." The thing to do, says the youthful editorialist, is to save all your vituperation and all your hatred for the system that has made him what he is—and crush the system!"[53]

III

In October the system came calling, and the socialist editorialist found himself transported to a markedly different milieu. Randolph was inducted into the Army on October 13, 1917, and went for a soldier to Camp Funston, in Kansas, where he was assigned to Company F of the 353rd Infantry. In November he was transferred to Camp Pike, in Arkansas, where he found himself assigned to Battery F of the 334th Field Artillery.

The greater portion of Randolph's military career was spent in the hospital, where he recuperated from a truly dazzling array of maladies. By November 9, according to his medical records, he was undergoing treatment for a hernia. Writing to Ralph Church on November 16, Randolph noted that "Uncle Sam has tacitly admitted, after a month's time, that he cannot make an infantryman out of me. It was a famous victory. I am pretty sick now—I weighs 116 pounds, and can't walk much. If I catch any damn thing I will die sure as hell, and have the whole business done."[54]

His worries about catching something were well founded, since Camp Pike was troubled by outbreaks of spinal meningitis, and Randolph's letters speak repeatedly of being under quarantine. "It was a lot more dangerous in the hospital," he told an interviewer in 1955. "I would have been a hell of a lot safer at the front."[55] But Randolph was spared, though many were not—"Battery F has lost six men from meningitis, and is under quarantine again," says one letter.[56]

Instead, he got mumps, and "orchitis, acute, bilateral," according to the medical records. His own account is more colorful: "Mumps, by God! Port and starboard, above and below. Nuts look like these here Water-Wings." Another letter tells Church a similar story: "Next day I goes out to drill and ruptures meself, and now I have got a lump about as big as a cantaloupe just windward of my prick." The letters and interviews also mention a bout with influenza and a "big fight" in which "I comes out with a nose mashed tremenjous [sic]," but these afflictions are not noted in the medical record.[57]

The end result was an even more decisive victory for Randolph. Uncle Sam, already defeated on the infantry issue, capitulated altogether and awarded him a disability discharge on January 10, 1918. He had just begun to fight too. By 1920, when the Bureau of War Risk Insurance authorized compensation of $8 monthly "during the period in which you are partially disabled," he had initiated the lifelong dance with the Veterans Administration, the Federal Board for Vocational Education, and other federal offices that would gain him untold thousands in disability and rehabilitation compensation, hospital costs, and pensions.[58] For sixty years the dance continued, ending only with his burial in the National Cemetery at Fayetteville, Arkansas, with grave marker and U.S. flag provided, one hopes with a smile, by Uncle Sam, who should have been used to giving by then. No soldier ever gave so little, and got so much in return.

The joke wasn't lost on Randolph either, and he loved to talk about "the days when I answered my country's call." He used to read aloud with glee each round of communications with bureaucrats in various niches of the government, and he celebrated each victory—an increase in his stipend, a wheelchair provided at government expense—with a cackling pleasure in the hilarity of it all that left his listeners gasping and clutching their sides. "Just a handful of soldiers like me," he'd say, "and the damn government would be brought to its knees. Serves the sons of bitches right, too—I wasn't suited for this soldiering business at all. I tried to tell 'em—the first time I went the doctors looked me over and realized that it would be a great mistake to take me into the Army. But they got it messed up somehow, and the second time the doctors said I was OK."[59]

Randolph's time in the Army was not entirely given over to recuperations in the hospital. He also found time to read, play poker, and shoot craps. "Now I just lays in my bunk and reads and eats and shits. I have decided not to do no more drilling. I studies considerable French days, and nights when the boys come in we yarns and shoots craps."[60] He told an interviewer in 1955 that "poker playing was awful good. I took $100 in with me and came out with $700-$800. . . . I never did mind the Army very much."[61]

He also collected some folklore. *Ozark Superstitions,* published in 1947, includes a chapter on beliefs connected with death and burial. His source for at least one such belief came from his days as a soldier: "A falling star is supposed to be somehow connected with the death of a human being; in 1917 I sat one night with a fellow soldier at Camp Pike, Arkansas, and as several stars fell the boy remarked gloomily that he reckoned 'they must be a-killin' fellers right now, over thar.'"[62] Several songs printed in *Ozark Folksongs* are credited to informants at Camp Pike.

His letters from this period—the ones that survive are to Church—display the same rollicking irreverence that will later enliven his Haldeman-Julius booklets on philosophical and religious topics. Writing of his transfer from Camp Funston to Camp Pike, he reports that he has arrived in the company of "about seven hundred of the lame, halt, blind, syphilitic and illiterate of the Famous Sun-Flower Regiment—the Fighting 353rd! Praise Gawd." He does, however, note the presence of "one Patriot. He is a Philippino [*sic*], who came over here to join the Regulars. He says he is 'fighting for liberty and justice, with equality for all.'"[63]

When his discharge came, Randolph evidently returned to Pitts-

burg for a time. "When I gets loose, I runs direct home," says a letter
to Church, "altho I feels for looking into New Orleans."[64] He left
Camp Pike just months before a young pitcher and slugger named
Babe Ruth came in with the Boston Red Sox to entertain the soldiers. "The game was rained out but the storm held off long enough
for the players to take batting practice before a huge crowd of soldiers. Ruth put on a spectacular show by hitting five balls over the
right field fence."[65] If he visited Kansas City before the end of April,
he may have crossed paths with a young *Star* reporter named
Ernest Hemingway.[66] The next three years would see him looking
into a wide variety of spots, New Orleans among them. He was
twenty-five years old, still very much a radical in his political
views—his letters to Church are filled with such questions as
"What vote did Hilquit [sic] poll?" and "How goes the *Appeal?*"—
and he was ready to hit the road.[67] "Hallelujah, I'm a Bum" had
been for many years a staple of the IWW red songbook, and Randolph seems to have done his wandering in accordance with its
guidelines much as young men fifty years later would stick out their
thumbs with visions of Kerouac's Dean Moriarty in their heads. He
fit very nicely with *Solidarity*'s description of the "nomadic worker
of the West," whose "anomalous position, half industrial slave, half
vagabond adventurer, leaves him infinitely less servile than his fellow worker in the East."[68]

By fall he was in California—he told an interviewer in 1955 that
he'd been in San Francisco when the armistice was signed. He
seems first to have stayed in the south, in San Diego or perhaps Los
Angeles. An undated letter to Church mentions "six kinds of hum-
mingbirds here," and also speaks of "dirty pelicans" and ground
squirrels "big as cats" that are used by the natives for "chilli [sic] &
chop suey." He seems to have been sick here too, since the same
letter tells Church about "this here flu." "Last week they figured I
was going to die, and wanted to wire the folks; now they say I am
entirely out of danger. I feel very bad. In a few days, tho, I am going
to get up and go to Frisco, where I know a guy who will get me some
light job on one of them fruit ranches."[69] There's an interview, too,
published in 1936, which has him journeying to California "to work
in the shipyards at Long Beach." This article has him "in a hospital
when the armistice was signed."[70]

No further mention of the fruit ranches has survived, but a letter
dated December 28 from the Park Hotel in San Francisco tells
Church that the writer "washes dishes mostly nowadays." These
letters are filled with news from radical circles—Randolph seems to

have spent much time at the Jack London Memorial Institute, which he describes as "a kind of school and library, modeled after the Rand School." One letter is written on a program of a play put on at this institute by the People's Players. The program is dated December 14, 1918, and the playlist is headed by "The Future: A Tragedy." An earlier letter notes that "I works now in the janitor business. Of evenings me and one of the elevator-girls goes to the Penny Dance. This is quite an achievement, you have no notion of the social chasm that yawns between janitors and elevator operators."

The janitor job didn't last, however, as Randolph notes in the letter written on the People's Players program. "How many a blooming odyssey has been nipped in the bud by some head janitor or other!" he writes, having noted that the loss of this "merry janitor job" has interrupted the writing of his life story. Another letter comments on economic affairs: "Prices is down. You can live here now on five dollars a week—room, board and beer. But you can't get the five! . . . I don't work no more—just sets in the Jack London Memorial."[71]

By February, 1919, he'd journeyed on north and east to Sacramento, where he worked for some time as a gardener at the Ben Ali Country Club. "It was a middle class country club. . . . I had a nice room, hot bath. I ate in the kitchen, good food. I painted some benches and prepared for spring. Raked some lawns. When spring came, I quit."[72] The last surviving letter from the California trip is undated and unplaced, but Randolph thought it might have come from Truckee: "I have beat my way to this god damned village and worked here two days on account I went to Frisco and spent her foolish. Am going to try to make Reno tonight." The same letter says, "I lays to come back pretty soon," and even mentions employment: "I would admire for to git back on the *Appeal*."[73] In 1955 he remembered his trip home. "When I left there [Sacramento], I went to Ogden and Salt Lake. I was 26, just out of the Army. I guess I was pretty young."[74]

By midsummer he was back in Kansas—several songs from *Ozark Folksongs* were apparently collected from July through October—but it wasn't long before he was on the road again. This time he headed east, evidently going first to Memphis and then traveling by boat to New Orleans, where he reportedly "spent two enchanting weeks in the Vieux Carré."[75] From New Orleans he tramped on through Mobile and Pensacola, and by December 27 he was in Tallahassee, Florida. A journal has been preserved that documents his trip from this point until he arrived in Atlanta on January 23, 1920.

The whole trip except for the final two days was spent in Florida, and Randolph's trampings covered a great deal of the state. From Tallahassee he hitched and walked east to Jacksonville, where he stayed a week in a Salvation Army Social Center before heading south all the way to Miami, crossing the state to Tampa on the west coast on the way. Except for the week in Jacksonville and two days in Tampa "answering ads," Randolph kept constantly on the move, hitching rides with salesmen and farmers and eating fruit bummed from packing houses; in one instance "I ate two grapefruit which I had picked up on the road, where they had been jolted out of some passing truck." Walks of fifteen to twenty miles in a day were not uncommon, and one journal entry, for January 19, includes a brief note on the rigors of tramp life: "Have walked thirty miles today, over sandy roads with bad ruts, and I am tired, and my feet are very sore."

The interest in radical politics so prominent in the California letters is absent from the Florida journal—the IWW is mentioned only once—but Randolph continues to identify himself proudly with the life of the hobo on the road. The boy from the town's center had moved to the edge with a vengeance, and there's an obvious pride in the way he displays his knowledge of hobo lore and slang. On the road just north of Miami, for example, he notes that the "east coast road is the best in the state, but is in bad repute with the fraternity because the people who use it are mostly northerners, and won't never give nobody nothin'." Coming into Tampa he notes "a lot of bums along here—practically the first I have seen walking in Florida—I miss the blanket-stiff so common in California at this season." On January 13, headed back north along the east coast road, Randolph is offered a second ride by a couple in a Dodge road-ster and accepts despite his embarrassment—the car isn't really big enough for three—because "they are of mine own people, and the only ones I have met since New Orleans." (The couple are peddling yarn to drygoods stores, and the man has been a hunter "in the Glades.") Throughout the journal there are references to "hitting the gumbo," and a note saying that in Daytona "the dicks were watching us and we had to put in somewhere quickly, so we took a double room at the unheard of figure of one dollar each."

But the most persistent note in the journal, the subject that oc-cupies far more space than celebrations of hobo life or even the ob-servations of folkways which will later make Randolph famous, has to do with the plants and animals he sees, the changes in the char-acter of the landscape. "About eight miles out of Okeechobie I saw my first bald eagle," he writes, adding that "he did not appear larger than a buzzard—bronze, with white head, neck and tail. I sat on a palmetto log and watched him for a long time." Another time, near Fort Pierce, he "saw a butterfly that fairly took my breath away— brilliant metallic blue it was, with flashes of orange from the inner margins of the hind wings—which I later identified as *Eumaeus atala*." An especially spectacular bird or tree or snake could set the tone for an entire day, as happened once when Randolph lost his temper when "a silly ass barber shaved my neck." He left town "in a very bad humor, but about five miles out something happened which quite set me up again. I saw the famous Florida Jay (*Aphelocoma cyania*), which is peculiar to this part of Florida and is found nowhere else in the world."[76]

This is Randolph the young biological scientist, the high school teacher who struggled with his stammer and took his students on field trips, the M.A. in psychology trained in the behavioristic school of John B. Watson. Randolph's interest in entomology was strong enough to induce him to prepare and publish academic papers on butterflies—two articles appeared in the *Transactions of the Kansas Academy of Science* and one came out later (in 1929) in *Entomological News*. His popular writing on scientific topics was much more extensive, and continued throughout the 1920s. His work for Haldeman-Julius began in 1924 with Little Blue Books on scientific, philosophical, and religious topics. His first scientific titles included *Physiology Self Taught* and *Life Among the Bees*. But 1925 would be his biggest year with scientific booklets—he turned out ten titles for Haldeman-Julius, mostly on psychology (among these was *Freud on Sleep and Sexual Dreams*, his Clark master's thesis very slightly reworked) and entomology. *Life among the. . .*booklets on ants, butterflies, and dragonflies formed a part of this output. The year also saw publication of the first in the series of *ABC* student crambooks Randolph did for Vanguard Press in New York—it was *The ABC of Chemistry,* for which he adopted the pseudonym of Newell R. Tripp. Other *ABC* books followed in 1926 (on evolution) and 1927 (on biology, physiology, psychology, and geology).[77]

The hobo, then, who tramped the roads of Florida in December, 1919, and January, 1920, was a member of yet another great outlaw tradition. His political radicalism was on the wane—his *ABC of Geology* would include a brief glimpse of its author's views when it noted that the defrauding of the populace by geologists trained at state universities is "due not to any defect in the science of geology, but to the antiquated and vicious organization of society under which we labor at present," but such glimpses would be increasingly rare in Randolph's work.[78] His days on the *Appeal* and his flirtation with candidacy for public office on the Socialist ticket were over, but he was as enthusiastic as ever in his intellectual radicalism. In *The ABC of Physiology* he apologizes to the reader for utilizing "the teleological jargon of the vitalists," and makes his own position clear: "No one believes more firmly than I in the complete physico-chemical nature of all human behavior."[79]

The models for this tradition are no longer Debs or Mother Jones or Joe Hill or Frank Little, the IWW organizer whose lynching at Butte, Montana, Randolph remembered writing about for the *Appeal*. The heroes now are Spinoza and Kepler, Galileo and Copernicus, Bruno and Locke, the masters of thought who stand to the intellectual status quo as Debs and Frank Little to the economic status quo.

Like the union organizer and political radical, then, the scholar will be a figure of the margin, a gypsy. That Randolph viewed him in this way is clear from his earliest Haldeman-Julius booklets, where nearly every figure discussed finds himself at some point in danger, threatened with persecution and/or death at the hands of his neighbors. Heraclitus, for example, to start near the beginning, "was not regarded with favor by his fellow-townsmen," and Anaxagoras, "because of his friendship with the radicals and his outspoken contempt for the official religion, . . . was driven out of the city at the beginning of the Peloponnesian war." The case of Socrates is more famous—Randolph says that his method "was said to be dangerous to both religion and government, and Socrates himself was accused of a great variety of moral delinquencies."[80]

The theme of exile, as in the instance of Anaxagoras, the frequency with which scholars and scientists are literally forced to "hit the road," is often stressed in Randolph's accounts. Spinoza, for example, is described in such terms: "The Jews expelled him from the Synagogue, the Catholics put his works on the Index, and he was finally driven out of his native Amsterdam." Here is Randolph on the tribulations of John Locke: "Because of his liberal views in religion and politics he was expelled from the university and persecuted by the authorities until he fled to Holland."[81]

It was as a scientist, then, that Randolph tramped through Florida writing in his journal, a scientist whose singular understanding of his enterprise prepared him well for its rigors—for its lack of financial reward and its long failure to gain him honor in his own country. The scientific habit of mind as Randolph understood it, with its emphasis upon careful observation and systematic record-keeping, would characterize his own approach to documenting the folk traditions of the Ozarks. As late as 1936, with his reputation as an authority on Ozark life already established by his first two book-length studies, he was identifying himself to interviewers as "primarily a scientist."[82]

One tenet of scientific method as it was understood by Randolph may have been especially significant in its effect upon his ethnographic fieldwork. During his years as a graduate student in psychology, both at Clark and later at the University of Kansas, he was a devoted admirer of "the modern doctrine of behaviorism," which is synonymous with "objective, scientific methods" in this field, and is credited to Dr. John B. Watson. According to "Newell R. Tripp," whose *Behaviorism: The Newest Psychology* is first and foremost a sympathetic presentation of Watson's position, behaviorism, "while it is intensely interested in all of the functioning of these parts, is intrinsically interested in what the whole animal will do from morning to night and from night to morning."[83]

Fifty years later, assessing Randolph's own contribution to folk-lore studies, Herbert Halpert calls him "one of our earliest recorders of a complete folk tradition. With the development of interest in the context of folk genres, in function and performance, we recognize that Vance Randolph led the way."[84] His "animal" was the old-time Ozark "residenter" and his descendants, and he interested himself in what the "whole animal" did, from morning to night and night to morning. The patience and persistence he would display in his long career of collecting folklore in the Ozarks were already evident in the meticulous dream records he kept for his thesis work at Clark or in his early work with butterflies. After all, his first entomological paper refers to "six consecutive seasons of collecting,"[85] and his second, "A Preliminary Study of the Life History and Habits of Dione Vanillae Linn.," provides an astonishingly detailed record of his work. For example:

> The egg measures about 1.2 mm in height and .7 mm in diameter at the widest part, barrel-shaped, with fourteen vertical ribs. A brilliant yellow at first, it assumes after about thirty-six hours a reddish-brown color. A few hours later an irregular, whitish broken ring, not quite circling the egg, appears about one-third of the distance from the top. When within an hour or so of hatching the shell becomes very thin and transparent and reflects the light with a sort of frosted-glass effect. The large black head of the larva inside gives the upper one-third of the egg a black, metallic appearance, while the yellowish body may be

seen curled up in the lower part. The incubation period seems to vary
greatly with the temperature, from forty-seven hours (August 7, 1917)
to seven days (September 22, 1918).

And so on, for some ten pages. Randolph's commitment to his task
knew no limits either, as when he mentions tasting specimens of
both sexes of butterfly, "crushing the bodies between the teeth and
holding them in the mouth for some time." His own impressions of
the taste are reported—it was reminiscent of "the taste of the seeds
of the common sticktight (*Bidens frondosa*)"—but he regrets that
he is "unable as yet to check these results against the experience of
others, my available observers having refused their services."[86]
    A man willing to stand around with butterflies in his mouth "for
some time" is not likely to be deterred by "fox-fire lights" either, so
it's not really surprising to hear Randolph's account of his experience in "a little buryin' ground on Highway 123, between Spokane
and Walnut Shade, in Taney County, Missouri." He'd been told of a
"bluish light" that appeared among the gravestones and then slowly
crossed the road, moving at about the pace of a man walking. "After
listening to these tales I went to this graveyard myself and waited in
the dark for hours on three consecutive nights but saw nothing out
of the ordinary."[87]
    By early 1920, then, as Randolph hitched into Atlanta and pre-
pared to head back to Kansas, he was ready for the work that would
occupy the rest of his days. He had all the tools—the observational
skills of the scientist, the resourcefulness of the hobo, and the re-
portorial gifts of the writer. He'd been to the Ozarks before, of
course—that vacation visit to Noel, Missouri, with his family in
1899 had been his introduction to the region—but now he was
ready to stay awhile. Before the year was out he'd buy a cabin and
ninety-seven beehives near Pineville, Missouri, from an old man
named Ed Wall. He'd soon get rid of the beehives, but Pineville and
the nearby town of Galena would be home to him, except for brief
visits to Pittsburg and not much longer sojourns in Hollywood, New
York, and the University of Kansas at Lawrence, for twenty-five
years. Ed Wall would tell him stories. The future Mr. Ozark was
about to hang out his shingle.

PART TWO

Who Will Recognize Them?

Who will recognize them? None but you.
To the rest without definition but to you
each a thing in itself, delicate, pregnant
with sudden meanings.

—William Carlos Williams
In the American Grain

4

Getting Started

The only house I ever loved was a shanty of rough
oak boards, perched on a little hill overlooking the
Big Sugar Valley. . . The roof leaked, the chimney
smoked, the doors rattled, the floor sagged. But it
was the only building that ever really pleased me,
the only house in which I ever felt at home.

—Vance Randolph, "To Hell with Honey"

I

Pineville when Randolph lived there in the 1920s was a town of just
over 400. It was what was then called an "inland town"—it had no
railroad service. It must have been, for a man just returned from
New York, San Francisco, New Orleans, and other such metro-
politan spots, an isolated place. "The nearest good bar," he wrote, "is
in the Connor Hotel at Joplin, thirty-eight miles as the crow flies."[1]

But he didn't arrive as a stranger. Noel, Missouri, after all, was
right down the road from Pineville, and Noel was the home of the
O-Joe Club, where Randolph had vacationed in 1899 with his parents on the trip that introduced him to the Ozarks. He'd wandered
all over the area with Vernon Allison in the summers before they left
Kansas for Clark University, too, and Joplin is cited in *Ozark Folksongs* for songs heard as early as 1909. He reports hearing "The
Hell-Bound Train" from a man in Joplin on September 5, 1911, and
adds that several months later "I heard the same song shouted in a
revivalist's tent near Seligman, Mo."[2]

In *Ozark Superstitions* Randolph says he "first came to Pineville,
Missouri, in 1919,"[3] and in August of that year, before leaving on his
Florida trip, he collected three songs in Pineville from Mrs. Marie
Wilbur. Eleven years later he would marry her, and her name would
appear again and again as the source of songs and stories in *Ozark
Folksongs* and the various folktale collections. As for Ed Wall, the
old resident who sold Randolph the cabin and beehives—the deed,

dated December 28, 1920, says that the one-acre property was sold for $300—he'd be remembered in a short piece called "To Hell With Honey," published in 1943 as a part of *Wild Stories From the Ozarks*, one of Randolph's booklets for Haldeman-Julius. Wall is described there as "an old bachelor with a formidable crop of ginger-colored whiskers," whose "shanty of rough oak boards, perched on a little hill overlooking Big Sugar valley" was the "only house I ever loved."[4] Wall seems not to have given Randolph any songs, but he is cited repeatedly in the folktale collections, and is remembered by name in the introduction to *Who Blowed Up The Church House?* "I shall never forget Ed Wall, the trapper who said seriously that 'a half-growed otter has got more sense than any man in Pineville.'"[5] Wall is pictured, though not identified, on the frontispiece of *The Ozarks* (1931), Randolph's first book on the region.

By the late spring of 1920, then, Randolph seems to have returned to Pittsburg from his East Coast wanderings—he was apparently in St. Louis on February 23—and evidently spent much of his time over in the Ozarks. There are song citations from May, June, and July, a three-month break in the late summer and fall, and then more citations for November and December. But more powerful than these dates are Randolph's own remembrances—the retrospective judgment that selects 1920 as the watershed year, with "all the value of my life" following it and "a wandering life" preceding it is one—which invariably focus affirmatively on the move to Pineville and understand the significant work of his life as originating in that decision.[6] The "To Hell with Honey" article is the major source here, for the ordering of life into legend is already apparent. Wall's cabin was "the only house in which I ever felt at home," and the three years in residence there were "the happiest days of my youth."[7]

In towns the size of Pineville and, later, Galena, Missouri, some forty miles east in Stone County, "news" is whatever your neighbors are doing. In the 1920s and 1930s every little country town had at least one and quite often two weekly newspapers, one for Democrats and one for Republicans. Thumbing through the pages of the *Pineville Democrat* (or the *Herald*) or the *Stone County News-Oracle*, one is frequently rewarded with such gems of information as "Mrs. Vance Randolph entertained two tables of bridge Friday afternoon in her apartment at the Mathes home."[8] Or: "Vance Randolph and M. V. Lamberson spent Tuesday and Wednesday in Pittsburg, Kansas."[9] One of the earliest notices involving Randolph concerns his purchase of Ed Wall's cabin: "Vance Randolph of Pittsburg, Kansas, bought the Ed Wall farm east of town Wednesday.

Consideration $900. Mr. Randolph contemplates building several bungalows before summer for rent to tourists." [10]

The plans for the bungalows never got off the ground, but Randolph's purchase did have ramifications beyond his meeting with Ed Wall and settling into life as an Ozark resident. He had the place surveyed as a part of his purchase, and this in turn introduced him to Jay L. B. Taylor, a man of many interests who would soon be involved with Randolph in an adventure that would bring several of the nation's most distinguished scholars hurrying to Pineville. This is, of course, the "Pineville Mastodon" story, related by Randolph in an article published some fifty-five years after the fact. The whole episode begins with Randolph and Taylor falling into conversation while Taylor is engaged in surveying the Wall farm (not a huge task, since the deed describes the land as consisting of "one acre, more or less"). Taylor was interested in Indian relics, and had dug up numerous "bones and stone implements" in Jacob's Cavern, a "V-shaped shelter" extending back about fifty feet from an opening approximately seventy-five feet wide. He invited Randolph to visit. [11]

On April 17, 1921, Randolph got out to Taylor's place, and the two men hiked down to the cavern. What followed is reported by Randolph in some detail:

> We had no tools for digging, but I began to scratch about with a stick near the northeast wall of the cavern. Taylor followed my example, and soon turned up a mussel-shell with two round holes in it. A few minutes later, fumbling in a wet spot under a roof-drip, I unearthed a piece of bone about four inches long. Like Jaybird's mussel-shell, this bone had two round holes drilled through it, and several deeply cut lines. Taylor sat down beside me, and we clawed with our fingers in the ice-cold mud and water till we had together eight of these pierced bones. The biggest one was the leg-bone of a deer, and bore an engraved figure which looked rather like an elephant. [12]

It was this last bone, of course, that caused all the furor. In fact, it was soon the only one left, for "three weeks after the discovery Taylor told me that seven of the eight bones had completely disintegrated." Randolph had made drawings of the entire lot on the evening of the discovery day—the drawings, retouched "so clumsily there was little resemblance to the originals," were later published in the December, 1921, issue of *Natural History*—but now the two men took steps to preserve the last bone. Taylor first coated it with linseed oil, but then Randolph, acting on advice from "Dr. Vernon C. Allison, of Pittsburgh, Pa.," decided to immerse it in melted paraffin. [13]

Thus protected, the bone sat on a rafter in Taylor's cabin until August, when Dr. Clark Wissler, curator of anthropology at the American Museum of Natural History came out to look at it. With him was "Dr. Vernon C. Allison, representing the Carnegie Museum at Pittsburgh," who was, of course, Randolph's old friend from Kansas and Clark University.[14] Wissler told Randolph and Taylor that the bone was of extraordinary interest to scholars—nobody knew, he told them, whether mastodons and men had lived at the same time in the New World. Wissler and Allison visited the cavern, did some digging of their own without notable result, and soon left town. The bone was eventually sent to Wissler for study at the American Museum, but not before a number of amateur archeologists came to Pineville to see the bone for themselves. One of these, a Dr. Charles Hunter, a Kansas physician, was certain that the bone was being viewed upside down by the experts. It was, he announced, a representation of four men in a boat, very probably Noah and his three sons.

After the initial flurry of excitement there was little activity until September, 1923, when the American Museum sent N. C. Nelson, Associate Curator of Archeology, to investigate. Nelson spent some three weeks at Jacob's Cavern, digging a trench from the rear wall of the cavern to the floor of the valley below, but the results were discouraging. "By way of results we found in the talus slope trench— down to an extreme depth of three meters below the surface—both well finished artifacts and skeletal material. In the trench inside the cave . . . we found nothing."[15] Things were looking bad for the Pineville Mastodon by now, and Taylor and Randolph were suspected as "a couple of fakers."[16] In December, 1923, at the meeting of the American Anthropological Association, Nelson gave it out as his considered opinion that the engraving was "a plain fraud," and Wissler, writing directly to Randolph on February 7, 1924, said that "some reasons for doubting its antiquity have been found."[17]

The whole matter might have died right there but for the interest of Randolph's old friend Allison, who subjected both the bone and a stalagmite (removed from the cave and shipped back to Pittsburgh for analysis) to exhaustive scrutiny and ended up convinced of the bone's antiquity. "It was a huge chunk of rock," Randolph remembered, "maybe weighed 1500 pounds. Lugging it out took four or five men most of a day."[18] Allison published his results in scientific form in 1926, in a forty-two page monograph, *The Antiquity of the Deposits in Jacob's Cavern*, issued by the American Museum of Natural History. Allison also collaborated with Randolph on a popular treatment, published on March 14, 1926, in the *New York Times Magazine* under the breezily confident title, "Ancient Man Is Traced in the Ozarks." The academy had little further interest in the matter though Nelson reviewed Allison's monograph in *American Anthropologist*, reaffirming his conviction that the bone was a fraud. Randolph did mention the "so-called Taylor-Randolph Mastodon" in his *The ABC of Biology*, published by Vanguard in 1927, and he discussed the whole episode in detail in his popular magazine article, "The Pineville Mastodon," which appeared in 1977 in The *Ozark Mountaineer*.[19]

But back in 1921, when the whole adventure was just beginning, with Wissler just departed and the bone on its way to New York, Randolph was preparing to leave Pineville for a while. He'd be back in time for Nelson's excavations in 1923, but in the meantime he would take his last sustained fling at the academic world, enrolling in the fall of 1921 at the University of Kansas as a doctoral candidate in psychology.[20] While there, he would learn again, and more definitively, that his work was back in Pineville.

II

Randolph's studies at the University of Kansas were, if anything, more rigorously "scientific" than his work at Clark. He enrolled in and completed a variety of courses in psychology (plus one each in anthropology and philosophy) during his two-year stint as a doctoral candidate, but his work focused on the study of learning processes in both animals and men. He did most of his work under the direction of Professor Walter S. Hunter—twenty-two of his forty hours—including the study of maze learning in Angora goats which was to serve as his thesis. Hunter, like Randolph's earlier mentor, G. Stanley Hall, was a considerable figure in academic circles. Himself a graduate of the University of Chicago, Hunter in the early 1920s was in the middle of a career that would take him to Clark in 1925 as G. Stanley Hall Professor of Genetic Psychology. He'd come to Kansas from his first teaching position at the University of Texas in 1916 and stayed until 1925, when he accepted the position at Clark. In 1936 he moved on to Brown University, where he directed the psychology laboratories until his death in 1954.

Hunter was also similar to Hall in that he was a prolific writer—he wrote a *General Psychology* textbook that went through two revisions and stayed in print for over ten years after its original publication in 1919, and he served as an editor for a number of academic

journals.[21] Two of Randolph's published pieces came out of his work
with Hunter at Kansas. The first, "Further Studies on the Reliability
of the Maze with Rats and Humans," was published in the *Journal
of Comparative Psychology* (where Hunter was an associate editor)
in 1924, with Hunter as senior author. This piece, as one in a series
of articles and monographs done during this period by Hunter and
his students, was concerned primarily with matters of method, with
the calibration of the instruments of laboratory work in psychology.
The goal, clearly stated in several places, was a more rigorously con-
trolled, scientific experimental environment. Specifically, Hunter
and Randolph were interested in "the dependability of maze data"
as a procedure for "studying the learning process."[22] The second
paper, "A Note on the Reliability of the Maze As a Method of Learning in the Angora Goat," appeared in 1926 in the *Pedagogical Semi-
nary and Journal of Genetic Psychology* with Randolph as senior
author. As the title indicates, it too is concerned with the dependability of maze experiments. The results of these and the other related papers were generally negative—the data generated by maze
experiments as currently conducted were judged not of sufficient
reliability to justify their use in quantitative studies. As Hunter himself made clear in a later article, the primary purpose of the whole
series of experiments was the raising of a question "sufficiently fundamental to warrant the expenditure of much effort in its proper
solution":

> If the present methods of training animals in the maze give data of low
> reliability, better methods should be promptly devised. If methods can-
> not be devised which will give results of a satisfactory reliability, the
> maze should be discontinued as a method of studying the problems
> affected. The primary principle is this: Students of behavior must cali-
> brate their instruments before using sets of measurements for quan-
> titative purposes. It is important to know just how gross the error of
> measurement is in studies of learning with the maze and with prob-
> lem boxes. No physicist would think of conducting experiments to
> find quantitative differences between groups of measurements with-
> out first carefully checking both his instruments and his materials.[23]

The reference to the "physicist" makes clear the basic milieu of
this work—Randolph is still a "scientist," just as he was when he
studied butterflies under Dellinger's supervision in Pittsburg, or recorded his dreams for Hall at Clark. But he was getting tired of rats
and mazes and Angora goats, although he continued to write about
psychology for Haldeman-Julius and for Vanguard. He wrote to
Church from New York in 1926 in high spirits over his successes

there: "If I can get Watson to write an introduction to my *Psychology* I'm a made man, and I verily believe I shall do it."[24]

Watson didn't and Randolph wasn't, and by that time he'd long since left the University of Kansas. "I just got tired of the whole business," he told two interviewers in 1977. "I could not stand any more of university so I just walked out of there."[25] There would be times when he would wish he'd finished, and settled into a comfortable academic career. There would even be times when he'd toy with the idea of returning—as late as the early 1950s, he was apparently taken with the idea of "going back to school"—and times when he would encourage in others the assumption that he had finished.[26] References to "Professor Randolph" and "Doctor Randolph" are not hard to find in Missouri newspapers, and even in more prominent publications, especially during the late 1920s and 1930s.[27] The three booklets on philosophical subjects issued by Haldeman-Julius in 1924—*Ancient Philosophers, Religious Philosophers*, and *Modern Philosophers*—have "University of Kansas" imprinted on the covers under Randolph's name, while the 1925 opus, *Zoology Self Taught*, has the name followed by an imposing array of academic credentials ("A.B., B.Sc., A.M.").

But the simple truth in 1923 was that Randolph was anxious to get back to work in Pineville. His most important experiences at the University of Kansas had been extracurricular. His first semester, in fact, had been greatly enlivened by a campus appearance of Vachel Lindsay, the then well-known American poet and "apostle of the gospel of beauty." Lindsay came to Lawrence early in December and addressed an all-university convocation. "College Yells Hope of Poetry—Lindsay" headlined the student paper's story, which explained that Lindsay had requested a performance of Kansas's famous "Rock Chalk" yell from the assembled students and, after hearing it, delivered the astounding opinion that "'The college yells of America are the nearest thing to American poetry that I ever have heard. . . . The hope of American letters and poetry is in the yell writer.'"[28]

Randolph was present at this convocation, and his reaction, especially in its conscious difference from the "student body," testifies again to his fundamental sense of himself as one apart. He identified more with Lindsay than with his fellow students:

> Vachel Lindsay was at convocation today. He wanted to hear the Rock Chalk yell, and they sure gave it to him. Then he reminisced a little about the time he came through Kansas begging, and preaching the Gospel of Beauty. Then he read us "The Santa Fe Trail" and "The

Congo." These readings seemed to tickle the student body so much
that it shook with laughter—*at* Lindsay—but they impressed me tre-
mendously. He sings—a kind of chant—like nothing on God's earth
that I have ever heard. He tramps about, throwing his head way back,
shutting his eyes, waving his arms, stamping his feet. . . .

    I don't know whether it is poetry or not—but I wish to God I could
hear some more of it.[29]

Impressed as Randolph was by Lindsay, the best was still to come.
In the spring of 1922 the campus was visited by Carl Sandburg,
who gave a program that combined a "lecturette" on new and old
poetry with readings from his own works and a performance of selected folksongs. The campus newspaper gave front page coverage
to the program, calling Sandburg an "outstanding poet of the twentieth century." The singing segment of the evening came in for special notice: "The third section of Mr. Sandburg's program was a
group of American folk songs, sung in an inimitable soft, drawling
voice that brought storms of applause." Several songs were reported
by name, including "the 'Frankie and Albert' song, a classic from
the gutters."[30]

Randolph attended Sandburg's program too, but he also managed
to meet the poet/singer and talk with him at some length. According
to Mary Parler Randolph, Sandburg "stayed at the K.U. frat that
hired Vance as a tutor for their members. Vance met Sandburg
there, and they got drunk together, I think."[31] Randolph's own recollections (with a tape recorder present that may have restrained his
embroidery—"In my old age I've turned name-dropper," he laughed
in another context. "I like to talk about the big shots that I have met
or known.")[32] are less specific:

    I met Sandburg and got acquainted with him at K.U.—Kansas Uni-
versity. . . . Sandburg came up there—he had a pretty girl with him
and he was playing a guitar and singing folksongs and old songs. . . .
He had several lectures—he lectured once on "Frankie and Johnny,"
and he sang a very dirty version of it with great lip-smacking enjoyment. He was a very poor singer and he was not a good guitarist either,
but the whole thing went over fine. He had a great effect, somehow;
he had personality. He was a very smart fellow.
    He was delayed there for some time, and I met him at several parties
around and talked with him. He got me interested in folksongs, and I
went to the library, looked at Child, read Percy and Scott. . . .[33]

Sandburg, of course, was an active folk song collector in his own
right, publishing an *American Songbag* in 1927 and a *New American Songbag* in 1950. The latter volume is of particular interest for

its extravagant praise of Randolph's own work—"Vance Randolph has done for Arkansas what Richard Burton has done for Arab lore and culture in seventeen volumes."[34] Sandburg's own work has been judged harshly by academicians—he seems most noted now for the bad influence he may have had on the Lomaxes, his own "cute" classification scheme being suspected responsible for the similar organization of their *American Ballads and Folk Songs*, published in 1934. D. K. Wilgus includes Sandburg's collections in a fifth category (after academic collections, running-comment collections, random-text collections, and singing books) that he calls "the portmanteau, a sort of valise stuffed with all sorts of goodies, often chosen with the tastes of a large public in mind." Bad business for sure. A man has the tastes of a large public in mind and you can be certain he's an impure fellow. What's more, "collections of this type either select their contents from other publications or are on other grounds not worthy of serious consideration."[35] Poor Sandburg! Sympathy rises up, after digesting these sniffy dismissals, to point out that if Sandburg led innocent folklorists astray with his classifications, his example also led Vance Randolph back to Pineville, where a long life's work awaited him. Randolph found in Sandburg (and in Lindsay) a romantic nativism he could respond to positively, even as his scientific background would focus its energies and his radical sympathies would halt its enthusiasm short of jingoism or xenophobia. It's pertinent, too, to remember that Sandburg was generous in his remarks about academic workers—the "Foreword" to the *New American Songbag* for example, praises the American Folklore Society by name, and applauds the work of such collectors as R. W. Gordon, Zora Neale Hurston, George Pullen Jackson, and Helen Hartness Flanders. W. K. McNeil's assessment, while as hard on Sandburg as any—his collections are judged "virtually useless as scholarly tools"—has the merit of focusing attention on his positive role: "his influence on Vance constitutes his major contribution to the field."[36]

That influence was cited in print by Randolph ten years later in *Ozark Mountain Folks*:

> While "settin' purty" in this comfortable seat of learning [the University of Kansas] I devoted some time to the literature of folksongs, examined the collections which Kittredge, Pound, Cox, Smith, Davis and others have made in various parts of the United States, and listened to some university professors who talked most impressively of balladry in general. I met Carl Sandburg, too, and heard the inimitable Margaret Larkin sing her songs of the great Southwest, to a skilled guitar ac-

companiment. All of these experiences combined to kindle my enthusiasm for the old songs, and I determined that when and if I returned to the Ozarks I should devote a large part of my leisure to ballad-hunting.[37]

There were other factors too, in addition to the inspiration of Sandburg, which encouraged the return to Missouri. He'd been spending considerable time down in the Ozarks anyway—in fact, the "lab work" on the Angora goat study was done near Pineville—and he was also busy with his ghost writing in Lawrence and Kansas City. Finally, in the spring of 1923, word came from the Federal Board for Vocational Education that he would be considered "rehabilitated" at the close of "the present school year," and would no longer be eligible for financial assistance.[38] He was, to sum it up, sick of school, short of money, and eager to collect folksongs. It was time to go back to Pineville.

III

The first fruits of Randolph's researches into the traditional lifeways of the Ozark mountain people appeared as articles in scholarly journals in the mid-1920s. He cast his net widely from the beginning, interesting himself in nearly everything said, done, made, or believed by his new neighbors. In *Ozark Superstitions*, published twenty years later, he gave a brief description of his collecting methods: "I carried scraps of newsprint in my pocket, and along with locals for the paper I recorded other things that interested me—folksongs, tall tales, backwoods jokes, riddles, party games, dialect, old customs, and superstitions. This stuff was later typed on cards and placed in a trunk which I had converted into a filing cabinet, indexed and classified so that I could put my finger on any given item at a moment's notice."[39]

Randolph's first article in the *Journal of American Folklore*, published early in 1927, dealt with folk beliefs. Beginning in February of the same year he produced a weekly folksong column in the *Pineville Democrat*. Twenty years later he would publish major studies in both fields, but in the 1920s and 1930s he first established his reputation in another area.

"I started in dialect studies, really. Louise Pound was at Nebraska then—I went to see her—and Percy Long at Harvard was editor of *Dialect Notes*. I corresponded with him. Pound encouraged my work. She even came down to Pineville once. You could say I was interested in dialect first, then in songs."[40] From 1926 to 1936 Randolph contributed, by himself and in collaboration with various co-authors, some sixteen articles to *Dialect Notes and American Speech*. Before long the contributors notes section of the latter journal was taking his reputation for granted: "Vance Randolph is well known to our readers through his papers on the Ozark dialect."[41] By 1936 no less a figure than H. L. Mencken, in the fourth edition of *The American Language*, was writing that the dialect of the Ozarks "has been the special province of Vance Randolph."[42] It should be remembered, too, that this work was begun while Randolph continued to produce the Haldeman-Julius booklets and crambooks for Vanguard that paid his bills. He was also, in the late 1920s, writing articles for hunting and fishing magazines. Nothing in Randolph's earlier background—except his attachment to George Borrow—would suggest any inclination toward languages or linguistic study. (There are perhaps hints in the love of tramp argot in the letters to Church from California, the snippets of German in other letters, and in the mention of studying French in the Army hospital.) His transcript from the State Manual Training School at Pittsburg shows not a single course in any foreign language. In 1926 and 1927, at the same time he was doing the dialect studies, he did include several language booklets in his work for Haldeman-Julius, and in one of these, *German Self Taught*, he expresses contempt for traditional pedagogy. "American students of the sciences," he writes, and it is clear from his own academic background that he writes as one such student, "long ago discovered a more economical system of language study than the one used in the regular college classes."[43]

Still, Randolph was throughout his life a man interested in languages. He "studied" Yiddish on and off for many years, sprinkled his letters with German phrases, and collected little aphorisms and witticisms in a wide variety of languages. Growing up as he did in a region of striking ethnic diversity, Randolph heard many different languages as a part of everyday life. He remembered his father giving speeches to miners that included little tags from their native tongues, and he mentioned in passing once that he was called "Boali" as a nickname by Lebanese and Syrian friends." Often, visiting him, one would be asked to translate things like *Nunc scripsi totum/da mihi potum/pro Christi* both as a test of one's own skills and an occasion for the display of Randolph's. He had, moreover, a deep and abiding interest in the argot of hoboes, tramps, thieves, and other groups whose marginality made them exotic and therefore eligible for celebration. Reviewing George Milburn's _The Hobo's Hornbook_ in 1931, Randolph assured his readers in magisterial tone concerning the accuracy of Milburn's work: "The glossary of hobo terms is adequate and authentic—a pleasant contrast to the errors of such writers as Vernon W. Saul (K. C. Smith) who once told us . . . that a _mush fakir_ is 'one who sits by another's fire and gathers no wood'!"[44]

The overall impression, then, is of a genuine if unsystematic interest in and appreciation for languages, especially for the slangs, argots, and dialects of "outlaw" groups which could be romanticized. Self-conscious doubts about his lack of formal training in foreign languages resulted in too forcibly phrased denunciations of traditional pedagogy and exaggerations of his own accomplishments much as Yeats, having once managed to learn the Hebrew alphabet (though little more), would solemnly lament the loss of "my Hebrew."[45] The true model, here again, is Randolph's great hero Borrow. Borrow, although his attainments in languages greatly surpassed Randolph's, also showed a leaning to groups beyond the pale and had a similar tendency to exaggerate his accomplishments.

Randolph's first article on Ozark dialect—it was his first published work on the Ozarks—appeared in _Dialect Notes_ in 1926. It was titled "A Word-List from the Ozarks," and it opened with an account of earlier studies. Prominent among these is a piece by one Jay L. B. Taylor called "Snake County Talk," which appeared in the same journal in 1923. Randolph's article singles out Taylor's work for particular praise—it is "by far the best treatment of this particular dialect." Randolph also notes that Taylor's material, despite the misleading title (there is no Snake County in Missouri), "was all collected in McDonald County, in the extreme southwest corner of Missouri."[46]

Pineville, listed by Randolph as his residence at the end of his article in the slot customarily occupied by the researcher's university affiliation, is the seat of McDonald County, and Taylor is, of course, Randolph's old friend from the "Pineville Mastodon" adventures. Turning to "Snake County Talk," one finds an introductory note, itself written in dialect, which begins, "Las' summer's a year ago, me an' Spike Randolph' . . ." The note goes on to credit Randolph with the whole idea of compiling the word list—after asking Taylor how long he's lived in the area (thirty years), and getting him to agree that the local speech has "'changed a right smart'" during that time, "Spike" suggests that "'some feller ortuh git up a word list for this neck o' bresh'"[47] The following list contains some 829 items, "but 350 of these are commonplace mispronunciations, grammatical errors, slang phrases, or vulgarisms."[48]

Randolph's own article is, as the title suggests, an alphabetized list of terms, with definitions and sample sentences demonstrating the term in use. Many, but not all, of these terms are reprinted in the ninth chapter of *Down in the Holler*, "An Ozark Word List." Randolph produced five such lists as articles, the first two for *Dialect Notes* (the second, titled "More Words from the Ozarks," appeared in 1927) and the last three for *American Speech*. The format for all of these is basically the same: a brief introductory note refers to previous scholarship, including in the later articles references to Randolph's own earlier pieces, and the terms that follow are listed alphabetically with short definitions and (usually) a phrase or sentence showing the term in use.

In addition to these word lists, Randolph produced a number of other dialect studies in the late 1920s. His first pieces for *American Speech* appeared in 1927—"The Ozark Dialect in Fiction" in March and "The Grammar of the Ozark Dialect" in October. The first piece was later supplemented by another study of the attempts upon Ozark dialect by novelists and short story writers, "Recent Fiction and the Ozark Dialect," which was published in the same journal in 1931. The material from both was utilized and elaborated upon in the sixth chapter of *Down in the Holler*, "The Dialect in Fiction." As might be expected, Randolph was not greatly impressed with the accuracy of the dialect he found. The 1927 article opens with an account of its own genesis: "One day I happened to pick up a novel dealing with the Missouri Ozarks, a story of the very county in which I was living at the time, and was astonished to find the characters talking an outlandish jargon altogether strange to me, without even a faint suggestion of the familiar speech of my friends and neighbors. Since that day I have read fourteen more of these Ozark stories, and the dialect in every one of them is very bad indeed."[49]

By 1931, concluding his second study of the Ozark dialect offered in fiction, Randolph was prepared to offer a general ranking:

> Beginning with [John] Monteith's *Parson Brooks*, published in 1884, I have examined the dialect in every Ozark novel that I have been able to find—twenty-two of them in all. The dialect in most of these novels is, in my opinion, very bad indeed. The worst of all, it seems to me, is found in a novel called *Sally of Missouri*, by Rose Emmet Young [published in 1903]. Incomparably the best Ozark dialect ever written in fiction, to my mind, is that of Charles Morrow Wilson. [Randolph refers here to Wilson's 1930 *Acres of Sky*, but he also admired Wilson's

nonfictional work, especially *Backwoods America* (1934).] The next best—although far below the Wilson standard—must still be sought in the works of the eminent Harold Bell Wright![50]

Down in the Holler, Randolph's last word on matters of dialect, does not alter these assessments to any significant degree, although there is considerably more matter from newspaper columns, non-fiction books, stage and screen comedians, and the like. Randolph praises the dialect of Wayman Hogue, Otto Ernest Rayburn, Marguerite Lyon, May Kennedy McCord, Isabel France, and a number of others. Many of these writers were personal friends and acquaintances—Randolph's published reviews are frequently efforts to publicize the work of his friends—and he may be making an extra effort to find something positive to say. Also special cases are the two instances where novelists sought Randolph's help with dialect and then showed their appreciation by dedicating the books to him. The better-known novel is *The Woods Colt* by Thames Williamson, published in 1933. Williamson's dedication to Randolph specifies his indebtedness: "Because he is the acknowledged authority on Ozark dialect, because we traveled them thar hills together, and because he twice went over this story in the painstaking effort to make it regionally perfect."[51] Randolph himself refrains from evaluating the dialect in *The Woods Colt,* citing his lack of objectivity: "Since I read this novel in manuscript, and most of my suggestions about the dialect were accepted by the author, there is no point in my criticizing it here."[52]

The other novel dedicated to Randolph for his help with dialect was *Girl Scouts in the Ozarks,* a 1936 juvenile by Nancy Clemens. "Nancy Clemens" was a newspaper reporter and prolific hack writer who collaborated with Randolph on several ventures during the 1930s, including two articles for scholarly journals. *Girl Scouts in the Ozarks* was actually published over the author's real name, Nancy Nance, and was dedicated to Randolph in terms similar to those used by Williamson. The manuscript was produced and marketed according to an "Agreement" signed by Nance and Randolph on July 30, 1934, which, reduced to essentials, required Nance to produce the manuscript and Randolph to revise and sell it. Costs incidental to the attempted sale—postage, typing—were shared, as were the proceeds, and Randolph could sell the manuscript as his work or as Nance's, at his discretion. At least ten such "Agreements" were signed, each of them calling for a 50,000-word manuscript to be delivered in one month's time, and at least one other book, *The*

Camp-Meeting Murders, published in 1936 by Vanguard with both authors' names listed, owed its existence to the Nance/Randolph collaboration.[53] Several booklets for Haldeman-Julius were also produced by Nance and sold by Randolph.

Another work by a personal friend that Randolph praised highly was Constance Wagner's *Sycamore* (1950). In both *Down in the Holler* and *Ozark Folklore: A Bibliography* he calls it "the finest novel . . . that has ever been published about the Ozark country."[54] Both these books were in print before Donald Harington's *The Architecture of the Arkansas Ozarks* was published in 1975, but Randolph enjoyed that book immensely, encouraged his visitors to read it, and told Harington he'd produced "the best Ozark novel yet."[55] (In Harington's work, in fact, the circle comes round, since Harington has credited Randolph in print on many occasions. He says in one place that he will no doubt steal from *Pissing in the Snow* "as I have stolen from many other Vance Randolph books in each of my novels.")[56]

The other early article for *American Speech*, "The Grammar of the Ozark Dialect," is noteworthy for the tone of its introductory remarks, in which Randolph stresses his lack of professional training. Opening with the claim that the Ozark dialect differs from "the standard vulgate" most significantly in "matters of prounuciation and vocabulary," he goes on to suggest that the dialect's "grammatical peculiarities" are "not altogether devoid of interest" and should be "investigated by some competent student." But no such figure is on the scene, so Randolph will "record some of my own observations" in the hope that "the publication of these fragmentary notes will attract the attention of some scholar."[57]

This is something new from the man who in 1924 and 1925 was attaching his academic degrees to his Little Blue Books and appearing in newspapers and the credits of other researchers as Dr. Randolph and Professor Randolph. That he confused even his friends is suggested by a strange little paper which appeared in *American Speech* early in 1929, "On the Ozark Pronunciation of 'It,'" in which "Dr. Vance Randolph" is taken over the coals for repeated violations of "his own unimpeachable rule" governing the conditions under which "the pronoun *it* is pronounced *hit*." The author of this item is none other than Vernon C. Allison, his stalagmite studies now evidently completed, who goes on to note that such errors are "incomprehensible to one familiar with Dr. Randolph and his meticulously scientific papers in his own field, which is, or used to be, experimental psychology."[58]

Allison's uncertainty is understandable, since "Dr. Randolph" was in fact only then coming into "his own field," and it wasn't experimental psychology. Increasingly, he would present himself as a worker outside the academy, and later as a "collector" instead of a "folklorist." In 1949 the "Work in Progress: 1948" section of the *Journal of American Folklore* noted that Randolph was hard at work on five books, one of which was to be titled *The Ozark Speech*. It was noted parenthetically that "he hopes to find 'some scholarly chap to collaborate on this one.'"[59] Still later, in 1955, he wrote to a prospective biographer correcting him concerning his proper categorization: "By the way, you should know that I am not a folklorist, but a collector of folklore. There is a great difference, as the terms are now used in the United States. Many of our most eminent folklorists— such as Stith Thompson and Archer Taylor—have never done any fieldwork at all."[60]

This "amateur" posture, then, partly defensive and in response to a perceived snobbery on the part of the academy, partly offensive in keeping with an already articulated celebration of marginal figures, was an enduring stance in Randolph's self-presentation. Even in his last years, those who knew him well came to expect occasions when the "I'm just a collector" speech would be dusted off, and would be prepared to reiterate their spirited demurrals. Such moments recur in the lengthy Randolph/Halpert correspondence, and it seems appropriate to understand the 1955 letter just cited in similar terms, especially since it ends with another specimen of humble pie that also recurred in Randolph's last years, with other interviewers and would-be biographers. "If you and Wanda should come to feel that a book about me is not worth the labor, why not just do a long magazine story on the subject and let it go at that? You won't hurt my feelings."[61]

But in 1927, in "The Grammar of the Ozark Dialect," the "amateur" note was new.[62] The study itself is straightforwardly descriptive, beginning with verb tenses and other verb usages and proceeding through pronouns, adverbs (including one heroic instance of multiple negation: "I ain't never done no dirt of no kind to nobody"[63]), adjectives, and prepositions. A later grammatical study, the second installment of an article prepared jointly by Randolph and Patti Sankee, "a high school teacher in K.C., Mo.,"[64] concerns itself exclusively with archaisms in Ozark grammar, and proceeds by citing identical usages in Shakespeare, Chaucer, Spenser, and other notables for every example taken from the speech of Ozark people.

Two other pieces among these early articles are exceptional for going beyond the purely descriptive presentation of observed usages that Randolph evidently found appropriate to his newly declared amateur status. "My purpose," as he puts it in *Down in the Holler*, "is to write down what I have heard the Ozark hillman say, how he said it, and what he meant by it." Theoretical matters, he adds, are best left to the "professors": "I am not concerned with distinctions between true dialect and other forms of substandard speech, nor with any of the scholarly disputations about such matters."[65]

Clear enough, but in "Is There an Ozark Dialect?" published in 1929 in *American Speech*, Randolph involves himself directly in just such distinctions and disputations, taking issue with such "grammatical pundits" as Krapp, Tucker, and even Mencken himself. Quoting these authorities for the notion that the United States is a nation without true dialects, but only "a general common speech, a *vulgate*, a *sermo vulgaris*, a *Volksprache* which serves the entire country," Randolph agrees with Mencken's claim that a street-car conductor from Boston could work in Chicago or San Francisco "without running the slightest risk of misunderstanding his new fares," but insists that "the Ozark region of Missouri and Arkansas is a different proposition altogether." Also of interest in this piece is a paragraph, of Randolph's own manufacture, offered as "a fair example of English as it is spoken by the old *residenters* in the more isolated parts of the Ozark highlands."[66]

"A Possible Source of Some Ozark Neologisms," published in 1928, is concerned with less controversial matters, but it goes beyond simple description to suggest that "mental defectives" may play a significant role in "the production of local peculiarities of speech."[67]

Almost all this material finds its final expression in *Down in the Holler*, although in most cases the treatment there is greatly expanded. "The Grammar of the Ozark Dialect" and the second installment of "Dialectal Survivals in the Ozarks" are seventeen pages long, taken together, while *Down in the Holler's* third chapter, "Backwoods Grammar," runs to thirty-three. The repeated material is often modified in some way; usually the change is a small matter of phrasing, but there is a striking and inexplicable tendency to moderation at work too, which sometimes works to the disadvantage of the later version. For example, the instance cited for the Ozarker's tendency to substitute *at* in situations where *to* would be expected is "*jes listen at th' dam' fool a hollerin'*" in "The Grammar of the Ozark Dialect" and "Just listen *at* the old fool a-hollerin'" in

Down in the Holler. If this seems mere prudery, another instance, where the article of 1927 asserts that "*Doesn't* is never heard, *don't* being substituted in every case," and the book of 1953 retreats to "Doesn't is very seldom heard, don't being almost invariably substituted," suggests no motive higher than timidity.[68]

The motivation for such alterations is difficult to reconstruct. Randolph was never, even in his eighties, a man afraid of "damn" or "never." In the early 1950s he wanted his collection of folktales to be issued by Columbia under the title of *The Half-Wit from Missouri*—he was alert, of course, to the obvious resonances such a title would have. "Maybe you're right about the title," he wrote in 1951 to Herbert Halpert, who had called it an "unhappy choice." "Still, I think *The Half-Wit from Missouri* would sell a good many copies, especially if it comes out in 1952, the year of a political campaign."[69] Randolph was overruled in this instance, and the book was eventually published (in 1952) as *Who Blowed Up the Church House?* Twenty years later, however, in 1973, he was successful in his urging that *Pissing in the Snow* be used as the title for his first volume of "obscene" tales, and in 1977 he sent poor Halpert, who had balked at *The Half-Wit from Missouri*, a story called "The Worn Out Pussy," with an accompanying letter identifying it as "the title story of my second book of bawdy tales."[70]

Randolph, then, is not on the face of it a likely point of origin for the numerous small hedgings and bowdlerizations of *Down in the Holler.* A more probable source is the "scholarly chap" listed as the book's co-author, Professor George P. Wilson. Wilson was an English professor at the Women's College of the University of North Carolina—now the University of North Carolina at Greensboro—whose reputation was grounded almost entirely upon his organizational and editorial work for the American Dialect Society and other academic bodies. His scholarship was ephemeral at best—Wilson's *Who's Who* entry for 1956–57, his final appearance, lists him as the author of "books in field" but names only *Down in the Holler.* (Earlier entries, prior to his involvement with Randolph, list two other titles: *Informal Oral Composition*, 1922, and *A Guide to Better English*, 1942.) Wilson also published several of his own articles in the Publications of the American Dialect Society series (PADS), which he originated and edited; see, for example, PADS NO. 1 (April, 1944), "Instructions to Collectors of Dialect," and PADS No. 11 (April, 1949), "The Value of Dialect." Wilson, in short, was an academic who went a long way on short accomplishments—he was in on the ground floor in a newly emerging field, and there he stayed, sitting on and sometimes chairing committees (the American Dialect Society's Committee on Regional Speech and Localisms, for example, which he headed from 1942 to 1952) until the sheer passage of time conferred a modicum of distinction.

The "scholarly chap," then, turned out to be not so much a scholar as a factotum. Ironically enough, Wilson's academic credentials were no better than Randolph's—he did his undergraduate work at North Carolina, graduating in 1913, went to Columbia for a master's degree (1919), and did additional graduate work at the University of Wisconsin from 1920 to 1923. Shift the dates and the institutions involved, and this record could be Randolph's—neither man completed the Ph.D. But credentials, after all, are a minor matter. A Ph.D. would not have transformed Wilson into the scholar that Randolph's dialect materials needed. The important thing to note is the crucial mistake in judgment. Randolph, recognizing his own lack of philological training, sought expert help in an attempt to present his materials in accordance with contemporary scholarly standards. Wilson, at first glance, must have seemed ideal—he was a prominent figure in the professional society devoted to dialect studies who had a special interest in regional speech and localisms.

Unfortunately for Randolph, "Wilson apparently had not kept up with advances in the methodology of recording and presenting dialect."[71] Randolph's own work in the field had ended in the 1930s; his last article-length study was "A Fifth Ozark Word List," which he did in collaboration with Nancy Clemens and published in *American Speech* in 1936. By the early 1950s the field of dialect study had changed markedly. In fact, the change is neatly marked by an event of 1952, the year before the publication of *Down in the Holler*. In that year the American Dialect Society appointed a new head to its Committee on Regional Speech and Localisms, replacing Wilson with Raven I. McDavid, a younger scholar who would play a leading role in the professionalization of the discipline. Two years later, in 1954, McDavid gave *Down in the Holler* its most searching critique. His *Journal of American Folklore* review praised Randolph's work but also noted the flaws which, sadly, defeated Randolph's whole purpose in seeking a collaborative effort and made the culmination of his long labors with Ozark speech outdated as a scholarly work on the day it was published.

Down in the Holler, said McDavid, "provides a great deal of evidence which the scholar can utilize for at least a preliminary interpretation of the position of Ozarks speech in relation to other varieties of present and earlier English." He then continues with specific attention to the work's shortcomings: "What the scholar misses is the framework to facilitate this interpretation. This omission is not Randolph's fault, for he does not pretend to be what he is not. But the book would be more effective if the statements about the position of the dialect had drawn on what has been learned in the last two decades about the regional and social varieties of American English."

McDavid goes on to detail the most important scholarly accomplishments of those decades, "the serious scholarship with which a writer on American dialect ought to be familiar." He does not directly criticize Wilson, though the explicit exoneration of Randolph surely comes through as suggesting Wilson's responsibility for the missing "framework." In fact Wilson is barely mentioned, dismissed in the first paragraph in a marvelously chilly sentence, a fine instance of that delicately venomous prose that academics strive for when they are having at one another. Randolph's work, says McDavid, "enjoyed the assistance of George P. Wilson of the Women's College of the University of North Carolina, an enthusiastic partisan of the amateur's interest in dialect study, and for eight years secretary of the American Dialect Society."[72]

There were other reviews, of course, in both the popular and academic press, and most of them were unqualified raves. The *American Speech* notice, for example, called *Down in the Holler* "as thrilling as any book of fiction," and pronounced it "the most interesting book about dialect that I have ever read." Wilson's contribution is characterized here as "not a small one": Wilson is "an old hand at dialect work, having been the mainstay of the American Dialect Society for a good many years." The chapters on grammar, pronunciation, and survivals are said to "owe much to him, as does the scholarly adequacy of the entire book."[73]

But the McDavid review was the one that counted, and Randolph knew it. He appreciated the positive remarks—McDavid had praised especially the "searching criticism of fictional representations of Ozarks speech"[74]—but he recognized the justice of his strictures too, and he blamed Wilson. His comments on Wilson's role were not kind ones, best summed up perhaps by his repeatedly stated wish that "I'd been hitched up with Mary Celestia before I got involved with Wilson. She'd have done a better job."[75] Mrs. Randolph remembered being around for the final revisions of the manuscript. "Wilson didn't do a thing for him," she said. "I cut out most of his stuff."[76] (These remarks are supported by Randolph's own prefatory acknowledgments, which credit his future wife for going over the whole manuscript and removing many errors and obscurities. "Without Miss Parler's encouragement the book would not have been written."[77])

But all these trials and triumphs were surely unanticipated in 1927, when the newly "amateur" Randolph of "The Grammar of the Ozark Dialect" was himself only recently departed from the ranks of the scholarly chaps. The year was in retrospect something of a turning point for Randolph—impressive in terms of the quantity of material he published and noteworthy as well for his first flurry of appearances in academic journals. He was still doing the hackwork for Haldeman-Julius and Vanguard, the booklets on scientific and philosophical topics he'd been turning out since 1924. For Vanguard he did four titles in the *ABC* series, guides to biology, physiology, psychology, and geology. For Haldeman-Julius he did two dictionaries, one German and one French. Both appeared with Randolph's own name, but the latter was advertised by Haldeman-Julius as the work of one "Gaylord Du Bois," and included a brief selection of French idioms featuring several entries bizarre enough to suggest playfulness on the part of the compiler. "Bruler la cervelle," for instance, is listed, and glossed as "to blow out one's brains."[78]

In March, 1927, Randolph began supplementing his income with articles for sporting magazines. The first to appear was "Old Pistols of the Ozark Mountains," which noted the continuing use of "obsolete firearms."[79] Two others appeared in 1927, including "Instead of a Holster," which describes in considerable detail a metal clip, first exhibited to Randolph by a "surly, taciturn animal" who operated "an unsavory resort" in Oklahoma, which permitted a pistol-wearing gentleman to appear in public unburdened by "holsters and auxiliary trappings."[80]

All of these, crambooks, dictionaries, and sporting articles, were done for money. But 1927 also saw Randolph publish a large body of work in various nonpaying formats. There were, of course, the three articles on dialect that, coupled with the first *Dialect Notes* piece in 1926, were his initial forays into that field. There was also his first *Journal of American Folklore* article, "Folk Beliefs in the Ozark Mountains," another piece on the butterflies he'd studied back in Kansas in the *Annals of the Entomological Society of America*, and an article done in collaboration with Vernon Allison on "Prehistoric Inhabitants of Crawford County, Kansas," in *American Anthropologist*.

Four books, two pocket dictionaries, three articles in sporting magazines, and six articles in academic journals—not bad for a

year's work, expecially for a man recently departed from academe.[81]
But one other bit of work in 1927, despite its obscurity at the time,
may have been the most important of all. Beginning on February 18,
1927, the *Pineville Democrat*, of weekly issue, began carrying a column titled "The Songs Grandfather Sang," which invited readers to
send in texts of "the old songs that our grandparents used to sing
way back in Tennessee, or Kentucky, or Carolinas, or whatever it
was they came from."[82] Inducement of a year's subscription to the
Democrat or $1 in cash, winner's choice, was offered for each song
printed. The instigator, editor, and judge of entries in this enterprise
was, of course, Vance Randolph, here appearing for the first time as
a student of folksong.

IV

"The Songs Grandfather Sang" was a modest enough enterprise in
itself, printing only eleven songs, but Randolph was happy enough
with the results to undertake a similar project two years later, in
1929, when Otto Ernest Rayburn agreed to open the pages of his
regional monthly, *Ozark Life*, to a column of the same title. Both
ventures were valuable beyond the published results for providing
Randolph with the names and addresses of potential informants.
The *Democrat* column, Randolph reported, led him to "about seventy local people who were interested in the subject," including
three of his most significant contributors to *Ozark Folksongs*. The
first prizewinner was a version of "The Cuckoo" submitted by Mrs.
Carrie Baber of Pineville. Randolph may have been priming the
pump in this instance, suggesting to readers the kind of songs he
was looking for, since he already knew Mrs. Baber, and in fact had
collected a slightly different variant of "The Cuckoo" from her in
1922.[83]

Of the ten later winners, five contributed songs to *Ozark Folksongs*, and two, Mrs. Lee Stephens and Miss Leone Duval, were
major informants. Mrs. Stephens, for example, who won her prize
with a version of "Young Edmond Dell," appears in *Ozark Folksongs*
in connection with more than twenty songs, while Miss Duval, who
won the column's last prize with a version of "The Jew's Garden"
printed on May 6, 1927, contributed almost fifty songs to Randolph.

Randolph provides minimal commentary on the texts printed as
winners. His introductory remarks for the "Johnny Randall" sent in
by R. H. Clayton, of Lanagan, Missouri, are the most extensive of
the series: "The ballad of 'Johnny Randall' was first sung in America

more than a hundred and fifty years ago, and some of the English and Scottish versions are older still. It used to be a great favorite in the Southern Appalachians, and was probably brought into the Ozarks by some of the early settlers who came west from Kentucky or Tennessee."[84] This note, brief as it is, is exceptional—most of the texts are printed without comment beyond identification of the reader who submitted them.

Far more space is given to exhortations by the editor. Randolph did not hesitate to tell readers he was interested primarily in old songs. "If we wanted such songs as 'Sweet Adeline,' 'After the Ball,' and 'On the Banks of the Wabash,'" he told potential contributors on February 18, 1927, "we would simply go to a Joplin music store and buy them."[85] Nor did he have any qualms about advertising his interest in specific songs. On February 25 he wrote:

> One of the ballads that we would like to print is about Lord Randall, or Johnnie Randal, who was poisoned by his sweetheart, and came home crying: "Mother, make my bed soon." Another old one is called "The Greenwood Siding," and tells the story of a mother who murdered her two little babes. Still another is about a little English boy named Hugh, who was killed by some Jews. And there are others older still—much older than any that we have published so far. The older a song is the better we like it. If you can't remember the whole ballad send in as many verses as you can.[86]

Two weeks later, on March 11, he had his "Johnny Randall," and "The Jew's Garden" would come in later, after he'd asked for it again on March 18, describing it this time as a song about "a Jewish woman who murdered a little boy, because he threw his ball into her garden."[87]

By 1927 Randolph had, of course, been collecting folksongs for most of the decade. Scores of songs in *Ozark Folksongs* were recorded before 1927 in Pineville alone, and by 1929 he was publishing "The Ozark Play-Party" in the *Journal of American Folklore* with extensive bibliographic annotations to the twenty-nine game songs printed. Randolph never said so, but it seems likely that the idea of using a column in the popular press as an aid to folksong research came to him from the example of Robert W. Gordon, who had edited a column entitled "Old Songs That Men Have Sung" in *Adventure* magazine since 1923, and subsequently used the list of informants and contacts provided by the column to organize the most extensive folksong recording expeditions yet undertaken in the United States. Randolph may not have known about the *Adventure* column in early 1927 (though he certainly knew it by 1946, when it was cited in the "Bibliography" of *Ozark Folksongs*), but it seems less likely that he would not have noted Gordon's series of folksong articles in the *New York Times Sunday Magazine*, the first of which appeared on January 2, 1927. Two additional installments appeared in January, and there were a total of fifteen articles before the series concluded with a piece on cowboy ballads on January 22, 1928.[88]

Whatever its source, the idea proved a good one, and Randolph was quick to use it again. His early interest in play-party songs, in fact, is apparent in the March 25 installment of "The Songs Grandfather Sang" when he departs from his usual practice of stressing his desire for the oldest songs—most of the songs he asks for by name are Child ballads—long enough to note that "nobody has offered any of the old play-party songs." He goes on to mention several of these by name: "It doesn't seem possible that all the old folks have forgotten such favorites as 'Shoot the Buffalo,' 'We'll All Go Down to London,' 'Roxie Ann,' 'Old Dan Tucker,' 'Waltz the Hall' and the like. There used to be dozens of these game-songs."[89]

This interest found its first printed form in Randolph's second article for the *Journal of American Folklore*, which was also his initial effort in the field of scholarly folksong study. And "The Ozark Play-Party," while it presents itself as the work of the same more or less casual amateur who made his debut in dialect studies, is nevertheless a paper clearly written with scholarly respectability in mind. It opens with a brief description of the play-party's social context and setting that reappears, virtually unchanged, as the headnote to Chapter Ten in *Ozark Folksongs*. This is followed by the "I'm an amateur" plea. Admitting that "I have read some books and papers about the party-games as played elsewhere," Randolph goes on to claim that questions concerning "the age and origin of the games, the changes which they have undergone in their successive migrations, the forces which have brought about these modifications, their obvious connection with balladry," and other like issues are "matters of which I still know very little."[90] But the twenty-nine texts which follow appear with the tunes (except for "My Pappy He Will Scold Me," where it is noted that the tune "seems to have been forgotten") transcribed, and the headnotes fairly bristle with citations. No fewer than thirty-three sources are cited, ranging from the works of major scholars—Gomme, Newell, Pound, Belden—to journal articles and specialized treatments—Leah Jackson Wolford's *The Play-Party in Indiana*, Edwin Ford Piper's 1915 article for the *Journal of American Folklore*, "Some Play-Party Games of the Middle

West"—to popular compilations like Carl Sandburg's *American Songbag* and Sinclair Lewis' *Our Mr. Wrenn*. Of special note are the references to popular records that begin to appear early on in Randolph's work. In the headnote to "The Girl I Left Behind Me," for example, one finds noted that "Dalhart has made an excellent phonographic record (*Columbia*, No. 437-D), but the words are very different from those of the play-party song."[91] In the February, 1930, issue of *Ozark Life*, as a part of his second "The Songs Grandfather Sang" column, Randolph's introductory remarks for a version of "The Butcher Boy" mention that "Bradley Kincaid, a radio singer (WLS, Chicago), has a slightly different version from the Kentucky Mountains."[92]

By 1929, then, the major outlines of Randolph's later reputation are already taking shape. He's in the academic world, publishing articles on folklore and dialect in professional journals, but not of it, since he lacks both a Ph.D. and an academic post. His work, while meeting the professional standards of the time, is already anticipating in some areas the standards of the future. In the 1930s and 1940s, let alone 1929, the commercial recordings of figures like Vernon Dalhart and Bradley Kincaid were generally considered beneath the dignity of scholarly attention. "In the decades before the fifties," writes country music historian Bill C. Malone, "the folklorist's rejection of hillbilly music was as strong as the urban folksinger's refusal to perform the music." Malone also reports that Charles Seeger's 1948 review of several hillbilly records in the *Journal of American Folklore* marked "the first time that the country's major scholarly folk publication had admitted the existence, or relevance, of commercial country music."[93]

By 1965, in a now famous "Hillbilly Issue," the *Journal of American Folklore* "blazed a new trail" which led to today's "liberal, modern scholarly concept of American folksong,"[94] and in one of that issue's articles Vance Randolph got some credit. "The only regional collector to use phonograh records extensively is Vance Randolph," wrote Ed Kahn. "Although his discographical references are not exhaustive, his documentation is generally accurate."[95]

Randolph's play-party article did bring his folksong work to the attention of academic researchers. If Louise Pound deserves primary credit for encouraging his dialect studies, the analogous figure in folksong scholarship would be H. M. Belden, of the University of Missouri, to whom he dedicated *Ozark Folksongs*, and for whom he wrote a warmly appreciative obituary notice in 1954. Belden, Randolph noted, had founded the Missouri Folklore Society in 1906, had edited the "monumental" *Ballads and Songs of Missouri* in 1940, and had edited and annotated, at the age of eighty-two, the ballads and folksongs in the huge Frank C. Brown collection from North Carolina. He "knew more about ballad texts than anyone else in America" and was "a great man and a brilliant teacher, with a wry sense of humor that is not too common among professors." Randolph closes with the resounding cadences he reserved for a handful of people—perhaps only Borrow and Debs are praised more effusively: "I count it a high honor and a privilege to have known him personally. He will be greatly missed and long remembered by folklorists everywhere."[96]

Belden and Randolph were corresponding by 1928, Louise Pound and he are in touch by 1927, and Ruth Benedict, as editor of the *Journal of American Folklore*, is being asked for her advice as early as the fall of 1927. In the July, 1930, installment of "The Songs Grandfather Sang" column in *Ozark Life*, Randolph concluded his introduction to a text of "The Sherman Cyclone" by noting that "I showed this piece to Professor J. Frank Dobie, of the University of Texas, and he says that it refers to a storm which swept Sherman, Texas, in 1896."[97] Belden, Pound, Benedict, Dobie, Mencken, Sandburg— these are large names, in and out of the academy. Randolph was getting known.

He was also building up his network of informants. Mrs. Carrie Baber, for example, who was the first prizewinner in the *Pineville Democrat*'s "The Songs Grandfather Sang" contest, had first sung for Randolph on December 7, 1920, when she performed a play-party song called "King William Was King James's Son." On July 6, 1927, she gave him "Fare You Well, My Darling." In between, on twenty different occasions, she gave him as many songs. Mrs. Baber seems to have specialized in songs; she does not appear in the notes to the folktale collections, nor is she cited for her beliefs concerning weather signs or home remedies. But other informants were more versatile. Mrs. Marie Wilbur, for example, who sang for Randolph as early as 1919, is still being credited with folktales in 1931. She gave him a rhyme about the destinies of children born on different days of the week that appears in *Ozark Superstitions*, and fourteen items in *Hot Springs and Hell*, Randolph's collection of jests and humorous anecdotes, came to him from her telling. All told, Mrs. Wilbur contributed sixty-four songs and nineteen folktales to *Ozark Folksongs* and five different folktale collections.

Mrs. Wilbur, who became Mrs. Randolph in 1930, is cited three times for her contributions to "The Ozark Play-Party." Mrs. Baber appears too, also cited three times, and Jay L. B. Taylor is credited twice. "I did not collect this stuff from strangers," Randolph wrote in his "Introduction" to *Hot Springs and Hell*, published in 1965. "My informants were old friends."[98] Still later, in 1977, he brooded at some length on the whole matter of researcher/informant relationships in a letter to Herbert Halpert:

> You know, I have always thought that a folklorist should do *some* fieldwork. It seemed to me that the reason you and Dorson are better than fellows like Archer Taylor and Stith Thompson was that you had done some collecting, and thus got closer to the *Volk*.
>
> Of late it occurs to me that one may get *too* close to the People. Maybe he can identify with his informants and lose his objective point of view. Sympathy becomes empathy, and leads to too goddamn *much* identification. Finally the collector finds himself a member of a crackpot fraternity, with secret signs and shibboleths and passwords—blood brother to the herbalist and the horse-leech, close cousin to the granny-woman and the witch.
>
> John Gould Fletcher knew about this, and I think Francis Lee Utley had thought some about it.[99]

In the late 1920s Mrs. Wilbur, Jay Taylor, and Mrs. Baber were still new friends, but Randolph was well launched on the path he would follow for the rest of his long life. His writing, by 1928, had taken on an increasingly Ozark focus—the dictionaries for Haldeman-Julius in 1927 were his last works in the Little Blue Book format until the hard days of the middle thirties, and the same year's Vanguard *ABC* guides on scientific topics were his last in that series. His next work for Vanguard would be his first major book and the culminating work of his first decade's labors in his chosen home. It would appear in 1931 as *The Ozarks: An American Survival of Primitive Society*.

Even the shorter pieces done for money were by 1928 increasingly centered upon Ozark topics. In that year he wrote five articles for sporting magazines, all of them devoted to the Ozark country. One of them, "Lost in the Ozarks," which appeared in *Forest and Stream*, relates the story of an urban braggart who offends his hosts with a know-it-all manner and then gets lost for nearly two days in "three mile o' timber." The story is notable for Randolph's obvious pride in the skills of his Ozark neighbors—it's his friend "Lem the tie-whacker" who can't believe that the slicker is in fact lost. "'He couldn't of got lost noway,' said Lem, 'a feller caint *git* lost in three mile o' timber, long's he's got th' moon an' sun an' stars t' looks at.'"[100]

Another *Forest and Stream* piece, "Jumping Bass in the Ozark

Country," is interesting for the violent imbroglio that followed its publication. The article itself is a reasonably straightforward account of an unusual (and illicit) method of taking game fish in muddied waters, known locally as "goosing" or "jumping." Randolph lets a fisherman named Fitzhugh describe the technique: "Whenever'n the river gits good an' muddy like, them 'ar linesides lays in th' weeds, an' if you-all runs in 'twixt them an' deep water hit skeers hell out'n 'em, an' they most generly allus jumps right spang in th' boat, an' caint git out noways!" Randolph's investigations convince him of "the deadly effectiveness" of the method—trailing behind a party of "young scoundrels" one night, he stays only a short time, watching them string "at least a dozen fine bass" before departing "thoughtfully and sadly." His tone is disapproving throughout, and the piece ends on a somber note: "the wonderful fishing waters of the Ozark country will certainly be seriously depleted unless this unsportsmanlike method of killing bass goes out of fashion." [101]

Nobody took issue with Randolph's conservationist ethic, but a number of readers wrote the editor impugning his veracity. Telling the story again a decade later, for *Esquire*, Randolph looked back on the furor: "I published a brief article on the subject in *Forest and Stream*, back in 1928, and was denounced and ridiculed from one end of the country to the other. Some people really became quite excited about it. An anonymous gentleman from Georgia wrote the editor that I was not only 'the God damndest liar ever heard of,' but also 'a scroundrel, son-of-a-bitch *and* bastard!' It was a very interesting letter. I have often wondered why he italicized the conjunction." [102]

His fishing stories weren't the only thing that got Randolph in trouble in 1928. That raucous and intemperate voices might be raised among the readership of hunting and fishing magazines is not really surprising, but appearing in the stolid pages of a scholarly journal devoted to dialect study would seem a safe enough enterprise. But such was not the case with "Verbal Modesty in the Ozarks," which examines verbal taboos in southwestern Missouri and northwestern Arkansas. The piece itself is one of Randolph's best, certainly the most entertainingly written of his language and dialect studies. The material in the article was reprinted several times, in *The Ozarks* in 1931 and again in *Down in the Holler* in 1953, and the appeal of the entire article was sufficient for it to be reprinted in 1981 in a general anthology of Ozarkiana. But in 1928 it was pretty strong stuff. Randolph had originally submitted it to Louise Pound for *American Speech*, but "an official of the printing company was 'terribly upset' and didn't want to publish such 'questionable material' without consulting the Attorney General of the United States!" Dr. Pound eventually "returned the manuscript to me" and "Percy W. Long finally published it in *Dialect Notes*." [103]

Randolph's troubles with "questionable material" would accompany him throughout his career, and even now, after his death, several of his major collections remain unpublished. When *Down in the Holler* appeared a number of reviewers in the popular press warned their readers of some "obscenity in the language that would offend some of the modest among us." [104] Randolph himself, with some relish, noted that a "nice old gentleman who teaches English literature in a college said publicly that *Down in the Holler* is 'the nastiest, filthiest book ever issued by an American university press.'" [105]

Any nice old gentlemen who were reading Randolph's work in 1928 would have found items in addition to "Verbal Modesty in the Ozarks" to disgust them. There was in the first place "Miriam," Randolph's second poem to find print, and his last, and in the second place a bizarre little piece entitled "A Survival of Phallic Superstition in Kansas." The poem, which appeared in a magazine of verse entitled *The Harp*, published in Larned, Kansas, is a brief excursion in the mode made famous by Dostoyevsky:

> So there we sat while the candles burned,
> And we talked of the girl that is dead,
> I thought of the dollars that she had earned
> And the mouths that she had fed—
> She was like your Christ in a way . . . she turned
> Her body into bread. [106]

The other piece, overtly jocular in tone, was published in the *Psychoanalytic Review*, and drew its inspiration from Randolph's days as a student at the University of Kansas. On the campus at Lawrence he had "seen a great many students, particularly women, step off the sidewalk in order to touch" a petrified tree stump embedded in the ground. This "pillar" was decorated with "two rounded stones" at its base, "and such stones are not common in this region." Randolph's inquiries elicited several sexually charged, if contradictory, beliefs—that touching the pillar somehow aided the acquisition of a husband "and healthy children," that "the touch of the pillar was supposed to have a contraceptive effect." His treatment is brief: "It is not practicable," he says, "for me to pursue the subject farther at present, but I am almost persuaded that here, in the pecksniffian state of Kansas, is something very like the phallic superstitions of medieval Europe—degenerate survivals of the great priapic religions of antiquity."[107] The article is greatly enhanced by the inclusion of a photo, the photographer unidentified (Randolph said he snapped it), depicting a young lady with her hand at rest on the monument's tip.

These are, of course, unimportant works, interesting at best for their hints at their author's continuing identification with archetypes of the margin—his "Miriam" is another of "mine own people" like the couple in the Dodge roadster in Florida, at home with Randolph's hoboes and gypsies and socialists and immigrant miners and bootleggers, admired by the goliardic scholar whose learned pieces twit the "pecksniffian" old gentlemen who rule at the center. By 1930 Randolph was well established in the Ozarks, but the allegiances and animosities of his Kansas days were still sometimes in evidence.

As the decade turned and the country headed deeper into the Great Depression, Randolph continued to gather songs and stories from his Ozark neighbors. His dialect studies were nearly completed—by the end of 1930 he'd published fifteen articles in *Dialect Notes and American Speech*, and would do only four more (the second piece on the dialect in fiction in 1931, a short note on the phrase "blackberry winter" in 1932, and two additional Ozark word lists, the fourth and fifth, in 1933 and 1936 respectively). In 1930 he was also involved with his second "The Songs Grandfather Sang" column. The April issue would be distinguished by the first appearance in print of Mrs. Emma Dusenbury, a figure who deserves volumes and songs of her own, a blind and impoverished woman clad in flour sacks who stunned all who saw her into the highest utterance each could command. Eventually she'd be recorded for the Library of Congress by several fieldworkers, and astonish the scholars with her vast repertoire of traditional song. To B. A. Botkin, chief of the Library of Congress's Archive of American Folk Song in the middle 1940s, Mrs. Dusenbury "seemed to have 'made a resolution to learn all the songs in the world.'"[108]

But in 1930 the world knew her only through the pages of *Ozark Life*, where five songs from her were printed between May and July. The first to appear were a version of "Edward," a Child ballad (No. 13) known to Mrs. Dusenbury as "Blood on the Point of Your Knife," and "Down by the Greenwood Side," a "very naughty ballad" (Child No. 20). She followed these up with a version of "Devilish Mary" (called "When I Was Young" by Mrs. Dusenbury) in the May issue, "The Guerilla Man" in the June number, and an untitled fragment that Randolph printed as a version of "Beware, Oh Beware" in *Ozark Folksongs* for the July column.

By 1930, then, Randolph was known to scholars in the world of folklore studies and dialect study. He'd completed a substantial body of work in the latter field, and had published two articles in the leading journal of the former. In his personal life, too, Randolph was moving ahead. On March 27 he married the former Mrs. Marie Wilbur, one of his most valuable informants and the daughter of one of Pineville's leading citizens, Dr. Oakley St. John. He was thirty-eight, she thirty-nine, and they would not be a happy couple.

Three months later, on June 20, Randolph signed a contract with James Henle at Vanguard Press in which he agreed to produce by February 1, 1931, "a book of approximately 100,000 words about the manners, customs, and folk lore of the Ozarks according to the outline submitted to the Publishers."[109] Vance Randolph, former etiquette book writer and producer of *ABC* crambooks, was about to write his first important book.

5

High Times

I wanted to be an anthropologist.

—Vance Randolph, 1980

I

The Ozarks: An American Survival of Primitive Society was published in September, 1931. It was a volume of 310 pages, with ten photographs by the author, and it received favorable attention in the popular press. Dorothy Scarborough praised it in the *New York Times Book Review*, and called it "a book to fascinate the folklorist, the collector of folksongs, and anyone interested in the history of social customs."[1] Stanley Vestal, in the *Saturday Review*, was more lyric in his enthusiasm. "No one with a taste for American folkways, no one who likes the tang of Shakespearean English, no one who has a trace of nostalgia for that America which passed so swiftly away at the coming of the machine and the immigrant, will lay this book aside willingly, once he is fairly inside it."[2]

But if *The Ozarks* was generously noted and praised in the general circulation press, its reception in the scholarly journals was a different matter. The *Journal of American Folklore* did not review it or its successor, *Ozark Mountain Folks*, when it appeared in 1932. Nor did the *American Anthropologist* take note of either book. Alone among the scholarly journals, the *American Journal of Sociology* and *American Speech* thought Randolph's first book-length study worth attention. The *American Speech* notice was by Louise Pound, who mentioned Randolph's "valuable articles on the dialect of the Ozark region," and added that he could have written "an authentic book" on dialect alone or on folksongs. Instead, *The Ozarks* demonstrates "that he is a student of other phases of Ozark life as well." Pound concluded with general praise: "The author's accuracy and thoroughness are well known to those familiar with his work. His book has had an enthusiastic reception from reviewers, and deserves it."[3] Robert Redfield, in the *American Journal of Sociology* review, stressed Randolph's "requisite combination of sympathy and objectivity." The Ozarks is more than a collection of "texts and quaint beliefs," said Redfield, though the work is "casual, and popular, and not formally ethnological, the folk tales and beliefs are set, to some degree, in their setting of social use and meaning."[4]

Randolph, reconstructing his own motives in 1980, placed *The Ozarks* in a context related to his old attempt to combine his work in the Ozarks with the pursuit of a Ph.D. in anthropology at Columbia. "Vanguard asked me to write a book about the Ozarks like Margaret Mead's *Coming of Age in Samoa*. I couldn't do it. She was much better. 'We want some kind of non-fiction about the Ozarks'—that's what they said."[5]

In this conversation, Randolph discussed *The Ozarks* and *Ozark Mountain Folks*, despite their differences, as written for one publisher in an attempt to accomplish one thing. "I tried to write the way I thought an anthropologist would. I didn't want to use folklore—for reviewers to see it as folklore—because it wasn't as popular as anthropology."[6] Asked about the subtitle, and told that Richard Dorson in a recent talk had chided his use of "survival" and "primitive," citing them as evidence of the untrained amateur's inevitable lack of theoretical sophistication, Randolph defended himself briefly and then returned to the matter of his purposes in the early 1930s. "Dorson's just being snotty," he said. "He's wrong—everybody used those terms then. It's no good now, of course. I was engrossed by 'survivals.' I had a notion once to go to Australia, or Canada—about 1932. If Boas had sent me to an English colony like that, I would have done it. I wanted to be an anthropologist, to write popular books on anthropology."[7]

These musings may be distorted, of course, since nearly fifty years separated them from the events involved; it seems likely, in fact, that the remark about Boas refers not to the 1930s but to 1915. It is, however, supportive of their general tenor to note that Randolph was writing to Boas as late as 1929, attempting to use his folksong collection as a doctoral dissertation. "Papa Franz" was not sufficiently impressed, however, and replied that he "could not accept a collection of songs as a dissertation."[8]

Knowing these things about the genesis of *The Ozarks* may make it a less surprising volume. If, as Herbert Halpert has noted, most folklore studies of the period "were text-oriented, and stressed historical and comparative investigations,"[9] one need look no further than Randolph's stated model to find a very different approach.

Coming of Age in Samoa was published in 1928, with a Foreword by Franz Boas. In a Preface written for a later reissue Mead described her book as "the first piece of anthropological fieldwork which was written without the paraphernalia of scholarship designed to mystify the lay reader and confound one's colleagues." Mead's book had a subtitle too: *A Psychological Study of Primitive Youth for Western Civilization.* "When this book was written," Mead's 1972 Preface continues, "the very idea of culture was new to the literate world. The idea that our every thought and movement was a product not of race, not of instinct, but derived from the society within which an individual was reared, was new and unfamiliar."[10] Mead wishes, of course, to emphasize the role of "social arrangements," the great variety of "patterns of life" produced under differing arrangements by an animal as malleable as man. Randolph, in turn, attempted to present the life of the Ozark hill people in terms of its own patterns and arrangements. "The interest and respect," writes Halpert, "with which Randolph presented the traditions of people with little formal education were also uncommon at that time. He tried to show how Ozarkers thought and felt about various aspects of their culture, rather than making 'quaint' characters of them."[11]

Mead opens her book, after a theoretical Introduction, with a descriptive, generalized account of a day in a Samoan village. Randolph opens his, after a historical and geographical introduction, with a descriptive, generalized account of "The Hill-Billy at Home" and "Womenfolk and Social Life." The second of these chapters, especially, might draw its inspiration directly from *Coming of Age in Samoa,* which focuses attention upon "the adolescent girl in Samoa."[12] Both writers occasionally manage a comparative viewpoint by unobtrusive means—Mead by calling attention at the outset to "the question which sent me to Samoa" (which asked whether adolescent disturbances observed in America are "due to the nature of adolescence itself or to the civilisation"),[13] Randolph by reference to the way Ozark scenes would strike "furriner" eyes. "Once inside the cabin," he writes, "the 'furriner' is usually struck by the untidy state of affairs." In a later section dealing with diet, he notes that the "Ozarker's table is often a shock and a despair to the hungry traveller."[14] But despite such moments of comparativist perspective—Mead tends to cluster these in separate chapters, such as her Chapter XIII, "Our Educational Problems in the Light of Samoan Contrasts," while Randolph distributes them throughout his text—both books are in the main straightforwardly descriptive accounts, written in a style that is always vivid and often openly impressionistic. Mead wrote later that *Coming of Age in Samoa* was not written as "a popular book," but "I tried to couch it in a language that would be communicative" and "not wrapped up in technical jargon for specialists." [15] Randolph's own Preface noted his desire to "interest the general reader," and the appeal of his book to this same widespread fellow is remarked by both Pound and Scarborough (though the latter calls him "the average reader"). [16]

Finally, *The Ozarks* and *Coming of Age in Samoa* are similar in that they conspicuously do not address the subjects of their investigation. Mead, writing in 1972, acknowledged that "young Samoans who read this book will feel somehow not included, because this account of young people two generations ago was written about them, but not for them, as I would write such a book today." [17] Randolph for his part is clearly addressing outsiders, since *The Ozarks* itself records his observations concerning the reading habits of his informants: "the ordinary hillman reads nothing at all." [18] The trouble, of course, begins when Samoans and Ozarkers, unintended audiences, open the books and sense themselves, as the case may be, excluded, patronized, misrepresented, romanticized, or exposed to ridicule.

Randolph moves with some care in this area. In the first place he stresses at the outset his exclusive interest in a specific subgroup (as does Mead, in fact: "because I was a woman and could hope for greater intimacy in working with girls," and because "our knowledge of primitive girls is far slighter than our knowledge of boys, I chose to concentrate upon the adolescent girl"). [19] *The Ozarks*, as the author points out on his first page, "is not concerned with the progressive element in the Ozark towns, nor with the prosperous valley farmers." Instead, it concentrates its attention upon "the 'hillbilly' or 'ridge-runner' of the more isolated sections." [20]

The Ozarks, then, does not present itself as a comprehensive treatment of the region, but this distinction is easily forgotten once the book is under way and the reader encounters phrasings of glib generalization in surprising contexts. "Every mountain girl," Randolph writes in his "Signs and Superstitions" chapter, "knows that if she puts a drop of her menstrual fluid into a man's liquor he is certain to fall madly in love with her." Later in the same chapter there is a no less astounding claim: "Sexual acts between human beings and domestic animals are rather common in the Ozarks, and nearly every native believes that these unions are sometimes fruitful." [21] Such "diverting and picturesque" details, like the discussion of the Samoan *moetotolo*, "in which a man stealthily appropriates the favours which are meant for another,"[22] were no doubt "likely to interest the general reader." But they were not calculated to please other residents, those "prosperous valley farmers" and members of "the progressive element in the Ozark towns" who resented the general opprobrium which they felt must result from such an unflattering portrait. After *The Ozarks*, if not before, there were people in the Ozarks who were unhappy with Vance Randolph.

Some of these were prominent citizens who felt that Ozark writers in general and Randolph in particular were giving the region a bad name by emphasizing the attitudes and actions of a backward and ignorant minority. These people today have nothing but praise for Randolph, since his work is now perceived as both good advertising for the region and good glorification of our sturdy forebears. The difference is that today's boosters have usually read only a small fraction of Randolph's work; their impression of him is mostly gleaned from brief references in newspaper columns or from such popular reprint booklets as *Vance Randolph in the Ozarks*. But in 1931 and 1932, these people were reading *The Ozarks* and *Ozark Mountain Folks*, and they were not entirely happy with what they saw.

This is not to say that Randolph did nothing to please such tastes as he understood them—there are passages in these early books calculated to gratify even the most assertively celebrative of tastes. Observe, for example, the bumptious racism masquerading as patriotism which closes the introductory chapter of *The Ozarks*:

> It is only in such isolated places that we find the traditional American nowadays, neither refined nor corrupted by the influence of European and Asiatic civilizations. There are not many real Americans left now, and we do not understand them any more. The Ozark hill-billy is a genuine American—that is why he seems so alien to most tourists. In a sense it is true that the American people are making their last stand in the wilderness, and it is here, if anywhere, that we must go to meet our contemporary ancestors in the flesh.[23]

It is not difficult, glancing at the work of other "Ozark writers" of the period, to find similar sentiments, expressed in the same thumping prose. In the March-April, 1930, issue of his monthly *Ozark Life*, Randolph's good friend Otto Ernest Rayburn announced that he was moving his operation from Kingston, Arkansas, to Winslow. The move, he explains, is an economic necessity—he needs to be located on the railway line—and in no way indicates a disregard for the citizens of Kingston. It is a wonderful place, he says. "Its people have the purest Anglo-Saxon blood to be found in America today."[24]

Every region, no doubt, has its own plague of loud praisers of an idealized past. Surely there are magazines and newspaper columns given over to *New England Life* or to the celebration of "real" Westerners and "true" Southerners. The hero, of course, is always the same—he lives close to Nature, is God-fearing and hard-working. His word is his bond. His wrath is terrible. He is self-reliant. His blood is undiluted

Dreary stuff, in short, and Randolph knew it. But he was an Ozark writer, and if at his most ambitious he could model his first major book upon a work as fine as *Coming of Age in Samoa*, he was on the other hand subject to the same pressures that operated on such regional writers as Rayburn, whose magazine published his folksong column, and May Kennedy McCord, the newspaper columnist ("Hillbilly Heartbeats") and radio personality from Springfield, Missouri. Like them, he was forced to solicit the interest of "the general reader" in a way that went beyond the avoidance of jargon that distinguished Mead's work. She could acknowledge, at the beginning of her work, the National Research Council for the "award of a fellowship," her father for "the gift of my travelling expenses to and from the Samoan Islands," and Admiral Stitt and Commander Owen Mink, U.S.N., for "the endorsement of my work" that gained her "the cooperation of the medical authorities in Samoa."[25] Randolph, living in Pineville and ekeing out a hand-to-mouth existence with his writing, enjoyed no such aids, and if his work sometimes exhibited the flaws characteristic of the Ozark booster press, it is to his everlasting credit that he possessed the intelligence and talent to more often rise above these circumstances and produce a work which bears comparison with an acknowledged anthropological classic. It is also pertinent to note, in reference to the ignorance of theoretical and methodological considerations sometimes alleged as inevitable flaws in "amateur" productions, that *Coming of Age in Samoa* was considered a very innovative work in its day. Boas himself, in his 1928 Foreword, credits Mead's work with going beyond the usual "systematic description of human activities," which, while valuable for historical and comparative studies, falls short in that it provides "very little insight into the mental attitudes of the individual." Mead accomplishes more by "having undertaken to identify herself so completely with Samoan youth." In this, says Boas, she is nearly unique: "up to this time hardly any one has taken the pains to identify himself sufficiently with a primitive population to obtain an insight into these problems."[26]

Nobody noticed, perhaps because "primitive" populations were supposed to be darker and more distant, but Vance Randolph, down in the Ozarks, was following in Mead's footsteps. He was, if anything, too up to date, turning out in 1931 and 1932 what later folklorists would call "folk ethnology" or "folklife." Carl Withers, for example, writing an Editor's Introduction to a 1963 reprint of Clifton Johnson's *What They Say in New England*, praised both Johnson and Randolph for "brilliant glimpses of how irrational beliefs and practices function in people's lives."[27] Withers's remarks are directed to Randolph's work generally, with emphasis upon *Ozark Superstitions*, but in 1979 much the same point was applied specifically to *The Ozarks* and *Ozark Mountain Folks* by Herbert Halpert: "Today, since American folklorists generally have accepted the concept of folklife, we look at Randolph's Ozark books and acknowledge him as one of our earliest recorders of a complete folk tradition. With the development of interest in the context of folk genres, in function and performance, we recognize that Vance Randolph led the way."[28]

Halpert, like Withers, associates Clifton Johnson with Randolph, a grouping that rings true at least in terms of direct influence, since Randolph cited Johnson among the writers he admired early and long. Also included is George Korson, the Pennsylvania newspaperman whose work in the coal fields paralleled in many ways Randolph's labors in the Ozarks. These three men, "all of them writers by trade," are credited with having "pioneered the folklife approach, including the life history method." Of Randolph in particular, Halpert adds that it is "convenient" to see his "first two books as marking a kind of watershed in American folklore studies," with later works tending more toward investigations of "folklore in context, emphasizing its importance for the individual and the community."[29] With Randolph's recollections in hand, the club of pioneers must certainly include Margaret Mead, and Zora Neale Hurston, whose *Mules and Men* appeared in 1935 with a Boasian "Preface" identical in its emphases with that written for *Coming of Age in Samoa*. Like Mead, Hurston "entered into the homely life of the southern Negro as one of them" and was thus able "to penetrate through that affected demeanor by which the Negro excludes the White observer effectively from participating in his true inner life."[30] Randolph himself, reviewing J. Mason Brewer's *The Word on the Brazos* in 1954, called it "the best Negro story book I have seen since Zora Neale Hurston's *Mules and Men* appeared in 1935."[31]

Clifton Johnson, George Korson, Margaret Mead, Zora Neale Hurston, and Vance Randolph—good company, indeed, and the

similarities in their careers are sometimes striking. Johnson's work
was done markedly earlier, but *What They Say in New England*,
first published in 1896 and now hailed as "the first systematic collection of American folklore," was not noticed in the *Journal of
American Folklore* for fifty years (Halpert, once again, was on the
case before most of his colleagues—he praised it there in 1947),
even though Johnson knew of Newell's purposes and his book
"reads as if he had used the journal's call [for "Relics of Old English
Folk-Lore"] as an outline."[32] Korson's first book, *Songs and Ballads
of the Anthracite Miner*, published in 1927 at Korson's own expense, was likewise ignored. Hurston's troubles with the academic
world, represented mostly by the omnipresent Boas, are discussed
at length in Robert Hemenway's superb biography. In 1928, while
Randolph was recording "the tales that were told to me in backwoods cabins, around wilderness campfires, on long rides over
mountain trails, beside little stills in big hollows, at frolics and candy-
breakings and play parties,"[33] Hurston was in New Orleans, "knee
deep" in conjure, getting so intimate with the "power doctors" that
she ended up lying nude for sixty-nine hours atop a snake skin, getting her back painted with lightning symbols, drinking a mixture of
wine and blood, and participating in the sacrifice of a black sheep.[34]

Like Hurston, Randolph wrote fiction. Like Johnson, he wrote
books for children. Like Hurston and Korson, he was often short of
money. Korson's employer, the *Elizabeth Times*, went under in the
Great Crash, the bank that had some eight thousand dollars of his
money failed, and for a time he was so strapped he had to move his
family in with his wife's father.[35] Hurston's last brief fling with the
front pages which treated her so cruelly came in 1950 when the
Miami Herald published a "Famous Negro Author Working as Maid
Here" story. Like Randolph, Hurston spent her last years in a
"home"—"When she died on January 28, 1960, writes Hemenway,
Zora Hurston had "'lived in Sorrow's Kitchen and licked all the
pots.'"[36]

Of the five, only Mead had a wealthy father and solid academic
connections, and even she was a maverick within the groves, "rap-
ping" about race with James Baldwin and laying harsh words on the
republic's leaders in the Vietnam era. Other names and other disciplines could no doubt be added. In particular it would be interesting
to examine the place of folkloristic studies like *The Ozarks, Mules
and Men*, and *Songs and Ballads of the Anthracite Miner* in that
more generalized resurgency of interest in native scenes and traditions which was articulated in the theater by the "folk drama"

movement centered at the University of North Carolina (*Porgy* was first produced in New York in 1927), and in the arts by the work of the American Scene painters, headed by the Art Students League and the so-called Regionalists. Grant Wood, "our Hans Memling," produced his famous double portrait of his dentist and his sister, the dentist in overalls and holding a rake, in 1929.[37] John Steuart Curry's *Baptism in Kansas* is from 1928 and Thomas Hart Benton's *America Today* murals for the New School for Social Research were done in 1930–31. "I met all three of those fellows," Randolph said in 1980. "Benton, Curry, and Wood—Benton and I were pretty close. I rated all of 'em very high. I liked them better than any."[38] Benton in the 1930s would impress Charles Seeger with his "Ozark folksongs" in Greenwich Village, and in 1946 he would do the end-paper illustrations for *Ozark Folksongs*.[39] Poets were up to such doings too—Hart Crane published *The Bridge* in 1930, five years after William Carlos Williams' still undervalued prose masterpiece, *In The American Grain*. *The Ozarks*, then, is a book very much rooted in its own cultural and academic milieu. If Randolph's most basic models were the swashbuckling writer-adventurer-scholars of his youthful reading—George Borrow, Charles Godfrey Leland, John Aubrey, Charles Doughty—and if the fundamental predilections fostered by such a background were given additional stimulus and focus by his experiences with Sandburg and Margaret Larkin at Kansas, his additional good fortune (or good judgment) was to choose as his immediate formal pattern a work as excellent as *Coming of Age in Samoa*. His next book, following quickly on the heels of the first, would offer additional innovations.

II

Ozark Mountain Folks, appearing in the fall of 1932, received, if anything, even less attention than its predecessor. It was favorably noticed in such mainstream popular periodicals as the *New York Times Book Review* and the *New Republic*, but failed to gain the attention of academic reviewers. The book was published, like the first volume, by Vanguard Press. Like *The Ozarks, Ozark Mountain Folks* is divided into twelve chapters; the latter volume's 279 pages is close to the former's 310, and the second, like the first, is printed with photographic illustrations. While all the photographs in *The Ozarks* were taken by Randolph himself, and include five of identifiable informants (three are named in the captions, the woman using "The Old-Time Corn Grater" is Mrs. Jewel Lamberson, and "A

Singer of Ancient Ballads" is Mrs. Linnie Bullard), a number of the illustrations in *Ozark Mountain Folks* are credited to Charles Phelps Cushing. "He was a New York photographer," said Randolph. "I didn't know him. The pictures were put in by the Vanguard folks."[40] Two of the photographs are of Randolph himself—one is clearly labeled as such, and the frontispiece, captioned "On the Gander Mountain Trail," shows a young Randolph in the saddle, cigar in place (this photo first appeared in 1928, in the *Forest and Stream* "Lost in the Ozarks" article).

Despite these similarities, however, the two books are very different. In the first place, *The Ozarks* contains a great deal of material reprinted from Randolph's articles. A good portion of the first chapter, "Old Trails and Campfires," is given over to a recounting of the "Pineville Mastodon" story and to Vernon Allison's stalagmite studies. The material here comes mostly from the *New York Times* article of 1926. The fourth chapter, "The Ozark Dialect," is similarly indebted to the previously published dialect articles, especially "Verbal Modesty in the Ozarks," which is very nearly reproduced whole except for the references to other scholarship. The fifth chapter, "Signs and Superstitions," has a considerable infusion of new material, but it is basically a reprinting of Randolph's first *Journal of American Folklore* article, "Folk-Beliefs in the Ozark Mountains." Even the pieces Randolph wrote for the sporting magazines are mined for the pages of *The Ozarks*—the "Jumping Bass in the Ozark Country" piece, for example, which elicited such vehement response from the "anonymous gentleman from Georgia," reappears in the tenth chapter of *The Ozarks*, "Jumpers, Giggers and Noodlers."

All this is not to suggest, however, that *The Ozarks* is no more than a collection of previously published articles. Much of the book is new, including the fine sections on homes and furnishings, food and clothing, which make up the second chapter, "The Hill-Billy at Home," and the extended treatment of "Womenfolk and Social Life" in the following chapter. The discussion of moonshining in the eighth chapter, "Ways That Are Dark," and of tales of lost treasure in the eleventh, "Fools' Gold," are also new. Years later, Randolph once remembered, John Gould Fletcher told him he'd written his books "ass backwards—I should have written the other books first. Details (superstition, tales, ballads) then overview."[41] Right or wrong, and Randolph tended in 1980 to regard it as right, Fletcher's remark describes the overall effect of *The Ozarks* accurately enough. It is an "overview," a comprehensive introduction to the region's folklore and folklife, touching upon everything from geology and archeology to exploration and settlement, homes and their furnishings, the role of women, the organization of social life, speech, beliefs, play-parties, songs, moonshining, hunting and fishing, tales of hidden treasures, and the impact of tourism and sportsmen on the traditional culture.

Ozark Mountain Folks is also an "overview," but it differs markedly in its mode of presentation and it contains a noticeably smaller amount of reprinted material. The contract for the book was signed on March 15, 1932, and the manuscript was titled *Dreadful People*. Randolph tried at least twice to get a book into print with this title, which he took from H. L. Mencken. The Sage of Baltimore was, of course, famous as a critic of the South. His "The Sahara of the Bozart" had appeared in 1917, but Arkansas in particular had come beneath the lash in a later piece, "Famine," which ran in the *Baltimore Sun* on January 19, 1931. "Arkansas is perhaps the most shiftless and backward state in the whole galaxy," Mencken wrote. Then, warming to the task, he turned to first-hand experience:

> Several years ago I enjoyed the somewhat depressing pleasure of making a tour of the country lying along the border between Arkansas and Oklahoma. . . . Such shabby and flea-bitten villages I had never seen before, or such dreadful people. Some of the former were so barbaric that they did not even have regular streets. The houses, such as they were, were plumped down anywhere, at any angle. As for the inhabitants, it is a sober fact that I saw women by the roadside, with children between their knees, picking lice like mother monkeys in a zoo. [42]

Randolph quoted this passage (and more) in the final chapter of *The Ozarks*, and tried unsuccessfully to use the "dreadful people" phrase as a title for both *Ozark Mountain Folks* and *From an Ozark Holler*, the collection of short stories that appeared in 1933. And Randolph, despite taking issue with Mencken's description of the region, as he'd earlier disagreed with his opinions about the existence of American dialects, held his work in very high esteem, publishing three of the *From an Ozark Holler* stories in Mencken's *American Mercury* and finally dedicating *Down in the Holler* to him.

What is most striking about *Ozark Mountain Folks* is the extensive use of a narrative persona. Randolph speaks in his own voice in both books, but where in *The Ozarks* he uses only brief quotations from his informants and often describes them obliquely (as "a poor hill farmer" or "a hard-faced moonshiner"), his characteristic practice in *Ozark Mountain Folks* is to let his "characters" do most of the talking and to give them fictitious names. "No character in this book is the portrait of any actual person," he says in his Preface, adding that the village of "Durgenville" and the settlement of "Poot Holler" are also imaginary.[43] According to Randolph's later recollection, these "characters" are more properly "composites." "I knew three or four old men; I used material from several of them to make Windy Bill."[44] But he stresses in the Preface that what they say is "true in every essential detail": "It must be made clear, however, that the data here presented are not fabrications of mine. . . . The dialect used is the actual speech of the Ozark hillmen, among whom I have lived and worked for more than a decade. The descriptions of primitive ways of living, outworn handicrafts, old-time social activities and the like, are the sober reminiscences of elderly folk who know whereof they speak."[45]

Randolph is not completely consistent in maintaining this distinction between the two books, since the Clarence Sharp mentioned in connection with the chapter on hunting traditions, "Where the Fox-Squirrels Bark," was in fact his good friend and is named as such in *The Ozarks*. There is a photograph of Mrs. Ada Check, too, captioned "Carding Wool," which appears among the portraits of Randolph and the other photographs by Cushing. But the major roles in *Ozark Mountain Folks*—Bib Tarkey the blacksmith, and Ezry Breen the singing teacher, and Aunt Elvy, Windy Bill's wife, and Carrie Langley the ballad singer—are all "composites" created in the manner of Windy Bill himself. The "Snake County" reference goes back to the 1923 dialect paper by Jay L. B. Taylor where "Spike" Randolph appears as a character.

The result is a book written largely in dialect, something very different from *The Ozarks*, but beneath this obvious stylistic change Randolph is still very much about the business of providing an ethnographic "overview" of the region's traditional culture. His remarks in the first chapter contrasting the "village aristocrats" of Durgenville with the "tiny settlement called Poot Holler," where the people are "genuine old-time Ozarkers," are exactly parallel to the first volume's distinction between the "progressive element" in the region's towns and the "ridge-runner" of the most remote districts.[46] The sixth and seventh chapters, "Hill-Billy Homespun" and "Local Color," deal in considerable detail with the complicated and backbreaking labors involved in the "carding," spinning, and weaving of linsey-woolsey and other fabrics, and with the no less formidable tasks connected with the dyestuffs native to the hills. Randolph's informants here are women, of course, and these chapters add to the portrait of "Womenfolk and Social Life" provided in *The Ozarks*. Both volumes have chapters that center upon folksongs, and

"The Poot Holler Literary" and "Frolic up the Holler" from *Ozark Mountain Folks* complement the picture of traditional social events given in the first book's sixth chapter, "The Passing of the Play-Party." *Ozark Mountain Folks* also has a chapter on the informal vigilante groups known locally as "bald-knobbers" or "night-riders" (in 1944, writing as "Harvey N. Castleman," Randolph would produce for Haldeman-Julius a booklet devoted to the heyday of such groups in the 1880s), another on the subject of "Witches and Witch-Masters," a third on the old-time schools of the region, and a final chapter that presents in considerable detail the material covered in a typical "singing school." Of these, only "Witches and Witch-Masters" had been previously published in the 1931 issue of *Folk-Say*, an annual edited by B. A. Botkin at the University of Oklahoma.

But perhaps the most interesting new note in *Ozark Mountain Folks* is the ninth chapter, "Windy Hilltops," which marks Randolph's first venture into the world of folktale scholarship. It's a substantial chapter too, the second longest in the book (in both volumes the folksong chapters are the longest). It opens with a series of Davy Crockett and Ab Yancey stories, the latter yarns centering upon the exploits of "a frock-coated, long-haired gambler who held forth in the eighties," was reputed to have killed a number of men, "and was suspected of turning his talents to bank robbery on occasion." There are also several wild tall tales about enormous mosquitoes and a hunter who bent his rifle barrel so he could successfully shoot a huge buck "which always eluded him by running around a big knoll before he could fire." [47]

The longest single tale included is the one titled "Talking River" when it is reprinted in *Who Blowed Up the Church House?* Windy Bill Hatfield is the teller in *Ozark Mountain Folks* but Randolph's notes in the later volume credit the story to William Hatton and give the date of its telling as July, 1929. The story itself is a fine yarn in which one Charley Barstow, a "pizen mean" villain, is turned into a toadfrog by an elfish "leetle small dried-up ol' feller" (who identifies himself as "'th' king o' these parts'") before he can add the killing of his dumb brother to his list of crimes. The brother's speech is restored by the "leetle feller" too, but he is warned to keep silent about his brother's transformation, on pain of a punishment worse than his original affliction. "'If you ever tell a livin' soul whut you've saw hyar today, you'll never stop talkin' ag'in!'" The brother carries the secret to his deathbed but then calls in his family and tells them the story. Within an hour of his death a new stream emerges suddenly

in the hollow, to become known as "Talking River" because of its
continuing babble, but the local people have their own name for it,
of course: "'We allus called it Bud's Creek,'" says Windy Bill, "'An'
some folk still thinks Bud Barstow ain't what you might call dead
nohow.'"[48]

A number of the other tales in "Windy Hilltops" and "Witches and
Witch-Masters" are reprinted in one or another of the later folktale
volumes published by Columbia in the 1950s, and there they are
accompanied by annotations giving the name of each informant and
the date of the tale's telling. The enterprise is somewhat more speculative, but much the same thing can be done with the songs in
Ozark Mountain Folks that make up the eleventh chapter, "The
Sport of Ballad-Hunting." Thirteen songs are printed, all with music. The first thing to note is the obvious preference for "old" songs
already evident in "The Songs Grandfather Sang" columns—all
thirteen songs are Child ballads. As presented in *Ozark Mountain
Folks* the songs are provided by four informants—five by Zeke
Langley, three by his wife Carrie, two by Windy Bill Hatfield himself, and three by Jethro Tolliver. Checking the texts against the
variants of the same songs as these are printed in *Ozark Folksongs*,
it's often an easy matter to see who actually provided the songs. The
five songs given to Zeke Langley, for example, were in fact obtained
from five different informants, not one of them male. In four cases
the texts in *Ozark Folksongs* and *Ozark Mountain Folks* are virtually identical, the only differences being a tendency toward dialect
spelling in *Ozark Mountain Folks* and toward regularized orthogra-
phy in *Ozark Folksongs*. The third stanza of "Lord Bateman," for example, begins as follows in *Ozark Mountain Folks*: "In this hyar
prison thar growed a tree,/Hit growed so very stout an' strong." In
Ozark Folksongs the same stanza opens, "In this here prison there
grew a tree, thin /It grew so very stout an' strong."[49]

In one instance, however, a more striking difference occurs, and
it seems clear that in 1932 Randolph was not yet so systematically
opposed to the presentation of composite versions of songs and tales
as he was in the 1940s and 1950s. The song is "The House Carpenter," and Zeke Langley's version of eleven stanzas is quite clearly
the same as the one Randolph collected from Mrs. Carrie Baber in
1921, except that Mrs. Baber's version ends with the tenth stanza.
Zeke Langley's eleventh stanza, however, the moralizing conclusion which says that if only the unfortunate woman had stayed at
home with her babes and her house carpenter, "I'm shore he'd of
treated her well," is nearly identical with the single stanza conclu-

sion printed as the third variant in *Ozark Folksongs*.[50] Randolph got this stanza from his friend Lewis Kelley, the "singing teacher" pictured in *The Ozarks* and again at the reins of his covered wagon in *Ozark Folksongs*. Kelley gave Randolph the final stanza of "The House Carpenter" in August, 1931, just in time for its inclusion in *Ozark Mountain Folks*, and Zeke Langley in this instance is Mrs. Carrie Baber spliced with Lewis Kelley.

Randolph does not do this often, even in his earliest work—Zeke Langley's other four contributions are all identical in stanza length with the texts printed in *Ozark Folksongs*—but the possibility of this instance being simply a case of mistaken speculation is rendered less likely by the presence of a second example in *Ozark Mountain Folks*. This song, the last in the chapter, attributed to Jethro Tolliver and said to have "no local title," is a version of "The Farmer's Cursed Wife," as Randolph notes.[51] Tolliver's version has thirteen stanzas. Two versions of this song are printed in *Ozark Folksongs*, under the title, "The Old Man Under the Hill." One, obtained from Mrs. Isabel Spradley of Van Buren, Arkansas, in 1929, contains twelve stanzas, while the other, contributed by Miss Myrtle Lain of Linn Creek, Missouri, in 1930, contains seventeen. The *Ozark Mountain Folks* text uses Mrs. Spradley's version as its base, but breaks after the ninth stanza to finish with four stanzas from Miss Lain's version. Randolph tinkers with the latter too, since "The Old Man under the Hill" contains nonsense syllables in the second and final line of each stanza, and these syllables in Mrs. Spradley's version differ from those in Miss Lain's—the second line is "hi di diddle di day" in the former, "Hi ho dan do" in the latter. What Randolph does, of course, in order to make Jethro Tolliver's text coherent, is insert the nonsense syllables from Mrs. Spradley's version into the stanzas taken from Miss Lain's.[52]

The same procedure applied to the songs in the "Ozark Folk-Songs" chapter of *The Ozarks* gives very similar results, although more songs are printed and a much greater variety is presented. Of the twenty-three songs included, all with tunes as well as texts, only five are Child ballads, and native American ballads ("Oma Wise," "McFee's Confession"), outlaw ballads ("Cole Younger," "Sam Bass," "Jesse James"), what are called "Negro or pseudo-Negro" songs ("The Jawbone Song," "Mister Booger"), and temperance songs ("The Drunkard," "The Whiskey Seller") are all represented. Again, as in *Ozark Mountain Folks*, most of the texts match up very well with their reappearance in *Ozark Folksongs*, differing again mostly

in a greater tendency toward dialect spelling in the 1931 version.
But in at least two instances Randolph appears to have patched together two versions to obtain the texts printed in 1931. His "Barbara
Allen," for example, appears in *The Ozarks* in a version of eleven
stanzas, and is clearly based on the sixth of the fifteen variants
of the song printed in *Ozark Folksongs* (these are lettered, however, rather than numbered, so that the source version is the one
labeled F). This text, given to Randolph by "a young woman in
Joplin, Mo.," who requested anonymity, was obtained in 1924 and
ran ten stanzas.[53] (This version can be matched to the one printed
in *The Ozarks* with some confidence—they are matched in nearly
every detail, and no other versions share the line in the second
stanza where the servant sent to Barbara with the news of "Sweet
William's" serious illness announces that "Mosso's sick, an' sent for
you."[54]) The two versions differ only in the longer one's inclusion of
a stanza where Sweet William responds to Barbara's diagnosis
("young man, you are a-dyin'") by prescribing the conditions of his
own recovery:

> Oh yes, I'm sick, I'm very sick
>   An' death is on me dwellin',
> But never better will I be
>   Till I git Barbra Allen.[55]

In the *Ozark Folksongs* text Barbara proceeds directly from diagnosis to recrimination, reminding William of the time in the tavern
when he "slighted Barbra Allen."[56]

Two of the fifteen versions in *Ozark Folksongs* include the additional stanza, but one (the N text) was collected in 1941. Randolph,
then, added it from the other (the D text, obtained from Mrs. Judy
Jane Whittaker of Anderson, Missouri, in 1928), to present as one
song a composite text obtained from two people in two places at two
times four years apart.[57]

All this is, of course, unsurprising. By the 1930s the desirability of
unamended and fully documented texts was "a very ancient scholarly convention."[58] The standard rationale for departures from this
ideal seems to have been desire for "popular appeal." Randolph's
books, as the reviewers perceived, were clearly aimed at a wide market—they went into the world unadorned with bibliographies,
indices, footnotes, the standard garb of donnish swagger. It bears
emphasis, too, that these rare composites can be traced only by
comparison with Randolph's later work, which did aim for scholarly

respectability, and secured it so surely that the standard survey of American collections refers to his "towering" achievements, his "magnificent" collections, and his "thorough job" in providing "the background of the material."[59]

Randolph's great master here was, of course, Belden, but his influence is most evident in *Ozark Folksongs*. The earlier books, to the extent that they participate in any tradition of folklore scholarship, exhibit greatest similarity to that strain of salvage-oriented work rooted in the nationalistic romanticism of the nineteenth century. In the United States the announced concern was to preserve (by recording) "the fast-vanishing remains of Folk-Lore" generally, and specifically to seek these "remains" from four primary areas, the first of which involved "Relics of Old English Folk-Lore (ballads, tales, superstitions, dialect, etc.)."[60] It is this venerable tradition that joins with the influence of the boosterism of the local Ozark press to account for the "real Americans" passages of *The Ozarks* and *Ozark Mountain Folks*, and the same tradition is behind the elegaic strain that runs through both books. Randolph titles one chapter of *The Ozarks* "The Passing of the Play-Party" to indicate the disappearance of a particular kind of traditional lore, and concludes the "Signs and Supersititions" chapter with explicit statement of the need for immediate recording: "But the collecting of these superstitions must be attended to at once, before the entire body of Ozark folk-lore is driven into hiding by the laughter of the schoolmarms and tourists." The old-time shooting matches, too, are "now practically a thing of the past," and the same influx of outsiders "is rapidly wiping out the old folk-speech."[61]

Ozark Mountain Folks is identical in tone. Aunt Elvy's demonstration of traditional weaving practices ends on just this note: "'Us ol' folks is a-dyin' off mighty fast,' remarked Aunt Elvy as we left the weavin'-shed one day, 'an' thar ain't a young-un in these parts whut knows th' first thing 'bout rale weavin'. Two-three more winters, an' they'll be a-choppin' up the ol' looms for kindlin' wood. I reckon,' she added soberly, 'that this hyar's th' last piece o' linsey 'll ever be wove in th' Holler.'" Aunt Elvy dies soon afterward, and the book itself ends with the narrator's last visit to Poot Holler after the news has come of Windy Bill's death. The place is deserted. "Dead ashes lay in the fireplace now, dead leaves were drifted across the worn puncheon floor." The visitor walks around the small place a final time, "past the weavin'-shed, past the old springhouse, past the corn-crib Windy Bill built the year Jesse James was killed," then sits in thought "in my old place on the step-rock till the harvest moon came up over Gander Mountain." The book ends with his departure: "A little breeze sprang up as I rode down the trail for the last time, and Windy Bill's old chair rocked gently to and fro in the moonlight."[62]

There are, of course, more contemporary and more popular sources for this tone than Newell's prospectus, though it seems clear from Randolph's citations in his earliest articles that he had checked through the back issues of the *Journal of American Folklore*. The first piece he published in its pages, in 1927, included footnote references to articles as far back as 1892. But the most obvious inspirations for works like *The Ozarks* and *Ozark Mountain Folks* are the several "Southern Highlanders" volumes that had appeared in the previous twenty years. Prominent among these are Josiah H. Combs' *The Kentucky Highlanders* (1913), John C. Campbell's *The Southern Highlander and His Homeland* (1921), and Horace Kephart's *Our Southern Highlanders* (1913, revised and enlarged 1922). Randolph had cited all of these works by 1927, and there are hints of each in his own books, but the latter two, and especially Kephart's study, have the more obvious influence.

John C. Campbell was a teacher who came into the mountains before the turn of the century. His book, while similar to Randolph's *The Ozarks* in many ways, is dedicated to bringing progress and reform to the region's isolated people. His two concluding chapters are titled "Avenues for Contact and Progress" and "The New Basis of Appeal." Campbell's work was supported in part by religious interests too—"as principal of the school he was also superintendent of the Union Sunday school, and teacher of the men's bible class"— and this focus is reflected in his book as well.[63] Two chapters are devoted to "The Growth of Denominationalism in the Highlands" and "The Religious Life of the Rural Highlands." There is no chapter on folksongs, and while *The Southern Highlander and His Homeland* is engagingly written and clearly addressed to a general audience, there is none of Randolph's emphasis upon "such matters as seem to me diverting and picturesque." Campbell's book, like Randolph's, is provided with photographic illustrations; unlike his it has several appendices and statistical tables, a bibliography, and an index.

Randolph cites Campbell in his first dialect article for an example of the term "norate," but the most telling influence of his work comes from his seventh chapter, "The Rural Highlander at Home," which very probably inspired Randolph's own analogous chapter in *The Ozarks*, "The Hill-Billy at Home." The titles alone would be enough to suggest the connection, but there are in addition any number of echoes and details to confirm the relationship. On the matter of the constant subordination of women and girls, for example, Campbell writes that from babyhood on "the boy is the favored lord of all he surveys," while Randolph says that "from the cradle the male child lords it over his sisters."[64] Early marriages, too, are treated by both authors, with Campbell writing that a "girl is a spinster at eighteen, and on the 'cull list' by twenty," and Randolph reporting that when a woman "reaches the age of twenty-five she is on the 'cull list,' and at thirty she is definitely an old maid."[65]

Horace Kephart, like Randolph, had no grand purpose in mind when he turned his attention to the southern Appalachians. He was interested in hunting, not education or uplift, and he was by profession a writer, the author of numerous articles in outdoor and sporting magazines and of books on similar topics. The mark of *Our Southern Highlanders* is everywhere in Randolph, not just in his first books but in his earlier articles as well. Kephart's sixteenth chapter, "The Mountain Dialect," contains brief references to the mountaineer's use of archaic, recondite, and euphemistic vocabulary. An instance of quintuple negation is also included. *The Ozarks* and *Our Southern Highlanders* both have chapters on moonshining, and they have identical titles, "Ways That Are Dark." Kephart, like Randolph in *Ozark Mountain Folks*, makes frequent use of pseudonyms.

The books do differ in emphasis, with Kephart giving more prominence to hunting, moonshining, and feuding while Randolph devotes more space to the everyday lives of his Ozark subjects. But Kephart and Randolph were two of a kind—they had not only their writing, their interest in mountain people, and their devotion to field sports in common but also an attraction to "Indian relics" and an addiction to guns. For Randolph's article, "Instead of a Holster," there is Kephart's description of the "suspender holster" worn by the friend whose speed with sidearms gains him the name of Mr. Quick in *Our Southern Highlanders*.[66]

It is important to recall that Kephart's book was popular too, in both senses of the word, and to understand that Randolph, in emulating it, surely hoped that some of its success would accrue to his own work. Nowhere is this emulation clearer than in the prefatory remarks appended by each author. Here is Kephart, in the Preface to the revised edition, dated 1922:

> This book deals with the *mass* of the mountain people. It is not concerned with the relatively few townsmen, and prosperous valley farmers, who owe to outside influences all that distinguishes them from

their back-country kinsmen. The real mountaineers are the multitude of little farmers living up the branches and on the steep hillsides, away from the main-traveled roads. . .

No one book can give a complete survey of mountain life in all its aspects. Much must be left out. I have chosen to write about those features that seemed to me most picturesque. The narrative is to be taken literally. There is not a line of fiction or exaggeration in it.[67]

Comparing this with Randolph's own Preface to *The Ozarks* leads inescapably to the conclusion that it must have been written with Kephart's work immediately at hand, with changes of phrasing deliberately introduced to avoid bald plagiarism. Here is Randolph:

The Ozark country and its people cannot be adequately described in any one book, nor can any writer do justice to the subject in all of its fascinating aspects. I have chosen to write about such matters as seem to me diverting and picturesque, and likely to interest the general reader. This book, therefore, is not concerned with the progressive element in the Ozark towns, nor with the prosperous valley farmers, who have been more or less modernized by recent contacts with civilization. It deals rather with the "hill-billy" or "ridge-runner" of the more isolated sections, and it is based upon some ten years of association with people of this type. Every statement in the book is intended to be taken quite seriously and literally; there is not a line of fiction or of intentional exaggeration in it.[68]

Additional influences could no doubt be found—Jean Thomas, for example, a court stenographer from Rowan County, Kentucky, was already in print in 1931 with *Devil's Ditties*, the first in a series of astoundingly romanticized volumes in which her beloved "mountain children" (who could be in their eighties) were costumed in homespun, fitted with folksy names, and exhibited to an admiring public at the "Singin' Gatherin'" held annually at "Traipsin' Woman cabin."[69] Randolph, may all the gods forgive him, went so far as to praise one of these productions, *The Traipsin' Woman*, in the *American Journal of Sociology*, and he includes *Devil's Ditties* in the *Ozark Folksongs* bibliography, so perhaps Thomas's Jilson Setters, "The Singin' Fiddler of Lost Hope Hollow," or one of his Anglo-Saxon fellows immured in Thomas's fantastic notions of Gregorian chant and even "ancient Chinese music," had his effect upon Randolph's first books.[70]

But Kephart was his major source among the popular writers, as Mead was among the academics. In *The Ozarks* and *Ozark Mountain Folks*, then, Randolph attempted to balance scholarly respectability with popular appeal. The books had some success in the second area, very little in the former, but at least Randolph's name was now more widely circulated. As early as 1929 the local booster press in the person of Otto Ernest Rayburn was hailing Randolph in print as "the greatest living authority on the folk-songs of the Ozarks," at a time when that title surely attached to Belden.[71] But by the time his first two books had appeared and been reviewed, the "foremost authority" tag began to have a wider distribution. By 1933 Hollywood had heard of Randolph, and he would be summoned as an "Ozark expert" to work as a writer on *Comin' Round the Mountain*, an MGM script for Wallace Beery and Marie Dressler.

III

Before Hollywood called, however, Randolph had surfaced as a fiction writer—*From An Ozark Holler*, a collection of twenty-two short stories, had appeared in the fall of 1933 to generally positive reviews. The *New York Times*, identifying Randolph as "the recognized authority on Ozark language and customs," called his collection "thoroughly enjoyable and worth while, a volume of genuine Americana, of a sensitive literary quality."[72] Randolph's own Foreword simply reverses the emphasis of the Preface to *Ozark Mountain Folks*. The latter says that while the names of places and people are not real persons or places found on maps, the material itself is "true in every essential detail," while *From An Ozark Holler* is described as "scrupulously accurate in matters of dialect and folklore, but the book is a work of fiction."[73] The progression, in fact, moves nicely from the straightforward, first-person narration of *The Ozarks*, through the use of composite personae in *Ozark Mountain Folks*, to the overt "fiction" of *From an Ozark Holler, The Camp on Wildcat Creek*, and *Hedwig*. More than half of the stories in *From an Ozark Holler* are first-person narrations, and in many of these Randolph makes no attempt to disguise the identification of the narrator with himself. "The Feather-Grafter," for example, opens with a paragraph that sets the stage for a story told by a prisoner: "The prisoners in the stone jail-house used to sing a good deal, and I often sat on the court-house lawn in order to hear their old-time songs. My collection of these folksongs is the only one ever made in the Ozark country, I think, but I have never been able to find a publisher for it. But no matter—this is the story of Jube Halliday, who called out from behind the bars. . ."[74]

In another story, "It Sure Won't Do No Harm," Randolph introduces a tale of an old "granny woman" by reference to his own previous researches. "When I first came to the Holler I was very much interested in these hillbilly healers and their lore. . . . Later I wrote a solemn paper on the subject for the *Journal of American Folklore*, and used a lot of the same material in one of my books."[75] Windy Bill Hatfield, Aunt Elvy, and Bib Tarkey, among other places and people from *Ozark Mountain Folks*, make a second appearance in the pages of *From An Ozark Holler*, and the *New York Times* reviewer noted that where "the author leaves off and the folklore begins is sometimes difficult to determine."[76] Randolph, in short, was appearing before the public in a different guise—he was a fiction writer now—but he was peddling much the same wares as before. In 1978 Randolph was straightforward concerning his own powers and the considerations that motivated the move to short stories and novels. The tales in *From an Ozark Holler*, he said, were "either tales of what actually happened around Pineville, or else stories that were traditional in that neighborhood. I heard all of them." They were presented as fictions "because the publishers wouldn't print folktales then." With specific reference to *Ozark Mountain Folks*, he said, "I could never be a novelist . . . . I've got no inventive powers at all."[77]

In the middle 1930s, however, Randolph was in the process of testing his "inventive powers." *From An Ozark Holler* was planned as a collection of "Ozark short stories," according to the contract, dated November 15, 1932, and several of its stories appeared that same year in *Folk-Say* ("The Saga of Little Ab Yancey") and Mencken's *American Mercury* ("The Burying of an Infidel," "A Man of Letters," "A Saint on Earth").[78] In "The Saga of Little Ab Yancey" and in several of the other stories first printed in the *From an Ozark Holler* collection, Randolph the first-person narrator is addressed by a new name—Doc. "People called me that in Pineville and Galena," Randolph reported. "It didn't mean I was a professor or a physician—it was a term used for a small time gambler."[79] The same volume also represented his second and final defeat in the attempt to have a book titled *Dreadful People* (though it was announced under that title in the *Pineville Democrat*, with what local reaction one can only guess). He did succeed, however, in outraging decency by dedicating the book "To Agnes, Mable, and Becky." This allusion, now recondite, would have been widely recognized in 1933, according to Randolph, as referring to a well-known brand of condom.

With this debut as a fiction writer under his belt, Randolph turned next to a "story for boys," and produced *The Camp on Wildcat Creek* for Alfred Knopf in 1934. Durgenville, Bib Tarkey, and a younger Hatfield named Carney are characters in this opus, which is dedicated to one "Buddy" Kiehl, identified as "age fourteen, First Class Scout."[80] Randolph's second wife, the Mary Celestia Parler to whom *The Talking Turtle* is dedicated, called it "the worst book for boys ever written," and the work seems to have passed nearly unnoticed before the eyes of reviewers.[81] The story it tells is a simple one: Jimmie Dean and his friend Bob Nash, Chicago boys of high school age, summer in the Ozarks, watched over and guided in the ways of the mountains by Mr. Dean's old friend and fishing companion, Lum Evans. Fish are gigged, trees and animals identified, an eagle's nest visited, the habits of hornets painfully explored, squirrels and groundhogs shot, cooked and eaten, and tall tales told throughout by Mr. Evans. In one lengthy section "Doc" Sackerville conducts an archeological investigation in a nearby shelter and favors the boys with an account of the region's prehistory. Jacob's Cavern is alluded to, and considerable respectful attention is given to Allison's old notion of stalagmitic dating. Allison is mentioned by name. At the end of the summer the boys, sporting tans and exuding good health, bid farewell to Lum and depart for Chicago. *The Camp On Wildcat Creek*, it is gratifying to report, is one very clean book. In the first chapter Mr. Dean does suggest that they take some good clothes along in case they decide to go to a dance, but dances and girls do not surface again. Neither Jimmie nor Bob is reported to say an unacceptable word or have an impure thought. They even instruct poor Lum Evans in the need for proper garbage disposal.

The Camp on Wildcat Creek, then, while it might seem to justify Mrs. Randolph's harsh judgment, continues to present basically factual material with the thinnest of fictional veneer. It was also a milestone in Randolph's career in that it was the first volume for which he received a publisher's advance. The contract, signed on March 14, 1933, called for payment of "Two Hundred and Fifty Dollars as follows: Fifty Dollars on signing of this agreement and Fifty Dollars every thirty days thereafter for four months."[82] There is good evidence that Randolph encouraged his friends to believe his first books had enjoyed a financial success consonant with their critical approval, that substantial advances and royalties kept his skillet greasy and his pockets full. Sometimes his encouragement went further—on March 26, 1932, for example, he wrote from Pineville to his friend Margaret E. Haughawout, an English teacher in Pittsburg who had reviewed his first book in the Kansas City newspapers. The subject was *Ozark Mountain Folks*: "I finally sold my second Ozark book, but they only gave me $250 advance—little more than half what I got on the other one. You could of heard me holler clear to New York, but it didn't do no good."[83]

Bold posing, this, since the contracts for both books specify the 10 percent on the first 5,000 copies, 15 percent thereafter with no mention of any advance for either book. The letter to Margaret Haughawout goes on to adduce further complaints: "I have done some short short stories, and it seems to me that they are pretty good—no worse than my books, anyhow. Some day, when you aren't so busy, I wish you would read three or four of them, and tell me why I can't sell them to the magazines."[84]

By 1933 things were looking better. He had sold several of the stories to magazines, and had published a whole collection in *From An Ozark Holler*. The advance from Knopf was a real $250, too, unlike the money of 1932, and by 1935, signing the contract for *Hedwig*, he'd do even better. Meanwhile, in 1934 he was busy with other things besides the antiseptic adventures of Jimmie Dean and Bob Nash. *Ozark Outdoors*, a collection of twenty-four hunting and fishing stories by Randolph and Guy W. von Schriltz, a lawyer and sportsman from Pittsburg, was issued by Vanguard, another article appeared in the *Journal of American Folklore*, and *Missouri Magazine* published "Cave Bats and a Unique Industry," an account of Randolph's meeting with guano harvester Mr. C. L. Weekly.

Ozark Outdoors reprinted eight of Randolph's articles from the sporting magazines, and included two others printed for the first time. Most of the fourteen pieces supplied by von Schriltz had also been previously published. The book was dedicated to Missouri Senator Harry B. Hawes, "in grateful recognition of his untiring efforts toward the conservation of wild life," and was printed with nine photographs showing the authors and others in action against Ozark fauna.[85] The frontispiece is a picture of Randolph fishing, and there are at least two other pictures that show him armed and taking aim. One of the previously unpublished Randolph articles, "Rabbits and Rifle Guns," is interesting for its recounting of a hunting expedition with the novelist Thames Williamson, who had "put me in a good humor" by praising *The Ozarks*. The other new essay, "Ozark Mountain Coons," consists mostly of facts about the habits of raccoons as told to Randolph by Carney Peters. The piece ends with the successful killing of a famous coon, "Ol' Three-Foot." Windy Bill Hatfield returns in a supporting role.

The article in the *Journal of American Folklore* was "Ozark Mountain Riddles," which Randolph co-authored with Isabel Spradley. The "I'm an amateur" note is sounded again in two brief notes before and after a "fragmentary collection" of sixty-five riddles offered in the absence of other studies, lest the material "be lost forever with the passing of the present generation." It is hoped in conclusion that the paper "will attract the attention of some student who can make a more serious and exhaustive study of the matter."[86] (And in fact his riddle collection did attract the attention of scholars with a specific interest in the genre. In 1944 Randolph and Archer Taylor published "Riddles in the Ozarks" in the *Southern Folklore Quarterly*—the collection supplied by Randolph, the arrangement and annotation by Taylor. Later that year Paul G. Brewster published a collection of eighteen "'Spelling Riddles' From the Ozarks" in the same journal, using thirteen from Randolph's collection that he acquired via Taylor.) Isabel Spradley's name had appeared with Randolph's before, in a 1933 *American Speech* article, "Quilt Names in the Ozarks," and her help is acknowledged in both *The Ozarks* and *Ozark Mountain Folks*. As Mrs. Isabel France she conducted a weekly column, "The Hills of Home," in a Fort Smith, Arkansas, newspaper, which was addressed primarily to nature lovers and bird watchers. Randolph identified her as a "teacher and writer," and testified that "what she writes is always worth reading."[87]

The short piece devoted to the guano collector is of interest only for its autobiographical elements and for the announcement of a book that was never published. The article itself, according to a headnote, was "reproduced from Mr. Randolph's book, 'Ozark Trails,' which will appear next year." The first paragraph attributes Randolph's first acquaintance with Mr. Weekly to "Honorable Dewey Short," the congressman brother of bank robber Leonard Short, and admits that the author first thought his "old friend was spoofing." But the congressman knew "that I earn my daily bread by writing features," and his story of the man who lived by gathering bat guano turned out to be true.[88]

In the middle 1930s, then, Randolph was keeping his hand in among the academics by continuing to place articles in the professional journals, but was obviously centering his attention upon fiction. With a volume of short stories and a novel for boys behind him, he turned to his most ambitious fictional work. Actually, he'd had *Hedwig* in mind for some time—two Vanguard contracts exist for the book, the first one dated May 12, 1931, prior to the publication of *The Ozarks*. The second, under which the book was finally produced, was dated March 1, 1935, when the book must have been nearly complete (the contract called for delivery of the "final, corrected manuscript on or before April 1, 1935"). The advance was a good one: $150 when the contract was signed and another $150 when the manuscript was delivered.[89]

There was a third contract also involved in the writing of *Hedwig*,

though the book is not named. On April 5, 1934, almost a year before the second Vanguard contract, an accord was reached between
Randolph and his friend Ralph Church that made Church an inves-
tor in Randolph's career. The contract, executed with all the full-
dress rhetoric of those with the publishing companies, called for
Church to pay Randolph $800—"$100 per month, payable monthly
beginning with April, 1934, for eight consecutive months." In return Randolph agreed to produce by January 1, 1935, a manuscript
of "not less than 40,000 words" on a topic of his choosing, to "devote
his best efforts to obtaining a publisher for said manuscript," and to
"pay over to the second party all money paid to him on royalties on
said manuscript . . . until said second party shall receive the sum of
$800.00."[90] After that Church was to get 25 percent of additional
royalties.

Church evidently debated the matter for some time, since Randolph wrote to him on April 23 urging him to sign. The deal, Randolph said, was "really a pretty good proposition," and he went on to
describe his prospects:

> There is every reason to think that another year will see me getting
> into the money. I have done ten years of drudgery without much help
> from anybody, and I am just reaching the place where I can cash in on
> my work. I'm not slowing up, either—witness my two books now in
> press to appear this fall.
> I wish you would decide what you are going to do about this con-
> tract. As it is now, I'm a little up in the air. If I've got to drop my serious
> work and go back to the newspaper grind, I may as well know it now.[91]

The letter ends with an invitation to visit but notes again that the
author is a busy man on the rise. "I go to St. Louis next week to
address the National Folklore Festival, but I'll be back by Thurs-
day."[92] Church eventually signed, and Randolph's notation on the
contract certifies that the last of the $800 was paid in November,
but the investment turned out a poor one. *Hedwig* did fairly well in
the hands of reviewers, but it fared very poorly in the marketplace.
A year after its publication the book had sold just over 500 copies,
and the royalty statement for the first half of 1936 told the whole
story for Church: four copies had been sold in the six-month period,
garnering a total of 80¢ in royalties. The bottom line read "over-
drawn Balance $222.60," meaning that sales were far short of cover-
ing the original advance. Assuming that Randolph gave Church
the entire $300 advance from Vanguard, his investment cost him
$500.00.[93]

Hedwig was, as reviewers noted, a new departure for Randolph. The story's major character is a German-American woman, born in Russia, and her first-person account is done in a convincing dialect. Percy Hutchison, in the *New York Times Book Review*, said that the skills apparent in Randolph's "folk-books" also "reappear abundantly in 'Hedwig,' and combine to make the brief history of a girl born to poverty and reared in brutality a minor annal powerful in simplicity."[94] Stanley Vestal, in the *Saturday Review*, called attention to the book's humor and social criticism but added that "the dominant feeling is one of pathos, relentlessly impressed upon us by the girl's helpless realism. Hedwig was easily pleased, but she didn't have a good time."[95] Other reviews were extravagant in the book's praise. The *Chicago Daily News* called it a "little masterpiece," and even Mr. Hutchison mentioned Tess Durbeyfield in passing, allowing Vanguard's blurb writers to trumpet on dust jackets that Randolph's novel was "compared by the *New York Times* to *Tess of the D'Urbervilles*."[96]

There was one more measured comment, however, by an unidentified reviewer in *The Nation*, which may have suggested to Randolph the opinion he cited as fact in 1978—that he had "no inventive powers at all" and could "never be a novelist." The author of *Hedwig*, said the reviewer, "has both honesty and intelligence; he knows his characters, and he presents them with a certain degree of truth. Unfortunately—for he has chosen a subject which demands the utmost in artistic treatment—he lacks any kind of artistic sense."[97]

A decade later, in his "Peter Nemo" production, *Confessions of a Ghost Writer*, Randolph recounted two additional anecdotes with the same message. The first concerns his adventures with Too-Frantic: "I was not over-burdened with modesty in those days, but I knew that I lacked the inner fire that makes for originality in writing. I was a good student and a competent craftsman, but the little spark wasn't there. I laughed at poor Too-Frantic because of his difficulties with the English tongue, but I realized that he was the real thing, while I was only a glib schoolmaster gone astray." The second anecdote concerns a work Randolph read in manuscript. It had been written by a woman, and had been rejected by many publishers as "too morbid." His own reading convinced Randolph that the work was "a truly great novel," and the encounter humbled him: "It is because of this experience that I have been content to earn my living as a ghost and anonymous hack, and have never tried to write serious fiction under my own power. I believe I could turn out some pretty fair stories, but I know I could never write anything as good as *The Seed Grows Cold.*"[98]

IV

Whatever the combination of factors, aesthetic and financial, which influenced Randolph's decision, the fact is that after *Hedwig* he turned away from "serious fiction." *The Camp-Meeting Murders*, described on the dust jacket as "an exciting story with an eerie setting amid the gloomy Ozark hills," was published in 1936 as the shared work of Randolph and Nancy Clemens, but "Clemens" did most if not all of the work, and the book was marketed according to the provisions of the "Agreement" signed on September 30, 1935, by Randolph and Nancy Nance.[99]

But the years that saw all this literary activity—seven books in five years—were filled with other activities as well. In 1930 he married Marie Wardlaw St. John Wilbur, adding his own to the imposing array of names acquired by this adopted daughter of Pineville's leading physician and water witch, Dr. Oakley St. John. In the same year he went on a trip in a covered wagon with Lewis Kelley, his friend the singing-school teacher from Cyclone, Missouri. In 1932 he got lost in Gentry Cave with Otto Ernest Rayburn, and the newspapers had a good laugh at the expense of the "Ozark experts." In 1933 he went to Hollywood and made such an impression in a two-month stay that his exploits are mentioned in a modern history of the MGM studios. In 1934 he was actively involved in preparations for the first National Folk Festival in St. Louis, and an "Ozark Booster" wrote to him from Noel, Missouri, hoping that his forthcoming book would "not be so rough on us" as its predecessor. There wasn't a whole lot of money—the Great Depression had the "book business shot to hell"—but there was a good bit of notoriety.[100] The national newspapers reviewed his books, the regional dailies in Kansas City and Springfield published feature profiles about the man educated in Massachusetts who "looks very much like one of the hillmen he writes about," and the local weeklies followed his every move.[101] It was high times in the hills of Big Sugar valley.

The marriage of Randolph and Marie Wilbur, on March 27, 1930, was front-page news in the next day's *Democrat*. The groom was described as "a writer and author of considerable prominence," while his new wife was "one of Pineville's most cultured and intelligent ladies."[102] She was moreover an adventurous lady, since the same paper had carried, twenty-three years earlier, an account of her first marriage. "Wedding Bells in Old Mexico" was the head of the May 24, 1907, story reporting Miss Wardlaw's marriage "to Mr. Ralston Wilbur, at Monterrey, Mexico, May 14th." Her husband, according to the same story, "was reared in St. Louis but for the past two years has been in various places in Mexico . . . as a mechanical engineer, superintending the construction of large power plants." The story added that Wilbur was currently involved with such a plant in the state of Hidalgo, "where he and his fair bride will remain for several months till the work is completed."[103] Marie divorced Wilbur in 1911—her suit was granted by the McDonald County Circuit Court when Wilbur did not show up. According to Randolph's 1955 memory, Wilbur and Marie had met "in St. Louis in 1904 during the Exposition." He also recalled that Wilbur had been "a football player at Yale." The same interview elicited a capsule description of Marie: "She was interested in pioneer customs and local history. She was a great help in my early work. She knew everybody around there, especially the elderly women. She was not artistically inclined. She read a good deal and was pretty well educated. She was a smart girl, well travelled, and she could speak Spanish."[104]

The journey in the covered wagon took place some seven months after the marriage, in early November. Randolph often said that this trip went from Pineville to Little Rock and back, but this is unlikely on the face of it, since it would require a round trip of close to 500 miles. A fragmentary journal from this adventure in the Library of Congress indicates a roughly circular trip confined to northwest Arkansas, with stops near Eureka Springs and Fayetteville. Several photographs of Randolph and the wagon have been preserved—one is printed in *Ozark Mountain Folks*, and Lewis Kelley is pictured in the driver's seat in *Ozark Folksongs*—and the trip is mentioned in *Ozark Superstitions*. "I once traveled through rural Arkansas in a covered wagon with Mr. Lewis Kelley, of Cyclone, Missouri, an old-time mountain man. We camped by the roadside every night and slept in the wagon when the weather was bad."[105] One year later, in the fall of 1932, Randolph was in the papers again—this time as a fall guy in the Gentry Cave caper. The *Tulsa Tribune* ran it as a brief filler headed "Ozark Expert Lost in Ozark Cave":

Galena, Mo., Aug 6.—People here in Stone county are telling a good story about Vance Randolph, author of "The Ozarks," and Otto Ernest

Rayburn, Ozark feature writer and former editor of Arcadian magazine. It seems that Mr. Rayburn, who has a studio at Camp Ramona,
near here, had volunteered to guide Randolph through Gentry cave.
This cavern is not a particularly large one, but its complex network of
winding passages is admittedly confusing. After spending seven hours
in the cave, the two chief authorities on things Ozarkian were rescued
by C. L. Weekley, the owner of Camp Ramona and the cave, who found
them wandering through the upper levels in total darkness. Randolph
had fallen down and smashed their only flashlight, he said, and
Rayburn's supply of matches was gone before they could locate the
entrance.[106]

Very similar accounts ran in other papers throughout the region.
Reminded of the event in 1980, Randolph remembered it with a big
laugh: "True enough, we did. It was a great joke, too, because we
were both supposed to be big Ozarks experts. It wasn't a big cave
either."[107]

If the "expert" got his comeuppance in Gentry Cave, his prestige
was greatly restored at the end of 1933, when the summons came
from Hollywood. This was the big time—Randolph would be paid
$200 a week, the highest wage he would ever command. High spir-
its prevailed as the Ozarks expert, his wife and old friend Church in
tow, boarded the Chief for California. They were "drunk as bears all
the way," according to his 1957 recollection, and split up upon arrival, with Church in a "hotel uptown drunk" and Marie and Vance
in a "place in Culver City."[108]

"I was hired as a writer," he recalled on another occasion. "I didn't
know a damn thing about it. I went to Culver City. For the first week
or two I didn't do anything. . . . I was there because they were going
to do a movie about Ozark life starring Wallace Beery and Marie
Dressler, because of my book."[109] Randolph was issued his identification card by MGM on November 10, 1933, and went to work with
Dore Schary, another writer new to the business, under the direction of producer Harry Rapf. Church stayed two weeks, drunk all
the time—Marie "had to help get him in a cab"—after which they
put him back on the train in a wheel chair, bound for Dallas where
he was scheduled to attend an insurance meeting. "They took him
to the hospital in Dallas," Randolph remembered. "I didn't see him
for about a year."[110]

Marie had little to do, especially after Church's departure—before
that they'd gone "to Catalina together and drove around looking at
palm trees"—but "she liked it out there. She liked to go around and
look at the stars." Meanwhile, back on the lot, Randolph was trying

to learn how to work in Hollywood. "I didn't like it. I couldn't do anything with it because the way they worked seemed absolute foolish-
ness. There were half a dozen men working on one story with constant conferences and wrangling over nothing. I felt I was wasting
my time."[111]

Despite such obstacles, Randolph and Schary did succeed in
working up a script. "The Ozarks were Randolph's special area,"
wrote Bosley Crowther in his history of MGM, *The Lion's Share*.
"He and Schary wrote a comedy scene in which the speech of a
couple of Ozark characters had to be translated into English by an
interpreter. It was a very amusing situation, pungent and appreciative of the Ozark speech."[112] The script was taken to Rapf, who
"had a fearsome reputation among writers as a tough and cruel
master," according to Schary's own reminiscence.[113] Rapf didn't like
it, and he told the writers that the dialogue "lacked authenticity."
Randolph, who in Crowther's telling of the story is "a colorful individual, a charming rustic in Hollywood," finally replied to the criticisms.[114] But Schary, who was there, tells the story more fully:

> Vance, bestirring himself, delivered the following valedictory: "Mr.
> Rapf, I don't know if the story is good or not, but I am, sir, the country's
> authority on what is and what is not true about the Ozarks so you can't
> tell me that the story we wrote isn't authentic—so I tell you, you take
> that script and stick it in a hole the Good Lord provided for you." As I
> was beginning to recover from the first shock wave, Vance horrified
> me by unloading a stream of [tobacco] spittle onto Mr. Rapf's green
> rug. I watched in stunned wonder as the spot burbled, bubbled, and
> grew, hardly aware that Vance had left the office. I looked over at Mr.
> Rapf, who, pointing a long, bony finger at me, shouted, "You're fired."
> I believed him.
> By the time I got to Vance's office, he had tied up his high–laced
> shoes, packed his belongings, and was on his way to check out of his
> hotel. I walked with him. He wasn't angry. Rather, he was relieved.[115]

Crowther's account also includes the salient details—the green
carpet, the instructions from Randolph to Rapf, and Randolph's
sense of his reputation as an "Ozarks expert." In Crowther's rendering Randolph has "a cud of tobacco hanging slack in his cheek," is
said to deliver his riposte in an amiable drawl, and tells Rapf "they
tell me I know more about the Ozarks than any man alive—and I
reckon I do."[116]

All this is understandably absent from the newspapers, which
simply reported Randolph's arrival—the *Hollywood Reporter* for
November 24, 1933, carried a short item headed "Randolph to

Script" which noted that he'd begun work the previous day—and his return to the Midwest. The *Springfield Leader and Press* for December 29, 1933, included a four-inch story headed "Vance Randolph Returns to Ozarks from Hollywood." Less than six months later another new writer would arrive in Hollywood (on May 7, 1932) and be assigned "to producer Harry Rapf for a picture called *Flesh*." His relationship with the film mecca would be longer and more fruitful. His name was William Faulkner, and he got $500 a week to start.[117]

Randolph returned from his own adventures in Hollywood with little to show for his work. The script he worked on was never produced, and his considered opinion nearly half a century later was that the major results were material: "I had a new car and I had a loud overcoat."[118] Back in Missouri by the end of the year, the "Ozarks expert" would soon find himself embroiled in new trials. Over in St. Louis, plans were underway for a National Folk Festival to be held at the end of April, 1934, after a series of preliminary festivals.

V

The "folk festival movement" itself offers a challenging subject for investigation. No full-scale study has been completed, but several valuable articles have appeared and some tentative conclusions drawn. Timothy Charles Lloyd, for example, in his study of "Early Folk Festivals in America," suggests that "the major impetus behind the 'folk festival movement' in the United States during the first part of this century was provided by recreation organizations and personnel."[119] Since the last decades of the nineteenth century, in fact, educators, architects, sociologists, and other concerned citizens had been much exercised over what they termed "the problem of leisure." As Percival Chubb, director of festivals of the Ethical Culture School in New York City, wrote in 1934, the "more serious significance" of the first National Folk Festival "lay in its bearing on the pressing problem of developing leisure activities to fill the large increment of spare time now being forced upon the masses of laboring folk."[120]

This is on the face of it a comical situation—a legion of grave-faced professionals worrying about how their blue-collar neighbors were going to cope with an "increment of spare time" suddenly "forced" upon them! The phrasing suggests that the poor clods would rather be working. The eight-hour day was newly won in

Chubb's heyday, and his whole ilk were sufficiently removed from
the workplace to view it as an added burden. But they were there to
help, lest the unwashed proles be driven to drink, insanity, or increased procreation by the terrible presence of leisure. And so it was
that Americans in these years, in the name of wholesome and edify-
ing leisure, found themselves surrounded by a steadily increasing
number of parks, museums, and playgrounds, and addressed by a
proliferating variety of concerts, expositions, agricultural festivals,
parades, and civic pageants.

This last spectacle, the civic pageant, was especially significant in
the development of the folk festival idea. As conceived and written
by such stalwarts of the genre as Percy MacKaye, the usual pageant
was a historical panorama centered upon a particular city or event.
The curtain opened upon idealized redmen who cavorted briefly before being supplanted by equally idealized founding fathers, and the
presentation moved with ruthless chronology to the celebration of
more recent captains of industry and Christian principles. The virtues often took to the stage in person. A heroic past inspired a present all could be proud of even as it presaged an even more glorious
future. MacKaye, himself a Harvard and University of Leipzig man,
got the civic pageant ball rolling with *The Gloucester Pageant* in
1909. In St. Louis itself, twenty years before the first National Folk
Festival, MacKaye and Thomas Wood Stevens pooled their talents
to produce "a chronicle-poem-play, *The Pageant and Masque of
St. Louis,*" an extraordinary spectacle that must be described in
some detail to be believed:

> For four days the pageant, written by Thomas Wood Stevens, unrolled
> the history of the city from the time of the Mound Builders to the Civil
> War. The clash between Indians and French explorers, the Lewis and
> Clark expedition, the pioneers of the great West, and scenes from our
> wars were exhibited before dazzled audiences. St. Louis was repre-
> sented as a youthful crusader. Separated by an interlude came the sec-
> ond part, the masque, by Percy MacKaye. This part set forth in sym-
> bolic language the national and universal meanings underlying the
> pageant. St. Louis, a symbolic figure, moved among Speaking Persons,
> Choral Groups, and Presences to develop the theme of the fall and rise
> of civilization. Other allegoric figures, as well as pioneers, miners, and
> rangers, came and went as they chanted eloquently. Music played con-
> tinuously throughout the action. The play enlisted the services of
> 7,500 citizen-actors who performed on a huge stage erected in Forest
> Park. For many years the supercolossal performance served as model
> for community masques given in other cities.[121]

By 1923 MacKaye was on the boards with *This Fine-Pretty World*, his contribution to the "folk drama" movement. In preparation for this opus, MacKaye and his wife had visited the Kentucky mountains for a period of "creative research" and reportedly rode on horseback for miles along the Appalachian Trail. The play was quite popular in its day but soon fell from grace. By 1948 one commentator could dismiss it in a single garbled sentence: "This jumbled tale of the rich uncle and the poor nephew, of a husband's desire to put away his wife and marry the maiden, of adultery and charges of 'deefamation,' of a babe delivered in a sack, of a kidnapping, trial, public repentance, and jail sentence, are all tied up into one ludicrous knot."[122]

The whole folk drama movement, however, made an important contribution to the development of the folk festival. This movement, and the related "little theater" idea, are usually dated from the founding of the Wisconsin Dramatic Society in 1910 by Professor Thomas H. Dickinson of the University of Wisconsin. In the same year Frederick Koch, whose major fame came later in North Carolina, organized a Sock and Buskin Society among his students at the University of North Dakota in Grand Forks. Civic pageants were well known in the upper Midwest too—Thomas Wood Stevens had produced a *Pageant of the Old Northwest* in 1911 before heading down to St. Louis to collaborate with MacKaye, and in 1914 Koch's Sock and Buskin Society staged *A Pageant of the North-West*, written by eighteen students, which "required one thousand homesteaders, cowboys, and Indians to tell the story of the opening of the great Western empire."[123] But the major impetus for the development of the folk drama in the United States came from a 1911 tour by the Irish Players, a troupe out of Dublin's Abbey Theatre. Especially important were the plays of John Synge, which "suggested to young writers the need of exploiting our own native resources, our folkways, our local history and rural types." *Riders to the Sea* made a particularly strong impression and influenced a number of American productions, "even to the cadence of the lines. It is safe to say that Synge is the godfather of the American folk play."[124]

Frederick Koch had moved south to Chapel Hill, North Carolina, by 1918, where he established the Carolina Playmakers in connection with his University of North Carolina course in creative and dramatic writing. Koch's students—Thomas Wolfe and Paul Green were among the first—were encouraged to write plays with regional settings utilizing local history and folklore. The influence of Synge was obvious in such early Playmaker efforts as Patricia McMullan's

Cottie Mourns and Green's *Last of the Lowries.* The latter play apes
Synge's *Riders to the Sea* down to the detail of the grief-stricken
mother who keens in rolling cadence: "That's all that's left o' them I
loved . . . a bundle o' clothes to show for my man an' four grown
sons. . . . And you'll all sleep quiet at the last. . . . But they're all
gone, and what call hev I got to be living more." [125] For his part, the
young Wolfe, who once dreamed of writing a play on a scale worthy
of MacKaye at his grandest ("Some day I'm going to write a play
with fifty, eighty, a hundred people—a whole town, a whole race, a
whole epoch—for my soul's ease and comfort";), [126] wrote and sometimes starred in several "folk plays" under Koch's direction.

   The folk festival idea was also greatly stimulated by the various
"cult of the mountains productions" that flourished alongside the
"folk play" in the 1920s. Of these, the best known was the Mountain
Dance and Folk Festival, which emerged from the Asheville, North
Carolina, Rhododendron Festival under the direction of Bascom
Lamar Lunsford, a character who crossed paths with Vance Randolph in 1934. Lunsford was quite a figure in his own right, the son
of a Texas schoolmaster who had moved to Mars Hill, North Carolina, and married the granddaughter of one of Mars Hill College's
original trustees. Lunsford was born in 1882 and grew up to make
his living as a schoolteacher, lawyer, and politician, but he made his
real mark as a promoter and champion of Appalachian mountain
people and their music. In some ways his career resembles Randolph's own, though certainly Lunsford was far from being the collector or writer that Randolph was. Both men devoted long lives
to the preservation and popularization of the traditional culture of
one region—if Randolph was "the greatest living authority on the
Ozarks," Lunsford was the "Minstrel of the Appalachians." In 1934
the two men were rivals for the affections of an attractive woman,
Miss Sarah Gertrude Knott, "who must certainly be regarded as the
prime mover of the 'folk festival movement' in America." [127]

   Lunsford had been raised with mountain music and "had been
playing the fiddle and singing traditional tunes since he was eight,"
but his active involvement with collecting and presenting the musical heritage of the region dated from the 1920s. In 1925 R. W. Gordon came to North Carolina collecting songs for the Library of Congress, and Lunsford accompanied him as guide and introducer. He
later performed a similar service for Dorothy Scarborough, and in
1927 was asked to produce a program of folksongs and folk dances
in connection with the Rhododendron Festival in Asheville. Lunsford's program was so successful that it soon dwarfed and eventually

replaced the Rhododendron Festival altogether, and he continued to direct it as the Mountain Dance and Folk Festival for forty-six years, making his last appearance at the Saturday night finale of the 1973 festival on August 4, just one month before his death.[128]

Meanwhile, next door to the west in Kentucky, a parallel course was being followed as Jean "Traipsin' Woman" Thomas, with William "Jilson Setters" Day in tow, made ready with the aid of the governor's wife to preside over her own American Folk Song Festival. Thomas' productions, in their own way, were every bit as preposterous as MacKaye's civic pageants. Photographs printed with Thomas's *Ballad Makin' in the Mountains of Kentucky* show performers on stage backed by crossed American and British flags, with Thomas herself in full Anglo-Saxon regalia and various captive children close by. Another photo pictures "Harrison Elliott and Josephine Harkins Browning singing the first folk opera, *The Call of the Cumberlands*" in front of a cabin with a sign reading "Traipsin' Woman" above the door.[129] After "folk opera" it is surely time for the savage gods, but the folk festival idea was clearly taking hold at the turn of the decade, and by 1931 Virginia had entered the field with the White Top Folk Festival.

Out of such diverse developments, then—from civic pageants and folk plays, folk music and folk dance festivals and concerned efforts of community minded citizens for the wholesome recreation of newly leisured muckers and sweaters—the idea for a national folk festival took shape. The major shaper, as Lloyd's article indicates, was Sarah Gertrude Knott, director of St. Louis's Dramatic League and founder of the city's Strolling Players. It was Knott who, having attended the 1933 Mountain Dance and Folk Festival in Asheville, returned to St. Louis and sold the idea for a national festival to the Chamber of Commerce. On December 18, 1933, the committee of St. Louis sponsors held their first meeting with six members of the newly established National Advisory Committee for the festival. Jean Thomas and H. M. Belden, an unlikely pair, were among those in attendance. Other members included George Pullen Jackson, Constance Rourke, Benjamin Botkin, Arthur L. Campa, May Kennedy McCord, and Bascom Lamar Lunsford. Under the direction of these and other leaders, preparations were made for preliminary festivals to be held in fourteen states.

But everything was supposed to start in the Ozarks, with the first preliminary festival of all scheduled for Eureka Springs, Arkansas, on March 13–14, 1934, and it was in connection with this event and the other regional festivals in the Ozarks that Vance Randolph found himself involved. The person immediately responsible was Advisory Committee member May Kennedy McCord, a considerable figure in Ozark circles in her own right. Like Lunsford, she had her own subriquet, "The Queen of the Hillbillies," and was well known in the Springfield area for her daily column in the local newspaper, "Hillbilly Heartbeats." A radio program with the same title was broadcast on Springfield station KWTO in the 1950s and 1960s— she continued to do this program until she was in her eighties— and an earlier program, from 1942 through 1945, was carried by KWK in St. Louis. May Kennedy McCord knew Randolph well; he collected songs from her own singing and from manuscripts sent to her in connection with her newspaper column and radio shows. Her contribution to *Ozark Folksongs* is a large one, totaling more than seventy songs gathered on nearly forty occasions.[130] Contacted by Knott and her prominent friend Mrs. Geraldine Parker (who would later be involved with Randolph in his work with the Works Progress Administration) in connection with the preliminary festivals in the Ozarks, McCord agreed to help, and suggested that Vance Randolph, the well-known "Ozarks expert" recently returned from Hollywood to his working hideaway in Galena, Missouri, would be another good name to enlist. Knott and McCord were soon on their way to Galena, where the expert found himself affected with a sudden enthusiasm for the project, and more especially for its striking director, Miss Knott. In July, 1980, remembering his involvement with the whole folk festival movement, Randolph's memories centered more on his brushes with the Springfield Chamber of Commerce and his liking for Sarah Gertrude Knott than with the festivals themselves.

And great adventures they were too. Randolph was all over the papers, and his days and nights were filled with high living. The first festival, in Eureka Springs, Arkansas, went off without a hitch under the leadership of Sam Leath, a local tour guide, Indian enthusiast, and Chamber of Commerce president. Randolph, Knott, and the other folklore and regional heritage luminaries gathered on the roof of the Basin Park Hotel to join with some 800 spectators for the two-day show. There were various contests to select a ballad singer, banjo picker, and guitarist to represent Eureka Springs at the upcoming Ozarks-wide regional contest to be held at the Springfield festival, as well as demonstrations of such traditional skills as weaving, knitting, spinning, blowing the dinner horn, and husband calling.

At one point Randolph, already settling into his role as Mr. Ozarks,

was called upon to speak, and he broke out for the occasion a series
of brief remarks that had already seen considerable mileage, and
that he would repeat many times in the following weeks:

These folklore revivals are might good publicity for the Ozarks, and
especially for the resort business. The professional Ozark boosters
would do well to put more of this primitive stuff into their advertising,
and not talk so much about our splendid highways and excellent new
hotels. City people won't come down here simply to stop in a shiny
new tavern, because there are still plenty of comfortable hotels in Chicago and St. Louis, even Kansas City. They come to see rugged mountain scenery and quaint log cabins and picturesque rail fences and
romantic-looking mountaineers. It is this sort of thing and not mere
modern conveniences that pulls the tourist trade. One of Harold Bell
Wright's novels got more valuable publicity for the Ozarks than all of
the "booster" associations combined, and the Weaver Brothers have
probably brought more tourists into the Ozarks than all of the chambers of commerce in Arkansas.[131]

Down the road a bit, at the Springfield regional festival, the
boosters would have some words in reply to such notions, but for
the time everything was fine. Randolph and Miss Knott were getting along famously, and together they took in the other preliminary
festivals at Rolla, West Plains, and Aurora, Missouri. These too came
off successfully, though Randolph's visit to the Rolla festival was enlivened by a challenge from "an elderly colonel" who had been involved in the fundraising drive there. As Randolph remembered it
in 1980, the colonel, somewhat mistaking Randolph's own interests
of the moment, offered to fight him for the affections of Mrs. Geraldine Parker, the "amateur writer and society figure" whose connections with the powerful Pendergast political machine would soon
get her the director's job for the Missouri Writers' Project.[132] But
Randolph somehow managed to avoid the bellicose colonel in Rolla,
and after the Aurora festival on April 13 the cast of folklore dignitaries headed for Springfield, where the All-Ozark festival was
scheduled to open on April 17. Sterner tests were waiting.

In fact, trouble had been brewing in Springfield for several weeks.
Back in March the newspapers had reported a heated exchange between an unnamed "Chamber of Commerce official" and May Kennedy McCord, "the honorable district chairman." The Chamber of
Commerce man was having second thoughts about the folk festivals:
"the 'hillbilly' stuff should be eliminated, a lot of freaks should not
be selected to go to the national festival as representatives of the
Ozarks." The Chamber's man ended his remarks with plaintive

questions: "'Why call back the thing we've been trying to forget for 50 years? Why advertise to the world that we are ignorant?'"[133]

It was a volatile situation, then, that greeted the various chairmen and judges who assembled in Springfield's Kentwood Arms Hotel for a welcoming banquet on the evening of April 16. The dinner itself was a full-bore affair, with a big slate of local politicians and everybody who was anybody in the world of folk festivals in attendance. Springfield's mayor Harry Durst, Chamber of Commerce President John T. Woodruff, and "toastmistress" May Kennedy McCord sat down to break bread with Mr. and Mrs. Randolph, Miss Knott, Mrs. Parker, and other folklore promoters. Also in town for the occasion was the "Minstrel of the Appalachians" himself, Bascom Lamar Lunsford, who was to be Randolph's fellow judge at the upcoming festival and would soon be his rival as well for the attentions of national chairman Knott. But for the moment all was well, as Lunsford seemed to be centering his charms upon May Kennedy McCord.

Mayor Durst opened the evening by introducing all the honored guests and stressing how pleased the city of Springfield was to be hosting the first Ozark Folk Festival. Durst then turned the platform over to the Chamber of Commerce's man, John T. Woodruff, a local hotel owner who had decidedly different intentions. Woodruff stunned the gathered notables by immediately plunging into a blistering attack on Ozark writers. There were, he said, "'a lot of carpetbaggers who have come in here.'" Three writers in particular came under Woodruff's lash that night, but only one of them was present. As Randolph and his wife sat across the table, Woodruff dismissed Harold Bell Wright, whose schmaltzy *The Shepherd of the Hills* is still selling copies and being presented as a drama to tourists in the Ozarks, as a writer who "'hardly knew a thing'" about the region. What's more, he added, if Wright were to be "'measured by any standard of a literary man, he couldn't pass the third grade.'"

Woodruff then turned his attention to Randolph himself, saying that his fellow diner "'doesn't know much about the Ozarks—he has been consorting with some of the undercrust, and he took them as typical.'" But his harshest remarks were reserved for Thames Williamson, whose recent novel, *The Woods Colt*, had been dedicated to Randolph for his help with the dialect. "'The worst thing about Vance,' said Woodruff, 'is his association with the author of *The Woods Colt*.'" Woodruff castigated Williamson and his book in considerable detail, characterizing it as "'the rottenest, nastiest stuff I've ever seen in print, and I haven't understood why it was not suppressed long ago.'"

Having thus disposed of Ozark writers, Woodruff turned to the immediate subject of the folk festival. The Chamber of Commerce, he assured his by now reeling audience, was "'heartily in favor of this enterprise.'" Perhaps sensing some withholding of belief on the part of his hearers, he went on to insist that "'we are really your friends. . . . We will try to make you happy, and we wish you good luck.'" But then his worries surfaced again, and he put in a final plea for restraint: "'We are hopeful you won't go to St. Louis and stage any rough stuff.'"

Woodruff then concluded his remarks with praise for the "typical Ozarkian," who was no "hillbilly" at all but a "'high-minded, patriotic and God-fearing'" citizen. "'Never get the idea that is rampant today,'" he pleaded, "'that they are uncouth, illiterate and mean, and possessed of none of the finer sensibilities.'" Then, having testified most eloquently against his position by his own loutish behavior, Woodruff sat down. Several fellow banqueters made valiant attempts to defend Randolph and to repair the breach. May Kennedy McCord said that Randolph was "'the greatest authority on the Ozarks living today.'" Sam Leath, in from Eureka Springs, said that Woodruff's "'pioneering in the way of better roads'" deserved praise, but added that he was "'indebted to Mr. and Mrs. Randolph'" as well. Mr. Carl B. Ike, identified as a "West Plains poet," said that Abraham Lincoln, the "greatest man that ever lived," was a hillbilly. And Mayor H. A. Von Rump of Rogersville, Missouri, who described himself as a man "'gradually becoming a hill-billy,'" asked that those present "'not be ashamed of those who have gone before us— lest those who come after should be ashamed of us.'"[134]

Randolph, who later admitted that he was "a little set back" by Woodruff's attack, declined an invitation to speak in his own behalf. By the time he met with reporters afterward, however, the "Ozarks expert" had recovered his voice. He didn't defend his own work, reported the next day's papers, which gave the whole brouhaha extensive coverage, and he didn't really dart to Harold Bell Wright's side either, except to suggest that "his stories are certainly harmless enough, and they have brought a lot of tourist business into the Ozarks." What Randolph did do at some length was defend Williamson's work:

> "Of course," said Mr. Randolph, "if the Chamber of Commerce is going to set itself up as a judge of literature, why spend so much money on a state university? Our young people can go to the Chamber of Commerce and glean pearls of wisdom.
>
> "There were some exaggerations in 'The Woods Colt,' but that is no reflection on its artistic merit. Every man has a right to his own opin-

ion, but the writers who compose the board of judges of the Book of the Month club are eminent people, and I would prefer to take their opinions rather than those of Mr. Woodruff, who runs an excellent hotel.

"I don't claim to be a judge of moral matters, but I don't see how 'The Woods Colt' can be regarded as a dirty book, or a book that should be suppressed." [135]

On April 18, even as the festival itself was proving a great success, Randolph was back in the news with a brief signed article much in the vein of his remarks in Eureka Springs. He declared that his own ancestors "were all hillfolk" and stressed again that the festivals were "good advertising for Springfield and for the entire Ozark region." His own involvement, he said, was "entirely unofficial, but I'm for it—strong." He was careful to praise his colleagues in the festival enterprise as well: "Miss Sarah Gertrude Knott, Mrs. Austin Parker, and Dr. Bascom Lamar Lunsford have done more for this region than a lot of professional Ozark boosters. . . . The same may be said of the Weaver Brothers, and May Kennedy McCord, and others who have played up the so-called 'hill-billy' material of fiction and the stage. And if the local chamber of commerce doesn't appreciate this publicity, then so much the worse for the local chamber of commerce." [136]

By this time poor Woodruff was in tattered retreat. On April 20, after the festival's final night, the *Springfield News and Leader* carried a front-page story headed "'C.C. Always for Festival,' Leader Avers," in which Woodruff presented himself as "for the folk festival all the time" and argued that such a position was "perfectly consistent" with his earlier statements. [137] For his part, Randolph had put in yet another appearance in the newspaper, this time with a picture of his smiling face. "The Laugh's on Randolph's Face," was the caption, and the story below explained the cause of his mirth.

> The Ozarks' author might be laughing because the Ozarks Folk Festival, of which he was a judge, is all over and because it turned out to be a success. Or he might be recalling with amusement the excited fears of the Chamber of Commerce, which was afraid that Randolph and others connected with the enterprise would give the world a false impression of the Ozarks. As a matter of fact, however, he is laughing because some one asked him what he thought of folklore. He replied that it is a wonderful thing and that, like education, it should be taught in all the schools. [138]

But all the difficulties in Springfield were soon forgotten in the preparations for the upcoming St. Louis festival. Randolph's experiences in St. Louis were marred by his defeat for the attentions of Miss Knott at the hands of the white-suited Carolina charmer, Lunsford. As Randolph remembered it in 1980, he and May Kennedy McCord were both left by the wayside by the time the festivities got under way. McCord had an official role in the festival—the final act of the four-day program featured the performers from the Ozarks, and it fell to McCord to organize and introduce her fellow Ozarkians—but her partner in unrequited love, his enthusiasm for the whole festival business much on the wane, was left to console himself as best he could with the opportunities to meet with some of the other folklorists who had assembled for the occasion.

Of these there were many. Jean Thomas was there, of course, with Jilson Setters in harness alongside, as was Helen Hartness Flanders from Vermont, who had her own folkfind, Elmer George, in tow. Zora Heale Hurston, whose *Jonah's Gourd Vine* was just being published, was present with a group from Florida, and Arthur L. Campa appeared with Mexican-American students from Albuquerque to stage a performance of "Los Pastores." Other dramatic presentations were staged by Frederick Koch's Carolina Playmakers, including a play by Festival President Paul Green. George Pullen Jackson arrived with white spiritual singers from Tennessee, Constance Rourke contributed singing lumberjacks from Michigan, and Lunsford took time out from his wooing to oversee the appearance of seventy-five singers and dancers from his North Carolina festival. In 1980 Randolph recalled especially enjoying a group of retired sailors from New York who sang sea chanties and told tall tales. The festival also featured Kiowa Indian dances, cowboy songs, French-speaking Hoosiers and Missourians from Old Vincennes and Ste. Genevieve, and other attractions.[139]

All in all, the National Folk Festival came off as a resounding success, with enthusiastic public response, ample praise from the press, and supportive encouragement from participating folklorists. The *Journal of American Folklore* gave a page and a half to a report of festival activities by Lillian Freeman Wright, who concluded that the "riches of traditional folk songs and dances of America have never been more adequately represented than in this first National Folk Festival of America."[140] Plans were immediately underway for the 1935 festival in Chattanooga, Tennessee. By 1975 a total of thirty-seven National Folk Festivals had been held, with 1945, 1956, 1962, and 1970 the only unfestive years. From the academy itself the attitude toward the festivals was mixed; Ruth Benedict gave strong support while Stith Thompson (in 1938) held that they were of "dubious value for serious folklore."[141]

But Randolph was through with them after 1934. The combination of amorous defeat and a growing atmosphere of hucksterism—he recalled in 1980 that Jean Thomas had written to him in Hollywood about getting "Jilson Setters" and her other Kentucky characters into the movies—seems to have soured him for a long time. He'd escaped unscathed from the elderly colonel in Rolla and from the angry Woodruff in Springfield, but bad times were in the air. The blast from Woodruff had not been his first scrape with angry Ozarkers who saw him as an outsider who portrayed them "as a bunch of illiterates" for his own personal gain. In the fall of 1933 one round of such vituperation appeared in the *Joplin Globe* "Voice of the People" section. On October 26 Mrs. John Bishop, of Jane, Missouri, wrote to express her resentment of the same three Ozark writers later excoriated by Woodruff. The words of these men, she wrote, are "an insult to every one of us." [142] Three days later another letter, from R. H. Clayton, of Lanagan, Missouri, expressed enthusiastic support for Mrs. Bishop's views. Here too, Randolph had his defenders, and on November 12 a letter from Mrs. C. P. Mahnkey, of Oasis, Missouri, praised Randolph's work and said that Ozarkers should "be thankful that this almost vanishing phase of our hill life has been preserved so vividly." [143]

By the middle 1930s, then, Vance Randolph had been to the tops of the mountains—he was "the greatest living authority on the Ozarks," he'd worked in Hollywood, and his books were published and reviewed in New York. But he'd crossed some deserts too—the books had not sold well, the Hollywood venture had been brief and disappointing, the people he'd come to celebrate were sometimes resentful and hostile. And as the decade moved into its second half, it must have sometimes seemed as if the high hopes of the recent past were gone forever. The "book business" was "shot to hell," and *Hedwig*, his most sustained piece of "serious" fiction, had been a total bust. The only thing to do, it seemed, was hunker down in Pineville and Galena and "go back to the newspaper grind."

6

Hard Times

> Certainly, I suffered Gaelic hardship
> throughout my life—distress, need,
> ill-treatment, adversity, calamity, foul
> play, misery, famine, and ill-luck.
>
> —Flann O'Brien, *The Poor Mouth*

I

Galena, Missouri, in the 1930s was a town much like Pineville, some sixty miles west. Galena was in Stone County, on the James River, and was a favorite retreat for fishermen and other outdoorsmen. May Kennedy McCord had grown up in Galena, and Edgar Lee Masters had done some of his writing there. Randolph had been coming down to Galena to work since 1931, drawn most of all by the availability of good room and board at amazing prices. Galena in fact boasted two fine boarding houses and Randolph patronized both, but he wrote down his appreciation of the establishment operated by Fannie Mathes, wife of one of the town's leading citizens and farmers: "Lunch and dinner were served in good country fashion, with two great platters of fried chicken. There was cornbread, and mashed potatoes, and gravy, and green beans, and cole slaw, and sliced tomatoes, and cottage cheese. There was a choice of coffee or tea, and a little bowl of sliced lemon and sprigs of mint with the latter. There was a big dish of hominy, and a pitcher of real Ozark molasses, and some good American cheese, and great wedges of huckleberry pie by way of dessert." Breakfast was celebrated in similar terms, as was the room itself—a "big, airy front room it was, with a fine view of the village and the river."[1] The bill for such pleasures, in 1934, came to $1 per day.

But the dollar was more difficult to find after the palmy days of publisher's advances and work in Hollywood at $200 per week. By the fall of 1934 Randolph was writing to his old associate from the *Appeal to Reason* days, Louis Kopelin (both his names now leached to Lewis Copeland), to inquire about possible royalties from three "little books" sold to Kopelin/Copeland under a 1925 agreement and published by him in 1933. "If there is any money coming to me," Randolph writes, "for Gawd's sake send it to me by air mail, special delivery."[2] In February, 1935, as a result of this inquiry, a check arrived for $12.06.

Additional monies were generated at this time by a series of articles for *The Kansas Teacher* treating the history of various university campuses in Kansas. Randolph did five such pieces, beginning with "The State College at Hays" in March, 1935, and concluding with "The University of Kansas" in September of the same year. In the June issue he discussed "The Teachers College at Pittsburg," and included a good deal of personal recollection. By 1936 dollars were still scarcer, and while Randolph the Ozark expert stuck gamely to his work, publishing "A Fifth Ozark Word List" with "Nancy Clemens" in *American Speech* and "Ozark Mountain Party-Games" with the same co-author in the *Journal of American Folklore*, he was driven by economic necessity to less scholarly tasks as well. Under the name of Allison Hardy, the first term a tribute to his old friend and fellow mastodon enthusiast, Randolph turned out *The Autobiography of a Pimp* for Haldeman-Julius, whose operation had itself fallen from the idealistic heights of earlier days and was turning out a good deal of soft-core porn alongside the reprinted classics and socialist tracts. He also "edited, added a phrase here and there, and acted as agent"[3] for a companion *The Autobiography of a "Madame"* published the same year, while back in October, 1935, he'd turned out *How to Keep Your Virginity* (by "Elisabeth Hamilton"). "It ran 7500 words, and I got $25 for it."[4]

For ten years Randolph would make his living by writing articles and booklets like these. Between *Hedwig* in 1935 and the first volume of *Ozark Folksongs* in 1946, only one full-scale book would appear with his name attached, and this was the 1940 *Ozark Anthology*, a collection of stories by other writers with an introduction by Randolph. He did several other pseudonymous booklets for Haldeman-Julius in the late 1930s—*A Book of Amazing Confessions* came out in 1937, the product of several hands, though Randolph is behind Richard Gould's "Confessions of a Rapist," Louise Brent's "I Got My Lover Lynched," Elizabeth Hamilton's "Are Today's Girls Competing with the Red Light District," and the "Anonymous" "I Am a Scarlet Woman." He also acted as an agent and supplied chapter heads and occasional retouchings for "Martin Avery," whose *Confessions of an Abortionist* appeared in 1939. Both of these booklets were "Big Blue Books" (approximately 5 x 8½ inches) of some 100 pages. Producing them must have been a dreary task for the man whose future had seemed so promising just a few years before.

Randolph had known Emanuel Haldeman-Julius since 1917 at least, when both men worked on the *Appeal to Reason.* The two were near contemporaries; Haldeman-Julius was born in 1889, in Philadelphia, and didn't pick up the first half of his name until he married Marcet Haldeman in 1916. He'd come to Kansas in 1915 after establishing himself in the world of socialist journalism as a writer for the *New York Call,* the *Milwaukee Daily Leader* (where fellow worker Carl Sandburg failed to impress him), the *Chicago World,* and the *Los Angeles Western Comrade.* His marriage the following year allied him with Girard's leading family—Marcet's father was a banker who had been educated at the University of Leipzig, and her mother was Hull House founder Jane Addams's sister. Marcet herself took over as president of the family bank after a brief acting career, and it was she who provided the $25,000 loan which allowed her husband to purchase the *Appeal* in 1919 and put in motion the publishing enterprise that made him famous.

The first Little Blue Books were *The Rubaiyat of Omar Khayam* and Oscar Wilde's *The Ballad of Reading Gaol* (though from 1919–1924 they were part of the Appeal to Reason Pocket Series, the Ten Cent Pocket Series, or the People's Pocket Series), which sold for twenty-five cents each. Later, as the number of titles increased—there were five hundred by 1923—and the sales volume picked up, the price went down to a dime, then a nickle, and finally to 2 cents in a 1942 special offer. Haldeman-Julius's autobiographical pamphlet, *My First 25 Years,* which he published himself in Big Blue Book format in 1949, tells the story of the Little Blue Book idea:

Frequently I'm asked how the idea got started and how it got going. This is a hard question, but I believe I'm close to the truth when I say I got it when I was about 15 years old, in Philadelphia, my home town. I dropped into a small bookstore at 5th and Pine streets, run by Nicholas L. Brown. There, on a table near the door, I picked up a pamphlet edition of Oscar Wilde's "The Ballad of Reading Jail." I then went across the street into a small, bare park that covered a block. It was winter, and I was cold, but I sat down on a bench and read that booklet straight through, without a halt, and never did I so much as notice that my hands were blue, that my wet nose was numb, and that my ears felt as hard as glass. Never until then, or since, did any piece of printed matter move me so deeply. When I walked away, my heels hit the stones with sharp clicks. I'd been lifted out of this world—and by a 10¢ booklet. I thought, at that moment, how wonderful it would be if thousands of such booklets could be made available.[5]

By 1924, the year Randolph produced his first booklets and the series became known as the Little Blue Books, Haldeman-Julius was well on his way as "the Henry Ford of Publishing."[6] Prominent writers like Theodore Dreiser, Jack London, Frank Norris, Margaret Sanger, Bertrand Russell, Upton Sinclair, and W. E. B. Du Bois wrote essays and booklets for Little Blue Books. A Big Blue Books series appeared in 1925, and by 1928 Haldeman-Julius was ready to issue *The First Hundred Million*. By 1951 he had printed some 500 million booklets and published more than 6,000 titles. He had challenged the mighty on several occasions, speaking out against the Ku Klux Klan in the 1920s (his own *K.K.K.: The Kreed of the Klansmen* was published in 1924) and J. Edgar Hoover in the 1950s (in *The F.B.I.—The Basis of an American Police State: The Alarming Methods of J. Edgar Hoover*). And he had been many a writer's most dependable source of income in dry periods. George Milburn, writing to Randolph in 1930, put his own indebtedness on record: "I told you, didn't I, that I worked for a couple of years in Chicago, hashing up joke books and gelded classics for H-J? That was one thing about the old boy, say what you will (and I can contribute a bit of fancy vituperation, if we ever get on the subject), he did pay promptly. I used to mail a ms from Chicago early one morning, wait a day, and the next day a check would be back from Girard."[7]

Randolph's work for Haldeman-Julius falls into three periods. From 1924 through 1927 he wrote twenty-three booklets himself and collaborated with Church on *The Essence of Catholicism*. The 1924 titles are dominated by religious and philosophical topics, those of 1925 by natural science and psychology, and the three booklets of 1926–27 are dictionaries and *German Self Taught*. Randolph signed nearly all of these with his own name (and often with his academic degrees), though *The Essence of Catholicism* is credited to Church, and "Anton S. Booker" and "Newell R. Tripp" wrote *Freud on Sleep and Sexual Dreams* and *Behaviorism: The Newest Psychology* respectively.

From 1928 to 1935 Randolph did nothing for Haldeman-Julius. These were the glory days of the first Vanguard books on the Ozarks, the short story collection and *Hedwig*, the Hollywood venture, and the speeches in connection with the folk festivals. Then, in the last years of the 1930s, he contributed writing and editing to nine of

Haldeman-Julius's sleazier efforts, none of which appeared with his name attached. Six of these were issued in 1936, with Randolph contributing little but editing and polish to such works as *Confessions of a Gold Digger, How to Get a Husband,* and *The Autobiography of a "Madame."* His contribution to *The Modern Sex Book* was more substantial; the final chapter, "Sex and the Whip," attributed to Freudian scholar Booker, was "all my own" according to Randolph's 1978 recollection.[8] But the only work of the entire period that was primarily his was *The Autobiography of a Pimp* of 1936, which "sold very well for a time" but was finally "suppressed by the postal service" according to Randolph.[9] One letter from this period, to George Milburn, describes the way he was working at the time, piling up the folklore material even though it wasn't selling while making ends meet with hackwork for Haldeman-Julius:

> I'm working like hell just now and turning out a lot of stuff. I've written more material in the last year than I wrote in all the years I spent at Pineville. Maybe it isn't as good stuff—I haven't sold much of it yet— but at the same time I feel as if I were getting somewhere.
>
> I've done four blue books recently for Haldeman-Julius, and am now working on a Big Blue Book to be called *The Autobiography of a Pimp.* Some sixty thousand words. God help us all.[10]

Randolph was involved with only one Blue Book in 1937, doing some writing and editing on *A Book of Amazing Confessions,* which came out as the work of "Various Authors." In 1938 he collaborated with his friend Nancy "Clemens" Nance again on *American Bandits,* a Big Blue Book which was published as the work of one "Anthony Gish." Here, as with *The Camp-Meeting Murders,* Nance did most if not all the writing and depended upon Randolph to market the manuscript. She seems also to be behind the "Elizabeth Hamilton" contributions to *A Book of Amazing Confessions,* and may even have had her hand in *The Autobiography of a Pimp.* In the world of hack writers Randolph was known as a quick worker, but even he was something of a plodder in comparison to Nance.

There were personal problems, too, in the years after 1935, to go with the professional woes. The marriage to Marie was not working out—she had liked Hollywood, but had little to do in Galena when her husband holed up with his work. All her friends and family were in Pineville. Marie Randolph was older than her husband too, and people who remember them together repeatedly stress the surface incompatibility of the marriage. Quite often the sympathy in these recollections is decidedly with Mrs. Randolph, especially around

Pineville, where the "Ozarks expert" is even today widely regarded as an interloping carpetbagger who married "our Marie" for her money and social position. Also stressed is the disparity in physical appearance. Randolph in the 1930s was "an extremely attractive man" who was "fastidious about his grooming" and "a witty conversationalist."[11] A reporter who interviewed him in 1936 described him as "a well-built, good looking man with short clipped mustache, light hair slightly graying at the temples, and horn-rimmed glasses, through which he looked at me with appraising eyes—a man of the world."[12] Pictures of Marie reveal a woman plain by contrast with such a glossy husband, and this contrast was evident to those who knew them both. Gossipy accounts can be collected—of Marie Randolph smoking continually and taping her fingers with brown paper to ward off nicotine stains, of Randolph himself washing out his mouth with Listerine and spitting it on the floor to irritate his wife, of squabbles over money and public scenes involving charges of impotence and infidelity.

But nothing is gained by dwelling on such things. It is clear enough that the marriage did not prosper, and that the husband, increasingly troubled by the failure of his growing collections to find a publisher, was more often and for longer periods absent from his home. On October 16, 1934, Marie Wardlaw Randolph, as she signed her name to the document, ordered made a last will and testament in which she bequeathed to her husband Vance Randolph, of Pittsburg, Kansas, "from whom I am permanently estranged, and pending divorce, the sum of one dollar only."[13] No divorce was ever pursued, but the will remained in force until Mrs. Randolph's death from cancer on February 19, 1937, after a year's illness. The will was probated on April 11, 1945, in Pineville, Missouri, where Marie Randolph is buried.

Her husband did not attend the funeral; in fact, he denounced it with a passage of invective worthy of Mencken himself, a passage that is easily the most vehemently negative he ever wrote about the traditional lifeways of the Ozarkers: "An obscene clown of a country undertaker, trundling my wife's body into their lousy little churchhouse. An ignorant rube preacher braying his filthy nonsense over it. A group of grubby farmers' daughters bellowing their unspeakable hymns, holding their silly music in one hand, scratching chigger-bites with the other."[14]

What the husband did, in addition to penning this vicious diatribe, was get drunk, as he had been doing with increasing frequency of late, and with decreasing pleasure. Randolph had always enjoyed drinking—he and Ralph Church had become friends back in Randolph's undergraduate days by spending their afternoons drinking beer. But by the middle 1930s his drinking had lost its exuberance and become a threat to his health. On December 1, 1936, he wrote to Church from Galena about his troubles: "The doctor tells me now that probably I can never have another drink as long as I live, and that beer is much harder on the old gut than either whiskey or wine!"[15]

By the fall of 1937 things had gotten worse, and Randolph, like his father before him, went off to Dwight, Illinois, to undergo the rigors of the then famous Keeley cure. According to the thinly disguised first-person account of "Felix V. Rinehart," whose *Confessions of a Booze-Fighter* was issued by Haldeman-Julius in 1943, the immediate cause of the trip was a post-bender warning by an old doctor in Hot Springs, Arkansas: "It is only about 600 miles from Hot Springs to Dwight, but I was four days on the road. Some of my friends came along with me, just for the hell of it, and we threw quite a party in Springfield, Missouri. The trip through Illinois is still a little vague to me, although I remember crossing the Mississippi at Quincy, and having some small difficulty with the police in Peoria."[16]

Randolph was in fact accompanied on this trip, as on his previous jaunt to Hollywood, by his old drinking buddy Ralph Church. In 1957 he told the story of their trip in his own voice:

> Ralph and I went to the Keeley Cure together. We crossed Illinois drunk and saw a cornpicker sitting out in a field. Ralph says, "I believe to God there must be a man inside of it. It can't be done." So we got out and went over to look at it.
> When we got to the Keeley Cure we were drunk. Ralph went in on tiptoes and I shuffled in like a bear on a chain. I have a diploma from the Keeley Cure with signed names of fellow patients. Nothing official. I swore to stay sober until I was 65.[17]

The Keeley Institute was a very big operation in its day. The founder of the whole enterprise, Leslie E. Keeley, who had opened his Dwight establishment in 1879 with much ballyhoo about a "Double Chloride of Gold" preparation, had died in 1900 as a Christian Scientist, but the business continued to prosper. In 1903 the institute had moved into new, more spacious quarters, and Teddy Roosevelt himself was on hand to throw the prestige of the presidency behind the opening ceremonies. In the previous decade the Keeley cure had been endorsed by such notables as Illinois Gover-

nor John P. Altgeld, WCTU founder Frances Willard, and Chicago
packing magnate Philip D. Armour, who said he had sent some 200
of his employees down to Dwight, about 70 miles southwest of the
City of the Big Shoulders, "and all have been premanently cured. I
do not think there is any one thing or any one man who ever did the
good to humanity that Keeley is doing with his cure."[18]

At the peak of his success Keeley's physicians were treating as
many as 800 patients at a time in Dwight, and the institute was also
operating branches in England, Canada, Australia, and each of the
United States. Business had fallen off, however, by the time Randolph and Church showed up for treatment, and "Rinehart" esti-
mated that there were usually about 100 patients in residence. The
"cure" lasted for four weeks, and cost $160 in 1937, exclusive of
room and board and attendant fees. Randolph's own bill, dated October 13, 1937, shows total charges of $339.30.[19] Two "medicines"
were used in the treatment regimen—one was the fabled "secret
remedy," though there was no talk of "Double Chloride of Gold" any
more, and the other was "a bitter yellow tonic" known as "soup" to
the patients and staff. The "secret remedy" was hypodermically in-
jected four times each day in a room called the "shooting gallery,"
while a spoonful of tonic with water was taken every two hours.
"The Keeley routine may be reduced to the following formula," writes
"Rinehart": "'Up at 7; shots at 8, 12, 5 and 7:30; tonic every two
hours from 7 to 9; meals at 7:30, 12:30 and 5:30; bed at 10:30.'"

"Rinehart" ends his confession on a strange note. First he says
that he's been sober for more than five years—not a drop "of any
liquid containing alcohol has passed my lips for 1,849 days"—and
then he claims that no real "cure" is involved. "Nothing has happened to me except that I have quit drinking. . . . I'm just a booze-
fighter on furlough." Finally, he stresses the costs of sobriety, quoting "one of my fellow alumni": "I haven't touched a drop for seven
years. . . . I'm in perfect health, I am happily married, and I'm making plenty of money. Everything is just fine, except—except that
the birds don't sing any more."

"Rinehart" vouches personally for the accuracy of this lament, in
terms that in a minor way suggest the greatest of all hymns to the
ecstasies and humiliations of drunkenness, *Under the Volcano.* "A
man who has known the high spiritual joy of drunkenness," asserts
this bush-league Geoffrey Firmin, "can never be quite satisfied with
the lesser, coarser pleasure of sobriety." The last pages of *Confessions of a Booze-Fighter* reveal his plans for the future: "But if I live
to be 65 I am resolved to quit work, and retire to an isolated place

adapted to my needs. And there, with appropriate ceremonies, I shall formally renounce this abstinence which has been forced upon me. I know that I shall never, even in my old age, be able to drink like a gentleman. But I intend to try it, anyway, and do the best I can. Hope springs eternal, and a man must have something to look forward to. Perhaps the birds will sing again, for a little while, before the final dark comes down."[20]

He lived far past sixty-five, and retirement never crossed his mind. That would have closed down the birds forever. Besides, he'd never had a "real job" anyway, not since his brief stint as a high school teacher in 1916–17. He was seventy-three when *Hot Springs and Hell* was published, and eighty when *Ozark Folklore: A Bibliography* appeared. *Pissing in the Snow* made him a heap of money when he was eighty-four. But he did in fact "renounce this abstinence," and for years and years in his seventies and eighties enjoyed his Scotch at the gentlemanly rate of about half a pint each day. If he could tell an interviewer in 1955 that his "weakness was drink, not women," by 1978 he was fond of referring to whiskey as "an old man's best friend."[21]

But the pleasures of moderate consumption were daydreams in the late 1930s, when Randolph returned to Galena as a Keeley "graduate" to resume his collecting and hackwork. His troubles were far from over, and another hard blow was soon to fall. In January, 1938, almost one year after his wife's death and less than six months after his return from Dwight, Randolph's mother fell seriously ill. On February 9, at the age of seventy, Theresa Gould Randolph died in the Pittsburg hospital. Her death was front-page news in her home town, where it was noted that she "was well known in Kansas library circles and had lectured to numerous women's clubs and other organizations in all parts of the state." The obituary also mentioned her two surviving sons. Gould, her youngest, was "a civil engineer connected with the Skelly Oil Company," while her eldest was "Vance Randolph, well-known writer, who has been making his home in Pittsburg recently."[22]

There is on the face of it little for extremities of grief or distress here; a son of almost forty-six is not perceived as an orphaned child, and a mother of seventy is hardly understood as cut down in her prime. Most of us, in desperate compacts we hope have been certified on high, agree to endure the loss of parents in the hope that we will be spared the loss of children. But Vance Randolph was closer to his mother than most sons. He may have lived in Pineville and Galena for extended periods, but his most stable address had

always been the "tall, prim looking house" at 303 West Euclid where
his mother lived for more than forty years.[23] Marie Randolph's will,
which listed her husband's address as Pittsburg, Kansas, was venomous but accurate. Even the Pineville papers, which chronicled
every move of the "well-known writer" in their midst, tended to
identify him with Pittsburg. It was "Vance Randolph, of Pittsburg,
Ks.," who in January, 1921, "bought the Ed Wall farm east of town
Wednesday," and nearly a decade later, in March, 1930, it was still
"Vance Randolph, of Pittsburg, Ks.," who is reported "visiting in
Pineville the past week."[24]

In 1936, two years before his mother's death, Randolph was the
subject of a biographical profile in *The Kansas Teacher* magazine's
"Little Journeys to the Homes of Kansas Authors" series. The "home"
in Randolph's case, appropriately enough, was his mother's house
in Pittsburg, and the article gives a nice glimpse of the relationship
between mother and son:

> For years I had wanted to meet Pittsburg's own brilliant scholar and
> facile writer, the aloof, unapproachable Vance Randolph. There seemed
> to be a little chance, however, for he was living in some mythical place
> in the Ozarks. He returned now and then, unheralded, for a day's visit
> with his mother, but was gone again before anyone knew that he had
> come. Sometimes this elusive young man spent a month here writing,
> leaving home early in the morning for a retreat in another part of the
> city, there to work undisturbed. Sometimes, too, he sat on the porch
> with his mother in the summer evening; I thought how interesting it
> would be to stop and talk with the two of them about new books and
> their authors, but I never had the temerity.
>
> Later I became acquainted with Mr. Randolph's mother, Mrs.
> Theresa Randolph, a woman of rare friendliness beneath an exterior of
> dignity and reserve, who has served as librarian of the Pittsburg Public
> Library for twenty-seven years. This was in 1931 soon after the pub-
> lication of Mr. Randolph's "The Ozarks: An American Survival of
> Primitive Society," which had been commented upon enthusiastically
> by every important reviewer in the country. Mrs. Randolph was to talk
> about recent publications to a group of university women. It would be,
> I knew, an unusual opportunity to hear a discriminating judge of
> books give an intimate review of the book which was being discussed
> by the intelligentsia everywhere. Imagine my utter disappointment at
> Mrs. Randolph's leaving "Ozarks" for the last six minutes of her talk,
> and then commenting on it with almost impersonal acumen. However,
> I found out since that Mrs. Randolph never bores her friends with a
> mother's tale of her son's achievements, but I still wonder how she
> kept from showing her pride that evening.[25]

If Randolph, then, was frequently in Pittsburg, where his mother's home remained his own, it is equally true that Mrs. Randolph was frequently in Pineville. The *Pittsburg Advertiser* for May 25, 1933, carried a short item headed "Mrs. Randolph Is 'Hankerin' for Ozark Hills—And a Visit with Vance, Her Famous Son," and the Pineville weeklies, for their part, noted with some frequency the comings and goings of Mrs. Randolph. In 1931, for example, the *Democrat* for July 24 reported that "Mrs. Theresa G. Randolph, of Pittsburg, Ks., spent last Sunday at the home of her son, Vance Randolph," while on June 19 the *Herald* informed its readers that "Mrs. Randolph and two lady friends, of Pittsburg, Ks., are spending this week with the former's son Vance Randolph and wife, east of town."

It's clear from all this that Theresa Randolph was an extraordinarily supportive mother, whose son depended upon her deeply and often. At times the extent of her aid, and his willingness to accept it, could seem excessive to other family members. "He imposed on his mother," remembered Mrs. Gould Randolph, wife of Vance's younger brother. "In the 1930s, when everybody was having a hard time, all he could eat was T-bone steaks for breakfast. That burned me up."[26] His fellow writer and frequent collaborator "Nancy Clemens" suggested in 1980 that she "always thought she [Randolph's mother] was the most important one person in his life, as far as influence was concerned."[27] If this is not strictly correct—George Borrow and G. Stanley Hall would be other obvious candidates—it is surely not much wide of the mark. In dedicating his second Ozark folklore book to "T.G.R." in 1932, Randolph was indicating his indebtedness as clearly as he did in 1946, dedicating *Ozark Folksongs* to H. M. Belden, or in 1947, dedicating *Ozark Superstitions* to Hall.

II

In his personal life, then, as well as his professional life, Randolph was taking a beating in the second half of the 1930s. The bibliography for these years consists mostly of shorter articles, with the softcore pornography for Haldeman-Julius providing the largest jobs. As early as 1935 Randolph seems to have recognized the situation accurately and put his short-term ambitions in line with the realities as he saw them. In October of that year he wrote to James Henle, his editor at Vanguard, explaining his work on what would be issued five years later as *An Ozark Anthology*, and outlining his general plans for the immediate future:

You do me wrong when you refer to my "putting time on books that can't possibly make any money, like *OZARK OMNIBUS*." I haven't put any time at all on *OZARK OMNIBUS*, except to write some authors whom I know personally and get permission to reprint their stories without any payment.

While I am forced to earn my bread by this miserably paid hackwork for Haldeman-Julius, it is my ambition to get one respectable book published, with my name on it, every year. That is why I am interested in this *OZARK OMNIBUS* thing.[28]

The "*OZARK OMNIBUS* thing" did eventually put in its "respectable" appearance in 1940 as *An Ozark Anthology*, with contributions by such old Randolph associates as "Nancy Clemens," Rose O'Neill, Thames Williamson, and William Cunningham. Thomas Hart Benton, who had provided a portrait of fortune teller Angie Paxton for Randolph's 1936 article, "The Witch on Bradshaw Mountain," and who would do the end-paper drawings for *Ozark Folksongs* in 1946, was represented by an essay titled "America's Yesterday." George Milburn, a good friend and steady Randolph correspondent since the early 1930s when Randolph reviewed *The Hobo's Hornbook* and publicized Milburn's quest for "Frankie and Johnnie" materials, contributed "Honey Boy," the volume's opening story. Altogether, *An Ozark Anthology*, which was published by Caxton in Caldwell, Idaho, only after Randolph signed a contract agreeing to purchase 100 copies, brought together fifteen short stories and essays. Randolph's brief Introduction lambasted portraits of Ozark life that erred at extremes of celebration and vilification, from Opie Read's "God's own people" from Newton County, Arkansas, "the garden spot of the New World," to Mencken's "dreadful people" and actor Gardner James's "savages," and vouched for the more moderate but accurate writers included in the following pages. These authors, he said, "have lived in the Ozarks" and "know their stuff."[29]

Perhaps the most promising professional opportunity of this entire period was the invitation, which arrived by telegram on August 6, 1936, to "go on Federal Writers' Project at once at salary discussed with Mrs. Parker."[30] The telegram was signed by Henry Alsberg, the national director of the project, and the "Mrs. Parker" mentioned was Geraldine Parker, who in 1934 had accompanied May Kennedy McCord and Sarah Gertrude Knott down to Galena to visit Randolph in connection with the National Folk Festival. Randolph had included Mrs. Parker among the festival luminaries who had "done more for this region than a lot of professional Ozark boosters" in his newspaper article after the Springfield preliminary festival, and it is clear that he had kept in touch with her from 1934 on. In fact, like so many other Randolph friends and associates, Mrs. Parker found herself party to yet another signed "Agreement" involving a literary undertaking. On March 30, 1935, Parker and Randolph agreed to collaborate in the writing and revising of "a three-act play dealing with a murder in the Ozark Mountain region, and tentatively entitled *Swan Holler Hanging*." Parker was to produce the first manuscript, Randolph was to revise it "and to devote his best efforts to obtaining a publisher." [31]

The play was evidently written—Randolph describes it in *Ozark Folklore: A Bibliography* as a "three-act play about murder, outlawry, and lynching in the Missouri backwoods"—but the best efforts of the second party were evidently insufficient, since the play was never published. [32] Randolph's important association with Mrs. Parker was extra-literary, and their acquaintance was apparently instrumental in landing him the position of assistant state supervisor of the Missouri Writers' Project. It would also, in a matter of weeks, land him in yet another fracas with politicians and chamber of commerce types; he would eventually lose the job, and his Ozark material would be "so badly edited and revised that I don't care to acknowledge it." [33]

The problems which plagued Randolph in his brief time on the Federal Writers' Project were similar to those that bedeviled the enterprise everywhere. The Federal Writers' Project was just one facet of the Roosevelt New Deal's most ambitious program, the Works Progress Administration, known as the WPA. Created by executive order on May 7, 1935, the WPA had by mid-summer articulated plans for "national projects intending to employ persons now on relief who are qualified in the fields of Arts, Music, Drama, and Writing." [34] The Federal Writers' Project was a reality by the end of July, and by April, 1936, more than 6,500 people were employed under its auspices. Henry G. Alsberg, the national director, had numerous shortcomings as an administrator and was eventually sacked in 1939, but he brought a varied background in journalism, politics, and theater to the job, along with what an insider historian of the project called "his passion for social justice." [35] In the New Deal era Alsberg was a Washington bureaucrat who looked very much the urbane administrator as he posed for a photograph with Eleanor Roosevelt, but fifteen years earlier he had been wandering around Russia with American money in his pocket, attempting to aid Jews impoverished and endangered in the wake of the revolution: "For seven months he traveled through southern and eastern Russia, riding in boxcars, sleeping in haystacks, and mixing with Russians of all kinds. Around him was a steady eruption of violence: arson, pillage, murder, and executions. In a pocket Alsberg carried some $10,000, which he was authorized to distribute to Jews in need."[36]

Woolly times, these, but there must have been times in 1935 and 1936 when Alsberg looked back to his Russian adventures as a period of relative order and sanity. The project's Washington office, following the lead of several inspirations and earlier examples, settled upon what became the American Guide Series with remarkable dispatch; each state project was to give top priority to the preparation of a state guidebook on the basic Baedeker format, with brief physiographic and historical data serving to introduce the "tours" that made up the heart of the volume. The next step was to establish offices in the various states (and in New York City, which was treated like a state in itself), and it was here that Alsberg's headaches began to multiply. Since the Federal Writers' Project was a department of the WPA, which already had state administrators in place, there was immediate conflict over who would appoint the state director for the Writers' Project. Political consideration frequently took precedence over editorial qualifications, with disastrous results.

Missouri was one of the worst. Alsberg's candidate for the state's top job was Jack Conroy, whose novel *The Disinherited* had just enjoyed a huge success. (Randolph knew Conroy: "He worked on the Missouri Guide in St. Louis. I knew him before that. Now he's called 'The Sage of Moberly'—his home town in Missouri. His father was a miner who got killed in an accident, I think."[37] In 1977 Conroy published a rave-up review of *Pissing in the Snow* in which he elevated Randolph to fellow Sage status, calling him the "Sage of the Ozarks and premier folklorist of the U.S.&A."[38]) But the power of Kansas City's Pendergast machine was such that "Alsberg was obliged to accept the machine's candidate with little or no discussion," and the position went to Mrs. Parker, "an amateur writer and society figure."[39] That Alsberg made the best of the situation by placing Conroy and short story writer and novelist J. S. Balch in second-level positions with the Missouri project only highlighted the incompetence of Mrs. Parker and made open conflict inevitable. The sorry history of the Missouri project gets extensive treatment in *The Dream and the Deal*, a history of the Federal Writers' Project by the man who served as its national coordinating editor. Mrs. Parker comes off very badly in this volume. She is pictured as sensitive only to the desires of "the political machine that had placed her in office," is scolded for "her prejudice against Negroes," and is reported to have forwarded all manuscripts submitted to the office of WPA state administrator Matthew Murray for censorship before reading them herself.

> Only after a manuscript was cleared was it sent on to Washington. Balch became incensed when the administrator's censor deleted from the guidebook material a large section dealing with miners in the Tiff region of the state who often died of silicosis poisoning. In another instance, the censor eliminated favorable references to Thomas Hart Benton, Missouri's most renowned painter. Neither Mrs. Parker nor Matthew Murray, the state WPA administrator, had any use for Benton's social realism. "I wouldn't hang him on my shithouse wall," Murray told a protesting delegation of Project workers. "Why don't you write about our beautiful roads instead? Now there's something really worth writing about."[40]

Shades of John Woodruff! Murray's position, had Randolph known it, would have been familiar. But in this instance Randolph was in the middle. He knew and liked Conroy, and would have shared the views of the protesters on the censorship of the Missouri guidebook. But he also knew and liked Geraldine Parker, who gave him a job when jobs were scarce and "simply told me to collect folklore material in the Missouri Ozarks," allowed him to travel "wherever and whenever I thought best," and permitted him to use "my own judgment as to methods of work."[41]

This cozy arrangement was put under considerable stress shortly after it began, when conditions in the St. Louis office reached the boiling point over Mrs. Parker's firing of a project worker named Wayne Barker. A subsequent inquiry vindicated Mrs. Parker in the particular instance—"the man should have been fired long ago," reported Reed Harris, Alsberg's administrative assistant, who had been sent to investigate the situation—but at the time Barker's colleagues rallied to his defense and soon called for a strike, the Project's first.[42] Randolph, out collecting folklore with outside support for the first time in his life, was soon embroiled in the middle. The strikers, of course, wanted Randolph's support, while the St. Louis office evidently had radically different plans. According to a letter he received from fellow worker Jean Winkler, in that office the "talk" was "that you will be called back here to take charge of the guide."[43]

Such talk evidently had some foundation, since a letter survives from Randolph to "Jerry Parker" which shows the writer desperately treading water, explaining to would-be rescuers on opposite banks

that the water is fine. He opens by assuring Parker that his partici-
pation in the strike is unthinkable: "You surely know that, if only
because of my personal loyalty to you, I could never join the strikers
who are picketing your office." Then, in the second paragraph, he
explains why it would be awkward for him to come to St. Louis: "I
want to remind you that I have been affiliated with organized labor
most of my adult life, that I belonged to the Socialist Party for many
years, that I was an editorial writer on the *Appeal to Reason*, that
I contributed to the old *Masses*, that I knew Gene Debs and John
Reed and Big Bill Haywood. Because of this background, it would
be mighty tough for me to work in St. Louis while the strike is going
on." In a third paragraph the swimmer offers to sink out of view:
"But I *should* probably resign because of bad health or something,
and go back to hacking for Haldeman-Julius."[44]

Randolph didn't resign; in fact, he outlasted Mrs. Parker herself.
But his tenure was short-lived. His letter of January 16, 1937, to
new director Mrs. Esther Marshall Greer, asking that she "be a little
patient with me" in the matter of required reports, was in fact written while his notice of termination of Employment, dated January
15, was in the mail.[45] Additional difficulties persisted through the
spring, with the St. Louis office evidently accusing Randolph of
goldbricking on government time. On May 17, writing from Pittsburg, Randolph defended himself vigorously in a letter to Murray.
He began by quoting the allegations from an earlier letter of Murray's: "You say that 'several persons in the St. Louis office have
stated that you submitted no copy to that office with the exception
of the Folklore essay which was sent to Washington.'" In the following paragraph Randolph says that "during my five months connection with the project I submitted at least twenty-five essays to the
St. Louis office." He goes on to list nine essays by title and length,
concludes that he is blameless if the "people in the St. Louis office
have somehow lost this material," and ends with a sharp paragraph
contrasting the accomplishments of the disagreeing parties: "If you
will look me up in Who's Who in America you will see that I have
written a lot of books for a lot of publishers, and have a fairly well
established literary reputation. Then look up the records of these
ladies and gentlemen who claim that I didn't do any writing while I
was on the Writers' Project, and see if you can find anything."[46]

The Federal Writers' Project, as Randolph wrote his letter to Murray, was just beginning to issue the first fruits of its labors in the
various states. The first state guide to be completed was from Idaho,
where state director Vardis Fisher reportedly wrote 374 pages of the

405-page guide by himself in a ten-month period. The Idaho Guide came out in January, 1937, and was quickly followed by a mammoth Washington, D.C., guidebook that ran 1,141 pages and weighed more than five pounds, all six New England state guidebooks, and a Cape Cod guide titled *Cape Cod Pilot*. The Massachusetts Guide provoked a storm of protest by devoting some thirty-one lines to the Sacco-Vanzetti case while giving five to the Boston Massacre, but the general response to the first publications of the project was overwhelmingly favorable. Lewis Mumford, in the *New Republic*, wrote that the guidebook series was one of the best "uses of adversity" yet discovered, an attempt to "make the country itself worthily known" to its own citizens. "Future historians," concluded Mumford, "will turn to these guidebooks as one who would know the classic world must still turn to Pausanias' ancient guidebook to Greece."[47]

The academic folklorists reacted to the Writers' Project with a caution reminiscent of their response to the folk festival movement a few years earlier. Strange people, not robed in Ph.D.s, were at large among the folk, and worry was evident when the scholars convened. The Council of the American Folklore Society debated the matter on December 28, 1937, at Yale, and eventually managed a statement as reported in the minutes:

> With regard to the Folklore material collected under the auspices of the Federal Writers' Project, it was agreed that no blanket endorsement of the material can be made without examination of it, and the following resolution was passed: The American Folk-Lore Society feels that the extensive folkloristic materials collected by the Federal Writers' Project can contribute effectively to folk studies only if their evaluation, supervision, and continuation were placed under expert guidance; we proffer our help in this endeavor. A committee consisting of the President of the Society and Dr. George Herzog was named to survey the Folklore archives of the Federal Writers' Project, and the Archives of American Folk-Song, Library of Congress, Music Division, Washington, D.C.[48]

According to *The Dream and the Deal*, Alsberg took all this seriously enough to replace John A. Lomax, the Project's first folklore editor, with Benjamin Botkin, who apparently "produced a favorable change of attitude on the part of the American Folklore Society."[49]

Alsberg was no doubt cheered by this success in placating ruffled scholars, but back in Missouri things were still stalled by political chicanery. Mrs. Greer, like Mrs. Parker, had been selected for the directorship by Murray, and she proved no more suitable for editorial tasks. Finally, after continued delays and reports that the Kansas City office was "manned by political lackeys of the Pendergast machine" and was functioning "as a gambling center for horse races," the Missouri project was eventually closed down for a time while the national office searched for a competent editor.[50] By this time, says *The Dream and the Deal*, "the Missouri Project had spent about $227,000 on salaries and expenses without having produced a single book." (Vardis Fisher, up in Idaho, had turned out his state guide at a cost of approximately $16,000.)

> Only once, during Mrs. Parker's reign, had the Project come close to publication. The Ozark Guide, prepared by Vance Randolph, an authority on that region, was completed and in page proof when its sponsors, the local Springfield Chamber of Commerce, decided that the book "played up the delinquencies of Ozarkians to an extreme degree, saying nothing about their good traits," and withdrew its contribution of $3,000 for printing costs. Murray, supporting the Chamber's stand, declared that the criminal elements described in the manuscript consisted of villains who had come to Missouri from neighboring states.[51]

The Ozark Guide was never published, and the Missouri state guidebook did not appear until 1941, after Charles van Ravenswaay, an able administrator and editor, was appointed to the directorship.

If Randolph's letter to Mrs. Parker during the St. Louis strike made private reference to his old socialist and laborite loyalties, he was soon bragging them up with similar exaggeration in a much more public forum. In January, 1938, he published "Utopia in Arkansas" in *Esquire*, of all places, and gave that magazine's sporty clientele an account of his visit to Commonwealth College, a "proletarian school" located near Mena, Arkansas.[52] Randolph had actually visited the school several years earlier—the *Commonwealth College Fortnightly* for July 15, 1933, carried a short item headed "Randolph Makes Visit" which noted that he planned to "return some time during the summer for a stay of approximately a month."[53] A history of the college included Randolph among a list of "writer friends," and added that he visited the secluded campus "time and again."[54] One of his good informants, F. M. Goodhue, who may have led him to the great singer Emma Dusenbury, was Commonwealth's mathematics teacher. The earliest date given for an Emma Dusenbury contribution to *Ozark Folksongs* is November 3, 1928, approximately three years after the college opened, so it is certainly possible that Randolph's acquaintance with Arkansas's experiment in labor education went back to the 1920s. It seems more probable, however, on the basis of the *Esquire* article, that his initial visit came after 1931, when founder Dr. William E. Zeuch was ousted from his post and replaced by Lucien Koch, "the present head of the college" in Randolph's account.[55]

While on campus, by his own report and that of the *Fortnightly*, Randolph addressed the journalism class taught by William Cunningham, soon to make a name for himself as the author of two novels set in the Southwest (*The Green Corn Rebellion* of 1935, hard to find but worth the effort, and *Pretty Boy*, published in 1936). In 1936, while Randolph gathered folklore under the auspices of the Missouri Writers' Project, Cunningham was working as the state director in Oklahoma. Cunningham was the brother of Agnes "Sis" Cunningham, who was herself a Commonwealth student before going off to New York and helping found the famous Almanac Singers (with the help of Lee Hays, an Arkansas native who also spent time at Commonwealth). During his talk, "which dealt largely with the practical mechanics of hack writing," Randolph dusted off his old radical credentials for what he hoped would be an appreciative audience: "I tried to impress these radical boys and girls by telling them I was once an editorial writer on the old *Appeal to Reason*, the pioneer Socialist weekly. I told them, too, that I knew Gene Debs and Bill Haywood personally, and that I had met Emma Goldman and John Reed. But they didn't seem much impressed. It made me feel very old somehow. Those were names to conjure with in my day, but doubtless young people have other revolutionary heroes now."[56]

Perhaps the "radical boys and girls" were troubled in their adoration by what must have seemed the obvious apostasy of the man who spoke to them of "hack writing" even as he invoked their gods. After all, Randolph's own account included mention of a "sad-eyed boy" who was "horrified when I said that, in my opinion, Jim Tully was a much better writer than Michael Gold!"[57] The young ideologues were correct in their suspicions, since the former Socialist party member had many years ago commenced the long slide toward the total political skepticism he articulated in the 1970s. "Now I've lost all interest in politics," he said in 1980. "I don't give a damn who gets elected." In the 1930s, midway on the journey, he was a moderately ardent New Dealer. "I thought very highly of him," he said of FDR. "He was a *folkmensch*. I voted for him twice at least and maybe three times. I was for him. Radicals were against him."[58]

III

Hospitals had been a part of Randolph's experience since his Army days, but it isn't until the 1930s that references to his poor health begin to appear with regularity. From 1933: "Vance Randolph, writer of Ozark stories who is rooming at the W. D. Mathes home in Galena, is able to be out again after a brief illness."[59] In 1936, during his time with the Missouri Writers' Project, Randolph was laid up for two weeks in a Springfield hotel with a bout of colitis. He managed to hide his illness from the St. Louis office only through the good offices of his fellow writer and collaborator "Nancy Clemens," who helped him write reports and generally nursed him back to health. A letter to Church on hotel letterhead describes the situation vividly (and also contains the information that Randolph was having another brief fling as an insurance salesman):

> I thank you for them fifteen dollars . . . I am still sick as hell, but don't tell the Librarian [Randolph's mother] this on account I wrote her I am coming on fine. . . . I was so groggy the day you and the liebe Katerina were here that I don't recall whether I told you or not. But the truth is that I have got a pretty good job from the Government, and my main occupation now is keeping them from finding out how sick I am, because if they find out they will can me sure. . . . And another thing is I don't want them sons-of-bitches in Pittsburg to know it, because if they found out I had a federal job they would holler so loud the Presdent [sic] himself would hear it in Washington, and then I would lose the job that way. . . .[60]

Again in 1938, scheduled to address the annual meeting of the Missouri State Historical Society, he wrote the society's secretary, Floyd C. Shoemaker, on April 7 to say he wouldn't be able to come: "I have had another of these damned attacks, and they are putting me to bed for another rest. There isn't a chance that I'll be able to speak at your dinner on April 14th."[61] On March 12, 1945, he entered the Veterans' Hospital in Fayetteville, Arkansas, and stayed there until April 18. He was back in the same hospital in 1962—the Eureka Springs *Times-Echo* reported on May 13 that Randolph had been hospitalized in Fayetteville "on Tuesday evening of last week, following a paralytic stroke suffered at his home."[62]

Now strokes and attacks of colitis are serious troubles indeed, and it would be a hard auditor indeed who could hear of Randolph's afflictions without sympathy. But it needs to be added, cold-hearted as it seems, that Randolph was a very shrewd man, and it seems clear that there was more than a hint of the valetudinarian in him. His brother's wife's barbed comment—"all he could eat was T-bone steaks for breakfast"—is addressed to this suspicion, as is the gentler remark of Richard Dorson in his 1954 *Journal of American Folklore* note, "A Visit With Vance Randolph." Dorson relates the eagerness with which he accepted an invitation to speak on Negro storytelling to a meeting of the Arkansas Folklore Society. He would, he thought, be able to meet Vance Randolph. "But Randolph was not at Fayetteville; ill health prevented his traveling the relatively short distance from his home at Eureka Springs." Undeterred, Dorson drove over himself and paid the house-bound man a visit. His first impression was surprise: "Tall, well-built, ruggedly good-looking, Randolph scarcely seemed the invalid. . . ."[63] No more is said, and Dorson, a hard man with a pen, is here and in other articles unusually subdued on the subject of Randolph.

Other examples could be adduced, but the point needs no belaboring. Randolph was a man who appreciated creature comforts and had a hearty aversion to physical labor, and his health problems, genuine as they were, were also additional weapons in his considerable arsenal of devices for getting assistance out of his friends. "I never saw Vance without a white shirt and dress pants," remembered "Nancy Clemens" in 1980, "even when he was most povertystricken. I never saw him do any physical work and I cannot picture him cooking or washing dishes or cleaning a room."[64] In 1949 Randolph had refined his "last legs, down for the third time" routine to the point where it could be seamlessly fitted into a real estate transaction with his brother Gould. A letter of July 5 offers to "dispose of my interest in the farm" and manages to include mention of "two heart attacks" in the first paragraph. The second paragraph outlines an "installment plan" and ends with "an agreement that you get my share anyhow, in case I die before the payments are all made." The third paragraph consists of one sentence—"This might be a good buy, since I may kick off any time now"—and the fourth opens with a dependent clause: "If I should last six years. . . ."[65] Brother Gould, unsurprisingly, made an offer in reply, but the dying man was sufficiently alert to his own interests to close the deal with a modest boost while at the same time conveying his acceptance of "your terms": "If you can make it $100 at once, and $30 per month for 48 months (that's only $40 more than your offer) I'll be glad to sell on your terms."[66]

By the 1970s, having survived into his eighties, Randolph continued unabashed and simply added his age to the list of infirmities cited. Rayna Green, writing to Allan Jabbour in 1972, was lured into the rash prediction that Randolph would surely die within two years, and Randolph's Fayetteville friends would occasionally be confronted at academic meetings by friends from other places who would press small checks into their hands and inquire (sometimes in terms strongly suggesting a nearly criminal hard-heartedness on the part of the listener) into the "scandalous" circumstances of Randolph's life.[67] At Christmastime many bottles and even cases of Scotch would arrive, suggesting that his benefactors imagined such depths of destitution and squalor as could only be mitigated by a boozy stupor. Randolph, of course, would happily squirrel each contribution away into what was often a very considerable cache of spirits. Among his many masteries, in short, was a truly awe-inspiring genius for "putting on the poor mouth" in the Gaelic and Anglo-Irish sense of "making a pretence of being poor or in bad circumstances in order to gain advantage for oneself from creditors or prospective creditors."[68]

IV

Financially, physically, and emotionally Vance Randolph had been through some hard times by the end of the 1930s. His marriage had soured and his wife had died leaving a will that denounced him, his drinking had gotten out of hand and forced him into a grudging abstinence, the mother who encouraged and supported him through all his ups and downs had died, his promising position with the Missouri Writers' Project had disappeared in a bureaucratic maze and he was reduced to hackwork for Haldeman-Julius and even to selling insurance again. His ambition of 1935, to "get one respectable book published, with my name on it, every year," had failed of fulfillment. "Here I am," he wrote in 1940, "with my people all dead, my health bust and two operations coming up, can't write worth a damn and the book business shot to hell anyhow, nothing ahead but chickenshit jobs, WPA, charity, and a lonesome finish in the Vets Hospital."[69]

But, he continued, "*I feel pretty damned good!* And the last two years have been far and away the happiest time of my life—worth all the rest of it put together. Three years ago I was despondent almost to the point of suicide, but if I had kicked off then I would have missed everything. A damned narrow squeak, and by God it'll be a lesson to me." He'd made some good friends in Galena, especially among the prominent Short family and with the town's physician, Dr. J. H. Young. Dr. Young was also the mayor, and it was he who solved Randolph's problems with some neighbors who complained about his pistol shooting. The Ozark writer, it seems, was fond of strolling down country roads taking potshots at rabbits and squirrels with various pistols (some of them, like the favorite old Colt .45 he'd had since his boyhood, quite noisy affairs). Dr. Young, remembered Randolph, told me not to worry about it, said he'd get me a permit. Well, it turned out he couldn't do that, there wasn't any procedure or anything where a citizen could get a permit to go around shooting pistols from the roads.

Old Doc Young didn't give up easy, though, and the whole business got him riled up after awhile. "By God," he said, "I'll make you a deputy sheriff!" And sure enough, that's what he did.

Randolph added that he "served for about a year, maybe a little more," and noted that the pistols were never needed in the discharge of his duties. "I did get a few dollars for serving warrants and other papers," he said, "but that was all." [70]

The relationship with the Shorts was more complex. Randolph paid tribute to the patriarch of the family, "Uncle Jack Short, in whose home I lived for more than a year," in the Introduction to *The Devil's Pretty Daughter*.[71] Leonard Short, to whom Randolph would dedicate a book unpublished at his death, had been killed on December 6, 1935, after he and five other prisoners shot their way out of the Muskogee, Oklahoma, "city-federal jail," fatally injuring a detective.[72] Accounts of Short's funeral in the Springfield papers make plain both the prominence of the family and the high regard many people had for Leonard Short himself. "Leonard Short died alone in the mud of an Oklahoma hillside," the story opened, "but 1000 of his friends yesterday saw to it he did not go alone to his grave." May Kennedy McCord was there, to play Chopin's funeral march, and Congressman brother Dewey Short was one of the pallbearers. The funeral was held at the Short home, and townspeople told reporters about Leonard Short's generosity. "'I remember how he used to take a whole gang of kids to the picture show,'" said one, while another pointed to an old woman with a handful of flowers. "'She walked seven miles to bring him that,'" the reporter was told. "'He did her a good turn.'" Two preachers praised Leonard Short briefly, in similar terms. The Reverend Joe Deatherage of Three Brothers, Arkansas, called attention to his "'noble deeds to little children, to the poor, to the neglected and unfortunate,'" and suggested that if such doings could be set to music they would rise to heaven as "'a requiem for Leonard Short that would eclipse the masterpieces of the ages.'"[73]

Vance Randolph was among the respectful mourners, his old admiration for the great outlaw tradition of Sam Bass and Emmett Dalton no doubt stirred by his friend's ascension to their company. Forty years later he still had the newspaper clippings, and in 1978 he described Leonard as "a very good friend of mine. He was the best man in the family. Uncle Jack Short, the father, thought so too."[74]

Randolph was also very much attracted to Lillian Scott Short, Leonard's widow. "I loved her very much," reads a note in his papers. "My idea was that we should get married immediately, but she said that marriage did not fit into her plans. I argued with her about it for two years."[75] It is possible, of course, for cynicism to raise its head at this, since Lillian Short occupied a position in Galena very similar to that of Marie Wilbur in Pineville. But the guess here, a naive one perhaps, is that cynicism is out of place. Lillian Short is described by those who knew her as a striking woman. She contributed more than seventy songs to *Ozark Folksongs*, even more than Marie Wilbur, and her picture is printed in the first volume. Among the papers that Randolph kept for himself even after giving the great mass to the Library of Congress were four small items, two pictures and two newspaper clippings. The pictures are difficult to identify, but one at least is clearly Lillian Short, and both clippings deal with her. One, of May 28, 1948, is a one-inch notice of her wedding on May 12 to a Mr. Deba Cline, and the second, dated July 9, 1948, is a two-inch report of a hand injury suffered by Mrs. Cline while mowing her yard.[76] A poor treasure, laughable in a hard or wrong eye, like the "broad fringe of white tissue pattern-paper" noted by James Agee on the mantel of the Gudger house. Read rightly, these things abash the cynic and direct the stunned attention to themes bottomless enough to sustain even Agee's prose in all seriousness: "how through so long a continuation and cumulation of the burden of each moment one on another, does any creature bear to exist, and not break utterly to fragments of nothing: these are matters too dreadful and fortitudes too gigantic to meditate long and not forever to worship."[77] One thinks of the old man in the nursing home, sleepless among the moaning and wandering rejects, in the light of his lamp, examining the records of a long life. He looks at the pictures and clippings, fastens them together again with a paper clip, and returns them to their folder. His experience is his alone, eluding even his own telling. How, after all, are we to "weigh absence in a scale?"[78]

Vance Randolph, then, endured the vicissitudes of the late 1930s with compensating pleasures. He found new friends and fell in love, and he continued to collect the songs and stories of his neighbors. He slowed the pace of his song collecting during the 1930s; in 1928, for example, over seventy-five songs from *Ozark Folksongs* were collected, as compared to fewer than five in 1935, and fewer than ten in 1936. The folktale collections reveal a different collecting pattern, however, for here the 1930s provided Randolph with more material than any other decade. There are a total of 489 stories in the five annotated folktale volumes, and 162 of them were collected during the 1930s. Even here, though, there is a falling off in the last years of the decade; for example, in *Who Blowed Up the Church House?* there are twenty-five stories from 1930–34 and only fifteen from 1935–39. By the end of the decade he recovered by his own account a considerable zest for living. The days of despondency "almost to the point of suicide" were behind him, the two years just past had been "far and away the happiest time of my life," and he looked forward with raucous good humor to whatever life had in store for a hack writer and "booze-fighter on furlough" about to turn fifty. "If a man could just lay in a good crop of hemmorrhoids," he wrote, "and go blind, and maybe get in the penitentiary, it looks like life would be a really blissful and hilarious business." [79]

PART THREE

The Big Books

I did not collect this stuff from strangers. My informants were old friends who straddled the ridges and knew more than any man can learn in schools. Most of them are dead now. But we were young then, and we laughed together when the moon rode high. That is a thing which cannot be forgotten so long as time lasts for any of us.

—Vance Randolph, *Hot Springs & Hell*

7

Songs and Superstitions

Meeting you is the finest thing that
has happened to me in a long time.

—Vance Randolph to Rose O'Neill,
June 6, 1938

I

Rose O'Neill's name is no longer a household word, but in the first quarter of the century she enjoyed considerable fame and even more fortune as a magazine writer and illustrator and creator of the "Kewpie." She was widely known too for the elegance of her lifestyle and the flair of her love life, though by the time Randolph met her she was nearly sixty-five and living in greatly reduced circumstances at Bonniebrook, her isolated home in Taney County, Missouri. Randolph was associated with her most obviously in connection with her autobiography, which she sought his help in writing, but their correspondence reveals a genuine intimacy which many took for romance. "Randolph's name was associated romantically with the artist's," says a 1975 article, "but he says they were never more than good friends." [1]

Rose O'Neill first saw the Ozarks in the 1890s, when she was nineteen. Her father had settled there from Nebraska after his daughter had made the family's fortune by winning a drawing contest sponsored by an Omaha newspaper and followed up her triumph by selling illustrations first to regional papers and magazines and then, at the age of sixteen, taking her talents to the larger and more lucrative New York markets. By 1901 she'd married and divorced "a handsome young Virginian" named Gray Latham, who evidently had a penchant for squandering his wife's earnings, and by 1909, after a second marriage (to writer and editor Harry Leon Wilson) had ended when the husband grew gloomy and objected to his wife's new "habit of using baby-talk," she'd hit upon the Kewpies and her fortune was assured.

The famous Kewpies made their debut as drawings in ladies magazines but soon were featured in comic strips, calendars, cutouts, and a wide variety of other formats as well. By 1913 the first Kewpie dolls were in circulation—they were manufactured in Germany and sold all over the world. The Kewpie was basically a more infantile Cupid, fatter and more benign, and identifiable in all guises by its topknot. According to the artist, the Kewpies first came to her in a dream: "They were bounding all over the coverlet, chirping their little newborn name. One perched in my hand like a bird. Its little sit-down wasn't warm like a human baby's; it was oddly cool. So I knew they were elves, but of a new kind. I had a strange impression that their intentions were of the best. In fact, I knew at once that they were bursting with kindness, that their hearts were as well rounded as their tummies."

Sit-downs and tummies were a big hit in *Woman's Home Companion, Good Housekeeping*, and other staple periodicals of Harding's and Coolidge's America, and their enterprising creator, who said she had "put all my love of humanity into this little image," was quick to enlarge the Kewpie tribe. The "Kewpie Doodle Dog" was soon on the scene, along with "Scootles, the Baby Tourist," and the town of Kewpieville appeared with the speed of a Klondike mining camp. The German factories were soon turning out the bisque dolls in nine different sizes, much as the Strawberry Shortcake family bred faster than rabbits in more recent times. The last big splash of Kewpiedom came in 1940 with the appearance of "Ho-Ho the Laughing Buddha."

The income from the drawings and the dolls was sufficient to fuel a magnificent lifestyle, with winters at Bonniebrook, summers at Cos Cob, Connecticut, and frequent visits to Europe, where Rose and her sister and manager Callista stayed most often on the Isle of Capri at a fabulously luxurious place called the Villa Narcissus. In the 1920s Rose also maintained a double apartment on Washington Square and "a large rambling house" near Westport, Connecticut, which they christened Carabas Castle "after the castle in 'Puss-In-Boots.'" Living in such style apparently insulated the celebrated artist effectively from the upheavals that troubled the lives of ordinary mortals—Rose was quoted at some length in one adulatory account about the impact of World War I: "'I lost many dear ones in it. They went down in the English Channel, poor things. I was so prostrated at the time that my life was despaired of.' When asked if they were relatives or friends she said, 'Kewpies! Bisque Kewpies! They were made in Germany and were on their way over to me when the whole shipload of them went down in the English Channel. Those terrible British torpedoed the lot of them. It is too awful to think about.'"[2]

By 1938, however, when Randolph met her, Rose O'Neill had returned to Bonniebrook to stay. The various Kewpie spinoffs had plummeted from grace, Carabas had been sold, and Rose was at work on her autobiography. Randolph obtained permission to reprint her short story, "The Hired Man," in his *Ozark Anthology*, and by 1939 she had enlisted his help in finishing her manuscript. In the last years of Rose O'Neill's life Randolph was a frequent visitor at Bonniebrook, and the surviving correspondence supports Randolph's contention that they became good friends but not lovers. O'Neill's flowery style might appear to suggest a more intimate relationship—she often addresses Randolph as "Dearest Boy" or "Dearly beloved Vance," and there is one letter from Santa Fe (from the home of Witter Bynner) in which she promises to return quickly in flamboyant terms ("That you love me and can't get on without me is *like a bugle*").[3] But counterbalancing these are Randolph's few surviving letters, which are brief, addressed to "Dear Rose O'Neill," and signed with "As always" or "Sincerely." The whole episode comes off as one reflecting credit on both parties. Randolph was obviously impressed by the older woman's accomplishment and style; she had been a great beauty and had been very famous. He was kind and gallant to her, and it seems obvious that he greatly cheered her last years. There is a fine photograph in the collection at the School of the Ozarks in Point Lookout, Missouri, of Randolph and Rose O'Neill seated in a bent willow chair at Bonniebrook, in which Randolph looks distinguished and greatly at ease while Rose sits formally beside him, turned into the crook of his arm.

It is easy, of course, to get several laughs out of the whole Kewpie business, and more especially to ridicule the silly cult of women running around organizing "Kewpiestas" and dressing up in Rose O'Neill drag today. But it's important to remember that the Rose O'Neill Randolph knew and admired was a considerably more human figure, a woman used to great beauty and unlimited wealth up against time and few dollars. Here is a picture never included in the tourist brochures:

> We used to carry some fifty or more Ho-Hos around in the car, trading them for ham and eggs. Rose had a little income from the Kewpie dolls . . . Callista made Ho-Hos in the house with rubber molds. Rose bought whisky or wine with the money from the sale of the Ho-Hos along the road. Owed about $2000 income tax from old days. Fellow come down, invited him in for a drink. Rose . . . said I'm ready to go to jail, I want to

change my clothes, I haven't got $500. We don't want to put anybody
in prison. I just want $500. Just finally gave up. I saw him when he
went out. He looked pretty abashed.[4]

Rose O'Neill contributed three songs to *Ozark Folksongs*, four
folktales are credited to her, and she sketched a fine portrait of Randolph that he was very proud of. The autobiography was never published—according to Randolph, "with the deletions demanded by
her family the manuscript, on which he had worked for nearly two
years, holds no interest for the publisher who had requested it in the
first place."[5] There is a manuscript in the library at the School of the
Ozarks, but Randolph maintained that even this copy was bowdlerized. The house at Bonniebrook burned in 1947, three years after
Rose O'Neill was buried on the property. Today there is a Rose
O'Neill Room at the Shepherd of the Hills Farm Memorial Museum. The sketch of Randolph hangs on the wall, and the entrepre-
neurs in charge have propagated the absurd notion that it was done
"the day before her death."[6] The shade of John Woodruff stalks
the land, and tourist traps and passion plays proliferate like mush-
rooms. Rose O'Neill had no reason to hope for better—anybody who
perpetrates a Kewpie and/or a Ho-Ho has earned the worst fate
tastelessness and avarice can contrive—but in her relationship with
Vance Randolph there is evidence of a dignity and a courage elsewhere obscured.

II

There are references in *Ozark Folksongs* to songs actually heard by
Randolph himself going back to "about 1897" (the singer here was
his father) and "about 1909," and there are at least two entries in
the standard "Sung by . . ." format dated 1911.[7] There are other citations from 1913–1919; "The Bonnie Blue Flag," for example, is
credited to Mr. Harvey Ross of Batesville, Arkansas, who sang it on
August 21, 1914.[8] On later occasions, too, Randolph dates his career
as a collector of folksongs as early as 1912—in a letter of February 4,
1938, to Ruth Benedict, he says he "began the collection of these
Ozark folksongs and folktales in 1912."[9]

But these early references are infrequent. Randolph's systematic
folksong collecting began upon his arrival in Pineville in 1919–20.
Before the end of the 1920s he had conducted his "The Songs
Grandfather Sang" in the *Pineville Democrat*, had launched the col-
umn of the same name in *Ozark Life*, had published his article on
"The Ozark Play-Party" in the *Journal of American Folklore*, and

had begun looking about for an opportunity to publish a whole collection. Louise Pound wrote to him on August 6, 1927, with the prescient suggestion that the songs might best be issued by "some state or local agency . . . as belonging to the history of the state."[10] In 1929 he tried unsuccessfully to interest Franz Boas in a Ph.D. dissertation worked up from his folksong collection—Boas replied that "a collection of songs as a dissertation"[11] would cut no mustard at Columbia—and by 1930 he was asking Ruth Benedict for her advice. After requesting permission to reprint the play-party article in "a book of Ozark folk-songs," he adds that he's "just finishing the typescript of the book—expect a lot of difficulty in finding a publisher for it. Do you think that the Harvard University Press people would consider another book of this type?"[12]

Benedict's reply encouraged Randolph but stressed the unpredictability of publishers—"My experience is that no one can ever tell what publisher will take a given volume"—and the manuscript was submitted to Harvard.[13] On January 23, 1931, "Vance Randolph, Esqu." was sent the bad news from Cambridge in a letter which stressed that the negative decision was "altogether a question of expense, as we could not have had a more favorable report on the quality of the work than we received from our reader."[14]

The exact size of the 1930 manuscript is a matter of conjecture, though there is a hint in Margaret Larkin's collection *Singing Cowboy*, published in 1931. Larkin, a poet, writer, and trade union activist who had met Randolph when both were at the University of Kansas in the early 1920s, printed versions of "Wandering Cowboy" and "Fair Lady of the Plains" obtained from Randolph in *Singing Cowboy*, and he returned the favor by praising the volume in an *American Speech* review. Larkin's headnote for "Wandering Cowboy" credits "Dr. Vance Randolph, who has collected more than three hundred texts and melodies in the Ozark Mountains, for his anthology 'Ozark Mountain Folks,' and other books."[15] By 1938 Randolph himself is referring to his collection as "very large" in a letter to Ruth Benedict, and in another letter of the same year he describes it as consisting "of some 400 titles, with several versions or variants of most of the items, and about 350 tunes."[16] He also, in the same letter, included a twelve-chapter organizational frame that would change only in its order when *Ozark Folksongs* finally appeared. There is also a letter of 1939 to Herbert Halpert, who had first been mentioned to Randolph by Ruth Benedict the year before, in which Randolph estimates his collection at "something over 1000 texts, and about 600 tunes."[17] By the early 1930s, then, if Larkin's headnote is accurate, Randolph had collected approximately 75 percent of what he had at the end of the decade. It would seem probable that his brief tenure with the Federal Writers' Project stimulated the collection of additional songs, but several factors suggest that the role of this position in Randolph's folksong scholarship might easily be overestimated. In the first place he held the job for less than six months, and he was sick in bed in a Springfield hotel for part of that time. There is also the letter in defense of his activities to WPA officer Matthew Murray, in which Randolph lists by title nine essays submitted by him to the St. Louis office, not one of these deals with music. There can be no doubt, however, about the importance of Randolph's work with the Archive of American Folk Song, which began in the fall of 1941. Put succinctly, the collecting and recording financed by the Library of Congress nearly doubled the size of *Ozark Folksongs*—Randolph's own recording log itemizes the preservation of 876 songs and fiddle tunes on 198 discs. A surprisingly high number of songs were recorded by Randolph himself—the Library of Congress surprised him by releasing his version of "Starving to Death on a Government Claim" in 1952—but most of these had been learned from earlier informants in the 1920s and 1930s, and these contributors are credited in the log. The man most responsible for Randolph's good fortune, of course, was Alan Lomax, who was an assistant in the Music Division of the Library of Congress in charge of the Archive of American Folk Song. When Lomax wrote to Randolph on behalf of the archive in February, 1941, he did so as the director of a going concern. The archive, established in 1928 with the private collection of first director Robert W. Gordon as its beginning, had prospered with the aid of private and corporate contributions and the great collecting forays of John and Alan Lomax during the 1930s, and by 1940 was able to produce a three-volume *Check List of Recorded Songs in the English Language in the Archive of American Folk Song to July, 1940*, which indexed some 4,000 records.

Lomax told Randolph that he'd long admired "your books about the mountains," and credited fellow worker Sidney Robertson with the idea of asking him to record for the archive: "now that Sidney Robertson is working in the office with me every day I feel that I almost know you. She has recently given me the list of titles you have collected in the mountains. It is an amazing job." Lomax went on to offer the loan of a recording machine and discs: "I should like to volunteer to help you in whatever way I can . . . we have machines and discs available for your use." Lomax then ended on a modest note: "All of this is purely by way of suggestion. I should like to hear from you very much."[18]

He heard from Randolph a week later, and mostly he heard about the writer's need for money. After brief thanks for "them kind words about my books," Randolph moved quickly to the heart of the matter:

> A few years ago I should have been glad to borrow one of your machines and make some Ozark records for the Archive. But I am broke now, and unable to do it unless you can get money enough to pay my expenses.
>
> These singers are my friends, and many of them live where no electric current is available. They won't sing for the Library of Congress or the WPA, but they'll sing for me personally. They don't want any payment for singing, but the least I can do is to bring them down to the village in a car, and take them back home when they have done their stuff. I can't ask some poor old mountain man to walk into town, sing his guts out, buy his own lunch and then walk home again at night.[19]

Lomax, undaunted, went after funds and by July was able to offer $1000 for "field expenses, including travel, living and reimbursement of singers, for five months." Lomax added that approximately $200 of the $1,000 "has been allocated for tips and gifts and outright payment by the hour for singers," but added that the archive would "leave this entirely up to you." Lomax asked Randolph to meet him in Knoxville, Tennessee, for "field instruction" in the operation of the recording machine.[20] Replying on July 20, 1941, Randolph conceded that $1,500 "should be ample" (an additional $500 had been budgeted for "mechanical costs" connected with the recorder) but complained that "it would be a real hardship to nurse my rattletrap Ford all the way to Tennessee," and suggested that he could get the hang of the recorder's operation without the bother of special instruction.[21]

Lomax subsequently went so far as to offer payment by the archive of Randolph's train fare to Tennessee, but the Ozark expert had by this time refined his "I'm a sick man" routine to a high art— a decade later he'd have Richard Dorson driving the forty miles from Fayetteville to Eureka Springs to see him—and by August the Washington office had capitulated completely and shipped the recorder to Missouri. All would seem to be well—he'd gotten $1,000, and he'd gotten the machine without having to stir from Galena— but still Randolph kept the archive on the defensive. On August 26, 1941, he wrote to Dr. Harold Spivacke, chief of the Music Division, to provide an account of his activities over the past month: "The recorder arrived August 8th, but no play back needles came with the machine. Mr. Wiesner wrote me that shadowgraphed acetate needles should be used, and that I could get them at any music store. I drove 250 miles, and visited 12 music stores, but was unable to get shadowgraphed needles. On August 10th I wrote Mr. Wiesner that these needles were unobtainable here, and requested that some be sent from the Library of Congress. I have received no shadowgraphed needles as yet."

Randolph goes on to assure Dr. Spivacke that he has, in spite of these formidable obstacles, put his time to good use. "I purchased 3 dozen cheap recording disks and some ordinary steel cutting and play back needles," he says, and by "experimenting with these I have become familiar with the operation of the machine." The letter ended on a note that must have seemed familiar to Lomax and company by then: "It's a bit awkward, my not being able to draw any of my $1,000 in advance. I am pressed for money, and hope that the Division of Music can get me some sort of payment as soon as possible."[22] (One should note here, as in the real estate dealings with brother Gould, the particular touches of genius—the "my $1,000," which establishes possession even as it ignores the $200 "allocated for . . . singers," and the "payment," which neatly transfers the entire sum from the "field expenses" category to something very much like wages. There will be additional examples of Randolph's flair for such matters, but in every case the thing most to be applauded is the absolute absence of anything approaching servility or even gratitude. The poor, it goes without saying, must always have a claim upon the attention of the comfortable, but it is the unbowed and unthankful poor who deserve our highest admiration and respect.)

Randolph, of course, got away with such tramplings of bureaucratic decorum because he astounded his sponsors with the quantity and quality of what he produced. The recording log lists 123 songs on thirty-five disks as his first efforts, with the notation in Randolph's hand, "sent 35 records September 27."[23] One month later to the day he shipped a second batch of twenty-five records, and then, only four days later, after marathon recording sessions centered upon May Kennedy McCord and Arkansas fiddler Lon Jordan, dispatched another twenty-four records on November 1. By the end of January, 1942, as the original five-month period anticipated as the duration of the project came to an end, Randolph had shipped nearly 150 records of more than 500 songs to Washington and was lobbying unsuccessfully for an extension of the project. Lomax, who replied with unfailing courtesy to Randolph's often peppery letters—"Is it the intention of the Library that I should live on the charity of my neighbors, like a damned backwoods preacher?"[24] he asked on October 5, 1941—was obviously much impressed by the material that was pouring into his offices in such quantity, and he evidently did apply in vain for additional monies on Randolph's behalf. As late as September 16, 1942, he is writing to propose "continuing your work under the terms of a Rosenwald Fellowship."[25]

After February, 1942, Randolph's collecting pace slowed markedly—he apparently had recorded 185 discs by the end of that month, and completed only thirteen more during the rest of 1942. On January 13, 1943, new archive director B. A. Botkin wrote to request the return of the recording machine and the forwarding of the remaining records; Randolph's cavalier attitude toward the library's accounting procedures had been a continuing problem. Back in June they had attempted to keep their records straight, writing to Randolph that their count showed "you should now have in your possession 91 blanks and finished records," only to hear in reply that "my record of the number of blanks received from you is not at hand."[26] Botkin, for his part, was informed that Randolph had received his letter and would "return the recording machine and records as soon as I can get them crated and hauled to a railroad station. The material is now at Rose O'Neill's place on Bear Creek, at some distance from either railroad or highway."[27]

The machine and the records were eventually sent, and Botkin, like Lomax before him, was sufficiently impressed by Randolph's work to overlook the fieldworker's inattention to institutional procedures and incessant panhandling. By early 1943, in fact, even as he assured Botkin that the recorder would soon arrive in Washington, Randolph was alluding to his own imminent death and attempting to touch the archive for the costs of copying his "large manuscript collection of Ozarks songs—perhaps 1500 tunes and 2000 texts."

I have no carbon of this manuscript collection, and only a few of the items have been published—some in JAFL in 1929, and a few more in my books dated 1931 and 1932. At my death the whole thing—if still unpublished—may very easily be lost. I have no near relatives, and my backwoods neighbors would probably use it to kindle fires. It seems unlikely that I shall be able to publish this material, but I should rather like to have it preserved somewhere.

If the Archive would be willing to pay the costs of having the collection copied, I would be glad to turn it over to you with the understanding that it remains my property during my lifetime, and that no part of it is to be published without my permission. If I die without finding a publisher for the collection, the whole thing becomes the property of the Archive.[28]

Botkin was unable to aid Randolph with the copying in 1943, but evidently he, too, was successfully added to the army of Randolph admirers and sympathizers, since Randolph wrote him a letter of praise and thanks in 1946, which asked his help with newer projects. "It was mighty kind of you to write me as you did," he begins, "and kind also of Mrs. Cowell to tell you of my difficulties." He then concedes that his affairs looked "a bit better just at present—I have sold both of the unsaleable books." The letter goes on to mention, with only one reference to his death, two additional manuscripts nearing completion, "a bulky manuscript entitled *Tall Tales From the Ozarks*" and "a book on *Folk Speech in the Ozarks*," and solicits Botkin's assistance in obtaining a publisher. "If you can get the University of Chicago Press people to look at 'em I shall certainly appreciate it."[29]

The two "unsaleable books" were of course the manuscripts which became *Ozark Folksongs* and *Ozark Superstitions*, the books that marked Randolph's long delayed admission to the respectability of the university presses and the review columns of academic journals. His folksong collection had grown considerably during the months of recording for the Archive of American Folk Song, and the flyer announcing publication by the State Historical Society of Missouri claimed a total of 882 titles, 828 tunes, and 1,644 texts. Randolph's pleasure in arranging for the publication of this massive collection, for which he apparently owed thanks to Dr. Belden again for urging Historical Society director Floyd C. Shoemaker to acquire the manuscript, is obvious in a letter to Church, written on March 16, 1945, from the Veterans' Hospital in Fayetteville: "I have finished up my big book of Ozark folksongs and found a publisher for it— two large volumes which will burn up the sons-of-bitches who have called me an idler."[30] Another letter, undated but evidently later, adds a third volume and centers the author's gloating upon another soon-to-be-burned-up critic: "Well it don't matter as I have got my folksong book off to the Historical Society and they are going to publish it next July in three volume, which it will burn up that so-and-so used to talk about my 'crack-brained industry' when I was collecting them songs, and it will be bigger & better as them silly little books he wrote, and I will still be setting in libraries in good company when there won't be a single son-of-a-bitch on earth will even remember what his name was."[31]

On November 15, 1945, Randolph wrote a much more temperate letter to Belden, thanking him again for past kindnesses and asking his help with the introduction and chapter headings. He was confident, he said, that "the collection proper is good stuff, and worth all the trouble it cost me." But he was "not so happy about my own remarks," and added that "it would be a great favor" if Belden would check these over "and blue-pencil anything that should be omitted."[32] In the Introduction finally printed, dated December 5, 1945, Randolph thanked George Lyman Kittredge and Louise Pound in addition to Belden, to whom the whole collection was dedicated, and also looked back in gratitude to Alan Lomax and Dr. Spivacke at the Library of Congress. If the "sons-of-bitches" who had scoffed at his labors were being burned up, the friends who had believed in him and given him their help were being thanked.[33] Randolph's difficulties with the introductions were not entirely based on his own doubts—on one page in the third of three unpublished "Ozark Songs" volumes he expresses contempt for Shoemaker, the Historical Society director in charge of arranging publication. The page opens with two paragraphs dealing with Ozark attitudes toward the private possession of and readiness to resort to revolvers, and contrasting attitudes toward "he who relies upon the law to protect him," as well as the relationship of these matters to "the hillman's singular attitude toward family life, feminine virtue, the marriage relation and other sexual matters." These are followed by a sentence that identifies their purpose and intended context: "The two paragraphs above were at the beginning of my chapter 'Songs About Murderers and Outlaws,' but that fool Shoemaker cut them out."[34]

As late as June 18, 1949, during preparation of the fourth and final volume, Randolph was writing Shoemaker to school him in the dos and don'ts of folksong editing. The controversy centered on "Two Little Girls in Blue," which Randolph recorded from Mrs. Lottie Barnett of Joplin, Missouri, on April 4, 1929. Mrs. Barnett omitted a line in the second stanza, and Shoemaker wrote to suggest its addition to the text. Randolph replied at some length:

> It isn't the thing for a folksong collector to add a single word or syllable that isn't pronounced by the singer. There are plenty of songbooks which reprint "Two Little Girls in Blue" exactly as the author wrote it. But to get a perfect text from oral tradition is very rare, and too many perfect texts in a folksong book is a sign that the whole thing is a fake. The lacunae and errors are often, from the ballad-hunter's point of view, more significant than the correct lines.
>
> Another reason for not changing a single word is that sometime

a scholar may check these printed texts against the microfilm and phonographic recordings which I have deposited in the Library of Congress. If he found many differences, it would look as if the editors (meaning you and me and Dr. Emberson) must have tinkered with the texts.

Probably this seems to you like a long harangue over nothing. But if you want to add the missing line, I suggest that you put it in a footnote; this will make it clear that the line was not sung by Mrs. Barnett.[35]

If these two examples are typical, then Randolph won some and lost some in his battles with Shoemaker. His headnote was expurgated, but Mrs. Barnett's song was printed as sung, with dots indicating the missing line.

The first volume of *Ozark Folksongs* appeared in 1946 and was accorded the same prominent notice in the popular press that had greeted the books of fifteen years earlier. Louise Pound in the *New York Herald Tribune Weekly Book Review* and Marguerite Young in the *New York Times Book Review* praised Randolph's achievement in glowing terms. But in addition to these, and unlike the books of the 1930s, *Ozark Folksongs* was noticed as well by the academic journals. Ruth Ann Musick, a personal friend who had collected in Adair County, Missouri, before devoting most of her career to work in West Virginia, wrote an appreciative review for the *Journal of American Folklore*. Randolph's work, she said, "is probably the most comprehensive undertaking ever planned for any single region." The Introduction is lauded as "a six-page gem," a judgment echoed thirty-five years later when W. K. McNeil called it "the best description in print of the function of songs in a community."[36] Archer Taylor added his voice to the chorus with a *Western Folklore* review calling the work "a veritable encyclopedia" and "a feast for the lover and the student of folk song."[37]

Subsequent volumes elicited similar encomia, often from the same reviewers. Louise Pound, for example, who had been urging Randolph's virtues upon her readers since the publication of *The Ozarks*, greeted the publication of the second volume in 1948 with another rave-up in the *New York Herald Tribune Weekly Book Review*. Her concluding paragraph, while it may contain yet another lash at the Brahmins of the Kittredge/Gummere/Gerould school she had so effectively routed in the great "ballad wars" of the 1920s and early 1930s, provides at the same time an appreciative estimate of Randolph's accomplishment:

Mr. Randolph is not just another armchair researcher or one who sits in a library and in old-time fashion compares texts gathered by others, leans heavily on his predecessors, and thinks his results authoritative. He takes to the open, goes from person to person among his scattered hillfolk (not all of whom are illiterate backwoodsmen), follows trails that allure him, importuning strangers, getting testimonies from many places . . . . He is nothing if not thorough, but he knows how to present his matter readably, often wittily, and he has an accurate eye for details. Over the years he has done a fine job for the record.[38]

Ruth Ann Musick, like Pound, wrote additional reviews (one devoted to volumes two and three, and a third for volume four, all for the *Journal of American Folklore*), and the appearance in 1950 of the fourth and final volume was noted by John Gould Fletcher, in a glowing review written shortly before the poet's death and published with a drawing by Thomas Hart Benton in the *New York Times Book Review*. Most reviewers were struck first of all by the sheer size of Randolph's collection—Pound's first review suggested that it might be "the largest assemblage for one region of comparable size yet made in the United States," and Taylor said it would "prove to be the largest single collection of American folksongs in print."[39] W. K. McNeil, introducing the 1980 reissue by the University of Missouri Press, remarks that the "first significant fact about *Ozark Folksongs* is its great size."[40]

The astonishment of reviewers would have been immeasurably greater had most of them been aware of the material that remained unpublished. In the first place, a great number of bawdy songs were withheld from *Ozark Folksongs*, and remain unpublished to this day. A 1,364-page typescript entitled "'Unprintable' Songs from the Ozarks," containing by Randolph's count 463 texts and 187 tunes, is available at the Library of Congress and a number of other depositories. There is also the three-volume "Ozark Songs" manuscript in the University of Arkansas library at Fayetteville, which carries Randolph's explicit note, "not used in my four-volume *Ozark Folksongs*," which contains 216 texts and 112 tunes in the first two volumes and a number of uncatalogued texts and fragments in the third.[41] Taken all together, Randolph's collections, gathered for the most part without institutional aid and encouragement, contain more than 2,300 texts, about one hundred more than the Frank C. Brown collection from North Carolina, the largest collection in the U.S. to be published as a unit.

But Randolph's collection had other virtues in addition to size. He was very much in the forefront, for example, in the inclusion of tunes for approximately half of his texts. McNeil notes that such a practice was "rare indeed" for the 1920s, when Randolph started collecting, and the magnitude of Randolph's achievement in this area is made graphically clear by D. K. Wilgus's table of "Tune Text Percentages in Representative Academic Collections" in his *Anglo-American Folksong Scholarship Since 1898*.[42] Wilgus reviews nineteen collections published between 1924 and 1950—the tune-to-text percentages range from 0 to 100 with the later collections generally featuring a higher percentage of tunes, and here Randolph's collection falls in the middle with a 49.5 rating. But in absolute terms Randolph's accomplishment stands out; no other collection in the sample prints more than 180 tunes, as compared with Randolph's 811. Randolph has also been praised for his widely inclusive definition of folksong—for his gathering of material from younger informants, his use of current hillbilly records to stimulate singers, and his inclusion of songs with obvious popular music antecedents and influences. Herbert Halpert observed that Randolph "accepted the broadest possible definition of folksong," while McNeil noted that he "perceived the value in recording everything sung by the folk." McNeil's 1980 general estimate would be shared by many—*Ozark Folksongs* is "unquestionably" the "magnum opus" of its maker, and is "one of America's most important folksong collections."[43]

Randolph did no more systematic collecting of folksongs after arranging for the publication of *Ozark Folksongs*, but he did publish several articles dealing with the history of "ballad hunting" in the region. The first of these was "The Collection of Folk Music in the Ozarks," done in collaboration with Frances G. Emberson, who had updated the headnotes and bibliography and performed other editorial tasks for the State Historical Society of Missouri in connection with the publication of *Ozark Folksongs*. Published in the *Journal of American Folklore* in 1947, this piece ranges backward in time from Randolph's own efforts to the pioneering researches of H. M. Belden, "who began the serious study of folk song in the Ozarks."[44] Of particular interest is the treatment of Mrs. Sidney Robertson's 1936 recording of Emma Dusenbury in Mena, Arkansas. Mrs. Dusenbury, who was paid "day wages to continue the series of recordings begun by Powell and Lomax in 1936," took her responsibilities seriously enough to insist upon an eight-hour working day. "Mrs. Robertson had to take the old lady into Mena for the sake of the electric current necessary to the recording machine, and get her back home in time to milk the cow at 4 : 30 P.M."[45]

Following this general survey of Ozark collectors, Randolph produced similar pieces devoted specifically to "Ballad Hunters in North Arkansas" in 1948 and "Folksong Hunters in Missouri" in 1951. The latter article was done in collaboration with Ruth Ann

Musick. In 1954 "The Names of Ozark Fiddle Tunes" appeared in *Midwest Folklore*, and in 1963 Randolph and his new wife Mary Celestia Parler provided notes for the Folk-Legacy record, "*Ozark Folksongs and Ballads Sung by Max Hunter*."

III

The second of the two "unsaleable books" mentioned as nonetheless sold in Randolph's 1946 letter to Botkin, was of course, *Ozark Superstitions*, the first Randolph volume to be published by a university press. Randolph's contract with Columbia, dated May 17, 1946, was a bit better than his *An Ozark Anthology* deal with Caxton—he didn't have to buy any books. But he didn't get any money either. There was no advance at all, and no royalty on the first 1,000 copies. Still, coming on the heels of the sale of the folksong manuscript, and coming after such a long dry spell with book-length manuscripts of any kind, the prospect of having his book issued by the university that had so persistently frustrated his doctoral ambitions must have pleased Randolph immensely. Unfortunately, "old Boas," who had frosted him back in 1929—"your subject matter is evidently, from an anthropological point of view, too one sided. We should have to require a knowledge of primitive culture"—had died in 1942.[46]

If Randolph's introductory remarks to *Ozark Folksongs* provide "the best description in print of the function of songs in a community,"[47] the Introduction to *Ozark Superstitions* gives one of Randolph's most extended descriptions of his own collecting methods. He begins by stressing the particular difficulty of gathering material relating to "superstitions":

> The collection of some types of folklore—riddles, party games, or folksongs, for example—is a comparatively easy matter, even in the Ozark country. If a hillman knows an old ballad or game song any reasonably diplomatic collector can induce him to sing it, or at least recite the words. But the mention of superstition raises the question of one's personal belief—a matter which the Ozarker does not care to discuss with "furriners." The stranger who inquires about love charms or witchcraft will meet only blank looks and derisive laughter.

Randolph adds that "Old-Timer" newspaper columns and questionnaires will fare no better than direct interviews in the attempt to collect this sort of material. "The man who wants to study the Ozark superstitions must live with the Ozark people year after year and gradually absorb folklore through the rind, as it were." This leads to a jaunty description of Randolph's own life with his Ozark neighbors, and a portrait of his collecting technique:

> I first visited the Ozark country in 1899, and since 1920 I have spent practically all of my time here, living in many parts of the region, sometimes in the villages and sometimes in the wildest and most isolated "hollers." I fished and fought and hunted and danced and gambled with my backwoods neighbors; I traveled the ridge roads in a covered wagon, consorting with peddlers and horse traders and yarb doctors and moonshiners; I learned to chew tobacco, and dabbled in village politics, and became a deputy sheriff, and solicited local items for the newspapers. By marriage and otherwise I associated myself with several old backwoods families, in both Missouri and Arkansas. I spared no effort to become intimately acquainted with Ozarkers of the hillbilly type, and succeeded insofar as such intimacy is possible to one who was born a lowlander.
>
> The Ozarker's wealth of folk material fascinated me from the very beginning. I carried scraps of newsprint in my pocket, and along with locals for the paper I recorded other things that interested me—folksongs, tall tales, backwoods jokes, riddles, party games, dialect, old customs, and superstitions. This stuff was later typed on cards and placed in a trunk which I had converted into a filing cabinet, indexed and classified so that I could put my finger on any given item at a moment's notice. I made no secret of the fact that I was gathering old songs and intended to publish a book of them some day, but the other material was collected more or less surreptitiously.
>
> The cards in the file marked *SUPERSTITIONS* accumulated very slowly for the first three or four years, but my neighbors gradually became accustomed to seeing me around, and began to talk a bit more freely in my presence.

The Introduction concludes with reference to the widespread sensitivity of Ozarkers concerning the alleged "backwardness" of such beliefs, and a closing opinion as to their underlying tenacity. Randolph singles out "civic boosters" and newspapers, especially in the smaller towns, as sources of the notion that "the persistence of the old folklore is somehow discreditable to the whole region," and mentions an occasion in Joplin, Missouri, when "an old gentleman cursed me at the top of his voice and even made as if to strike me with his stick, because I had published something about Ozark superstition in *Esquire*."[48] (Randolph published nothing about superstition in *Esquire*; most likely this refers to a brief item in the June 19, 1939, issue of *Life*, where Randolph introduces six posed photographs by D. F. Fox, a Galena photographer, with a glib letter that is not one of his more responsible efforts. "Some people speak with the Elizabethan dialect of Shakespeare's time," says the man identified once more as "an Ozarks expert." "And they still believe in medieval witchcraft."[49]

The "old gentleman," if this was the piece he had in mind, was not entirely unjustified.)

Ozark Superstitions was published in the spring of 1947, with a dedication to G. Stanley Hall, who had died in 1924. It reprinted material from both *The Ozarks* and *Ozark Mountain Folks* and from articles and booklets ranging from recent Haldeman-Julius titles back to the first *Journal of American Folklore* article of 1927, but much of the book is made up of previously unpublished matter. Both *Ozark Superstitions* and *Ozark Folksongs* were printed with indices and bibliographies; the latter provided three separate indices (to title, to first line, and to contributors and towns), while the former featured an annotated bibliography containing sixty-three published studies of superstition in the region and referring as well to a number of unpublished manuscript collections. As if to make amends for ignoring Randolph's earlier work, the *Journal of American Folklore* reviewed *Ozark Superstitions* twice, with Paul G. Brewster appearing first, in 1948, and Wayland Hand, overlooking Brewster's notice, following in 1954. Both reviewers were generally favorable. Brewster was especially impressed with the "genuineness and sincerity" of the book, and he contrasted Randolph's "straightforward, almost matter-of-fact, style" with "the sensationalism which mars the work of some other writers on the Ozarks."[50]

Hand's article, published some seven years after *Ozark Superstitions*, bestows its superlatives even more freely, calling the work a "classic collection" and referring to Randolph's "full coverage" and "indefatigable field work":

> As one would expect from such patient and methodical research, the material is authentic and unusually rich in detail. It is precisely this intimate recording, with every item in its full setting, that enables one to see possible connections with earlier strata of American folk culture and with many obsolescent customs and beliefs that still linger in our hinterlands. No other book in the field, save, perhaps, Puckett's *Folk Beliefs of the Southern Negro* succeeds in giving such a full picture of what underlies these manifold primitive expressions.

Hand's regard for Randolph's work is clear enough in all of this, despite the fogginess of "possible connections with earlier strata" and "manifold primitive expressions," but his review concludes with a more effectively phrased assessment that was the highest praise "the greatest living authority on the Ozarks" had yet received from anyone with Hand's academic reputation: "*Ozark Superstitions* is one of the great works on superstitions to appear in this or any other country. In scope and method, and in its complete integrity, Randolph's work is one of the finest ever to have come from the pen of an American folklorist."[51]

In the popular press, too, *Ozark Superstitions* made a big splash. It was reviewed in *Time*, and Carl Withers, who fifteen years later would write one of the finest general appreciations of Randolph's work, produced a generous notice for the *New York Times Book Review*. Like Hand, Withers called attention to the wealth of contextual information provided by Randolph:

> What distinguishes this book among American folklore compilations is the wealth of circumstantial detail and cultural background with which Mr. Randolph surrounds all the separate items. He relates fascinating tales of marvelous local happenings. He names places and people and reports many situations and conversations through which he "learned" a particular superstition or cluster of superstitions. Thus we can actually *see* the hillman's mind moving in the "tremendously involved system of signs and omens and esoteric auguries" which he follows instead of "the mental procedure the moderns call science."
>
> We hear people arguing and debating contradictory beliefs— people who feel that their crops, happiness, health, or very lives may depend on reading the traditional evidence rightly. As native skeptics, "modernists," and "defenders of the faith" rework their beliefs, we can observe the transmitted body of folklore changing under our very eyes. Mr. Randolph is no mere collector of antiquarian oddities; we are grateful to him for showing us so much about how folklore functions among those for whom it is meaningful.[52]

By 1963, writing his Editor's Introduction to the Columbia University Press reissue of Clifton Johnson's pioneering 1896 classic, *What They Say in New England*, Withers thought to compliment both men by comparing their work:

> Both Johnson and Randolph give us brilliant glimpses of how irrational beliefs and practices function in people's lives; how they have meaning and are actually utilized in work, illness, serious or playful forecasting of future events; how they are tested and abandoned or resanctioned, often in the face of adverse evidence; how they are transmitted in an on-going culture. Both give us enough commentary and surrounding social circumstance, and enough local talk and argument—at several dialectical levels—for us to perceive that in the homogeneous societies they knew so intimately there were believers, nonbelievers, partial believers, and those who had "spells of believing."

In the same way that Johnson's other New England books supplement *What They Say in New England* to give a substantial account of the folk customs and folk history of his home region, Randolph's long series of books and articles on Ozark life, folktales, folksong, language, etc., combine to form the most complete account yet presented of the folklore and folkways of any American region.[53]

Ozark Superstitions, then, was a great success for Randolph. It opened the gates of the university presses to his work—Columbia itself would eventually publish five volumes from his folktale collections—and was if anything more widely reviewed in popular newspapers and magazines than the earlier books or *Ozark Folksongs*. It stayed in press too, going into additional printings at Columbia and being kept in press through the 1950s at least, and then in 1964 appearing in a paperback edition from Dover, with later printings in this format altering the title to *Ozark Magic and Folklore*. With *Ozark Folksongs* and *Ozark Superstitions*, Randolph's reputation moved to higher ground. He'd been "the greatest living authority on the Ozarks" since 1930 at least, when Otto Ernest Rayburn and May Kennedy McCord crowned him in their pages and programs, but by 1950 he'd produced more than one work recognized as classic in even the most rarefied airs.

It changed him too. He still needed money enough to accept hackwork, but after 1940 even his hackwork managed to center upon topics of folkloristic interest. From 1939 to 1942 Randolph did nothing for the socialist crusader and soft-core pornographer Haldeman-Julius, but then, in 1943, the year after his work for the Archive of American Folk Song, he suddenly resurfaced with no fewer than eight titles, all of them entirely his own.

Not since 1925, when he'd turned out ten Little Blue Books, had Randolph written about anything that really interested him for Haldeman-Julius, and the collaborative efforts of the 1930s are for the most part a dreary lot. But the booklets of the 1940s are strikingly different—only one of the eight from 1943, *The Truth About Narcotic Drugs: Don't Be a Dope-Fiend*, is entirely silly. Another is the autobiographical *Confessions of a Booze-Fighter*, the alleged work of "Felix V. Rinehart," and three others are "old west" booklets (*Gun-Fighters of the Old West* and *Belle Starr: The Bandit Queen*, both by "William Yancey Shackleford," and *Wild Bill Hickok: King of the Gunfighters* by pimp expert "Allison Hardy"). Three others are signed as his own by Randolph, and one of these, *Funny Stories from Arkansas*, is a collection of anecdotes, traditional jests, and tall tales. It should be noted, in connection with the flamboyant titles of many booklets, that Haldeman-Julius himself was often responsible for this aspect of his enterprise, believing as he did that catchy titles could boost the sales of a booklet. Some of his title changes became quite famous: "when Guy de Maupassant's *The Tallow Ball* was selling only at a few thousand copies a year, Haldeman-Julius changed its title to *A French Prostitute's Sacrifice*, resulting in sales increases of over 50,000." He even rewrote his wife's titles, changing Marcet's *What the Editor's Wife Is Thinking About* to *Marcet Haldeman-Julius's Intimate Notes on Her Husband*.[54]

In 1944 there was more of the same—much more, as Randolph turned out sixteen booklets. One was another autobiographical piece, "Peter Nemo's" *Confessions of a Ghost-Writer*. Five were on Ozark topics—*Tall Tales from the Ozarks* and *Ozark Ghost Stories*, for example—and four of these were signed by Randolph (the exception was *The Bald Knobbers*, by "Harvey N. Castleman"). Five more were additional "old west" booklets and bandit biographies like *The Mormon Pioneers* ("Hardy") and *Sam Bass, the Train Robber* ("Castleman"), and two of particular interest focus upon Randolph's old hero George Borrow and Lafcadio Hearn, the once well-known chronicler of Japanese life. Both Borrow and Hearn were folklorists of sorts—as was recognized not long ago in Hearn's case when the *Journal of American Folklore* printed "Lafcadio Hearn, American Folklorist," a fine article presenting his work from a folkloristic perspective—and Randolph was attentive to this aspect of their careers. Of Hearn's *Gleanings in Buddha-Fields* "Tolliver" reports that "the most fascinating section . . . is that which deals with Japanese folksong."[55] His interest in Borrow is, of course, more intense, and here "Tolliver" ends his account with a generalized assertion of his subject's importance: "It needs no gift of prophecy to say that people will be reading *Lavengro* and the *Romany Rye* long after Borrow's more pretentious contemporaries have fallen to eternal oblivion."[56] In this contrast, of course, Borrow stands in much the same relationship to his "more pretentious contemporaries" as Randolph to "that so-and-so" who had poked fun at his folksong collecting. Borrow and Randolph would "be setting in libraries in good company" when these contemporaries and detractors were forgotten.[57]

Haldeman-Julius published four titles by Randolph in 1945 and four more in 1946. The 1945 issues include two of his most interesting booklets, *The Truth About Casey Jones, And Other Fabulous American Heroes* and *The Truth About Frankie and Johnny, and Other Legendary Lovers Who Stalked Across the American Scene*.

These bold claims to veracity appeared as the work of one "Belden Kittredge," as Randolph continued to pay his homages in playful ways. The fabulous heroes, in addition to Jones, include Johnny Appleseed, Davy Crockett, Roy Bean, and Mike Fink, while the legendary lovers (treated briefly, since most of the volume deals with the "Frankie and Johnny" ballad) are those celebrated in "McFee's Confession on the Gallows," "Henry Green," and "Fuller and Warren." With two booklets by "Gerald Harvey" on witchcraft, vampires, and grave-robbers (the latter, in one of H-J's inspired moments, was titled *Vampires and Grave-Robbers: Amazing Excerpts From the Literature of a Hideous Phase of Human Behavior*), and two others on buried treasure by "T. D. Barrett," Randolph closed out his career as a writer of Blue Books in 1946. All in all, from 1924 to 1946 he had written fifty-five booklets, had been involved in one way or another with ten more, and had done a few short items for the *Haldeman-Julius Monthly* as well. Much of this total, especially the collaborative efforts of the 1930s, is made up of work done solely for money. Randolph did such work well, putting to good use the skills he'd learned from G. Stanley Hall—"boiling down a long treatise into two or three paragraphs" and combining "a lot of brief items on cards . . . into a logical or pseudo-logical order so as to make a book."[58]

The booklets of the 1940s were made in much the same way—in most of them Randolph relied heavily upon information available in books or magazine articles, and worked up his own treatment by pulling his diverse sources into "a logical or pseudo-logical order." But the topics of the 1940s booklets were much closer, and in some instances were identical, to the interests Randolph followed in the work he did even when there seemed no way to make it pay. His Borrow material, for example, came largely from Professor Knapp's biography, as his Hickok booklet depended heavily upon a 1926 study by Frank J. Wilstach, but Randolph's personal devotion to Borrow amounted almost to hero worship, and "Allison Hardy" was interested enough in Hickok to include several first-person observations in his account.

For the most part Randolph's Haldeman-Julius booklets attracted little attention, though Herbert Halpert did review them very briefly in the *Hoosier Folklore Bulletin* in 1945.[59] Randolph himself, hiding behind his own pseudonyms, permitted himself an occasional pat on the back, as when he annotates the "Belden Kittredge" study of "Frankie and Johnny" in *Ozark Folklore: A Bibliography* as a "full account" and praises "William Yancey Shackleford" for his "factual account" of Belle Starr's career, adding that his book "offers several significant local legends."[60] The most searching analysis given any of these booklets, however, was that accorded the ones on western topics by Ramon F. Adams, in his *Burs Under the Saddle: A Second Look at Books and Histories of the West.*

Adams's assessment is generally a harsh one. Of the more than 400 books reviewed in *Burs Under the Saddle*, six (all pseudonymous) are by Randolph, and only one of these, the "Castleman" *Sam Bass, the Train Robber* elicits praise as a "fairly accurate account." Turning to the Belle Starr booklet, Adams opens by noting that "Shackleford" has compared "various accounts of Belle Starr in an effort to clear up certain matters." He then concedes that "some of his points are well taken, but others are not," and goes on to list nine errors of fact and allude to others. A similar procedure is followed for *Wild Bill Hickok: King of the Gunfighters*, where "Allison Hardy" gets credit for debunking "some of the legends concerning Wild Bill" but rebuke for repeating "many others just as untrue." Again, a list of many factual errors follows the general evaluation.

But it is *Gun-Fighters of the Old West*, another "Shackleford" opus, that really comes under Adams's lash. Since this booklet covers more figures, it contains more opportunities for error, and Adams's account of these slip-ups fills some six pages. The tone is openly scornful at times, but given the task of reading some 400 examples of melodramatic fustian and treacle passing as history, one might soon sympathize with Adams's exasperation. Here is Adams on "Shackleford" on Frank James: "After Frank James surrendered, 'they sentenced him to life imprisonment, but a few years of prison life ruined his health. He seemed to be dying of tuberculosis, and *some governor* pardoned him.' Frank was pardoned by Governor Crittenden as soon as he was sentenced and never spent a day in prison, nor did he have the tuberculosis that many writers want him to have." Adams concludes his review of *Gun-Fighters of the Old West* with an all-inclusive indictment: "Sometimes it seems too bad there is no way to keep such absurdly false accounts out of print."[61]

It should be added, however, in fairness to Randolph, that his sins against the facts were by no means exceptions. In fact, working as he did from printed sources, on jobs undertaken for money where the luxury of time for primary researches simply did not exist, it was inevitable that he would reproduce the errors of his predecessors. At the end of his massive survey Adams permits himself a marvelously succinct Afterword in which he comments on the state of the art as a whole. "The written history of our Western gunmen is a travesty," he begins, and ends just a page and a half later:

All in all, a great mass of absurdities has been written about most of the gunmen, and one writer has repeated another, compounding the glaring errors until they have become legends which refuse to die. And when one tries to correct these figments of the dime novelists' imagination, he surely makes an enemy of the romanticist. In spite of all this, however, I hope writers will begin to seek the truth behind the fictitious tales that have been so tenaciously recorded, and I hope this truth will receive proper emphasis and wide circulation. It is time to turn from fantasy to reality. That is why this book was written.[62]

Surely Randolph, if he knew of Adams's strictures, would have sympathized with his position. He too, in his own work, had earned enemies among the romanticists and those who in search of their dollars catered to their tastes. Woodruff had denounced him, the elderly gentleman in Joplin had threatened him with his stick, letters to editors had upbraided him for holding the region up to the nation's scorn, and back in 1934 he'd even received a note from an "Ozark Booster" warning him of reprisals if his future work continued "so rough on us folks as your others." "Say I will tell you one thing," continued the "Ozark Booster," "if you don't quit slamming us so much in your stories we are going to come over there and ride you on a rail."[63] Like Adams, whose concern was for the old gunmen of the West, Randolph undertook his own labors in an attempt to tell the truth about the traditions of the Ozark mountain people. On a smaller scale his articles on the dialect in Ozark novels may be seen as analogous to Adams's review of his own productions in western history.

But after 1946 there would be no more Haldeman-Julius booklets, no more bandit biographies hashed up from the works of others. The "great collections" were about to begin their parade into print. In 1947 he would move to Eureka Springs, Arkansas, where he would be close to Otto Ernest Rayburn's great Ozark library and be able to live with his old friend Church. He would live the rest of his life in Arkansas, where the state university would award him an honorary doctorate in 1951 and the governor himself would proclaim June 12, 1976, Vance Randolph Day. It would be a time of honor and recognition. In 1948 Herbert Halpert would be maneuvering (unsuccessfully) to get him the vice-presidency of the American Folklore Society, and in 1950 Randolph himself would be instrumental in the establishment of the Ozark (later Arkansas) Folklore

Society and would serve as its president in 1950. By 1978—it took almost twenty-four years for the *Journal of American Folklore* to start reviewing his books, so another thirty after *Ozark Folksongs* and *Ozark Superstitions* is probably par for the course—he'd been elected to membership in the Fellows of the American Folklore Society.

But all this applause began in the 1940s with the publication of the folksong and superstition collections, and as the decade turned and Randolph neared sixty he turned his attention to folktales and his dialect studies. Opportunity had knocked at last, the university presses had opened their doors, and his "trunk which I had converted into a filing cabinet" was full.

Vance Randolph's father John, in the 1880s.

Vance Randolph as a child in Pittsburg, Kansas, about 1895.

Vance Randolph as a university graduate student, early 1920s.

"A Man of the World" in Galena, Missouri: Vance Randolph in the late 1930s (McDonald County Library, Pineville, Mo.).

Vance Randolph recording "Deacon" Hembree's fiddling for the Library of Congress, 194 or 1942 (Lyons Memorial Library, The School of the Ozarks).

"Just Friends": Kewpie creator Rose O'Neill and Vance Randolph at Bonnie-brook, O'Neill's home in Taney County, Missouri (Lyons Memorial Library, The School of the Ozarks).

Participants in the Folklore Institute of America, 1958. Seated, left to right, on "The Liars Bench," are Richard M. Dorson, George Korson, R. D. Jameson, Vance Randolph, Archer Taylor, and Stith Thompson (photograph by Jan H. Brunvand).

Sketch for official Vance Randolph Day, in Arkansas, June 12, 1976 (George Fisher for the *Arkansas Gazette*).

Mr. Ozark, 1978 (photograph by Jim Simmons).

8

Tales, Talk, and Laughter

Have you collected any tall tales from the
Ozarks? I should be most eager to publish
a collection. Is there anyone who would
be interested in looking for them, or don't
tall tales flourish in the Ozarks?

—Ruth Benedict to Vance Randolph
February 1, 1938

I

The answer to Benedict's question was, of course, an affirmative
one—Randolph had been collecting folktales of all kinds since 1920,
along with songs, superstitions, and nearly everything else connected with Ozark traditional life. And here, too, as with the songs
he heard his father sing in the 1890s, his informal experience went
back much further. "It was in 1899 that I met Price Paine, a Cow-
skin River fisherman; he was the first storyteller I ever knew, and
one of the best."[1] His reply to Benedict gives some indication of his
progress by the late 1930s: "I was interested in your question about
tall tales in the Ozarks. We have plenty of them, God knows. I have
collected and filed more than two hundred of these, with the idea of
doing a book entitled *Ozark Folk-Tales*. But they are not now in
shape for publication."[2]

A more exact count can be obtained by going through the informant and collection data provided for *Who Blowed Up the Church
House?*, *The Devil's Pretty Daughter*, *The Talking Turtle*, *Sticks in
the Knapsack*, and *Pissing in the Snow*, although this will not include the tall tales in *We Always Lie to Strangers*, since they are not
systematically annotated. "I am sorry," says Randolph in his Preface,

that it is impracticable to credit each item to the individual from whom
it was obtained, as I have done in *Ozark Folksongs* and some of my
other publications. Several old friends and neighbors who helped me
in this enterprise do not wish to be mentioned here, and there are
other reasons for omitting many informants' names. Whenever it has

seemed permissible to identify the teller of a particular story, I have done so in the text. In case such identification was not advisable, I have named the village or the county where I heard the tale and let it go at that.[3]

A survey of the other five folktale volumes reveals a reasonably steady rate of collection, although the 1920s produced the lowest number (105) and the 1930s the highest (162). The distribution is even-handed from volume to volume, except for *Pissing in the Snow*, which had 40 percent of its stories gathered in the 1950s. *Sticks in the Knapsack*, for example, printed twenty-two stories collected in the 1920s, thirty-one from the 1930s, eighteen from the 1940s, and twenty-six from the 1950s.

Randolph's introductions to the various folktale volumes, in addition to explaining his attitude toward crediting informants, are noteworthy for their description of his collecting techniques. In *Who Blowed Up the Church House?* he begins by saying that folktales are not difficult to collect: "It is much easier to collect these items than certain other types of folk material, such as family ballads and superstitions."[4] In *The Devil's Pretty Daughter* he gives a concise description of his recording practice:

> In the early days of my collecting I was accompanied by a young woman who wrote down every word in shorthand as the storyteller spoke. At another period, when the Library of Congress employed me to collect folk songs, we used the Library's recording machine for stories also, and transcribed them from aluminum discs. More often, having neither stenographer nor recorder, I made notes in pencil and typed the story a few hours later, before the notes grew cold. My purpose was to record each tale just as I heard it. No item in this book is an exact literal transcription, but they're all pretty close to the mark. The tales are not retold or rewritten; they are not literary adaptations or re-creations. I did not combine different versions, or use material from more than one informant in the same text.[5]

This is repeated with slight variations in the other introductions, but the fullest statement of the rationale behind Randolph's practice is printed in the first of the annotated volumes, *Who Blowed Up the Church House?* Randolph begins by saying that he has added titles, changed some proper names, "and sometimes revised sentence structure in the sense of clarity." He then turns to the matter of dialect spelling: "I tried to keep the Ozark idiom intact, but made little effort to reproduce the peculiarities of pronunciation. Many of my neighbors say 'skeer' for scare, 'sass' for sauce, 'bile' for boil, and so forth. They make 'yonder' rhyme with gander, and pronounce 'onion' so that it sounds like 'ing-urn.' Most old hunters use a very long *a* in panther, and a *t* sound instead of *th*, but I do not believe anything is gained by spelling it 'painter' as the local-color novelists do." The same introduction gives examples where "it seemed best to translate dialect terms" like "durgen" (into "kind of old-fashioned"), "grub hyson" (into "sassafras tea"), and "woodscolt" (into "bastard").

Randolph next turns his attention to the matters of profanity and obscenity. Profanity was not such a problem:

> When an informant became too profane, I used the blue pencil freely. Cusswords are easily disregarded in conversation, but they grow monotonous in print, and clutter up the page to no useful purpose. I once persuaded an aged hillman to spin a yarn into my recorder, and played the record back without noticing any excessive profanity. But that night, when the typist got it transcribed, we found that *God damn* appeared twenty-seven times in a 900-word script. I left four attributive *goddamns* in the text to preserve the flavor of the old gentleman's speech, and deleted the other twenty-three.[6]

Obscenity, however, was a more difficult matter, and Randolph tended to feel that bawdy tales could not be successfully edited. "I prefer to omit unprintable tales," he wrote in the Introduction to *Sticks in the Knapsack*, "rather than risk spoiling them by expurgation."[7] He does mention, however, one instance where he "tried my hand" at editing such a story: "The man who told me about 'Hogeye and the Blacksnake' used a four-letter verb meaning copulate. Believing that this word could be eliminated without weakening the narrative, I cut it out. Probably I did wrong, but that's what happened."[8]

Such a *mea culpa*, of course, is not to be taken without salt; Randolph means to say simply that bowdlerized tales don't read well. The genuflection to academic insistence upon verbatim transcription is more formal than substantive, since Randolph knew better than most that "transcription" itself is a term describing an ideal rather than a practicable standard. Richard Dorson himself, when he chides Randolph's practice by calling him an "able collector-retoucher," knows how far even his own careful work with an informant like Julia Courtney falls short of anything like a "transcription." At the most obvious level the would-be transcriber must assume the "retoucher" mantle to even punctuate or paragraph his text.[9]

This is not to say, however, that Randolph's practice is above criticism. If few would quarrel with his decisions with regard to spelling, editing profanity, and omitting obscenity if printing it intact was impossible, and if most could approve of his decision to "translate dialect terms," there would still remain at least one passage where Randolph explains a practice that would make a great many specialists uncomfortable. In *The Talking Turtle*, his introductory remarks, while repeating his views on dialect spelling and profanity, extend into matters of syntax and editing:

> I have tried to retain the Ozark idiom, but if one sets down the hillman's exact words his peculiarities of speech appear to be exaggerated. The common query, "Whereabouts do you-uns live at?" fits the speaker's mouth perfectly and sounds all right on the phonograph record, but it looks too thick in print. So I generally write, "Whereabouts do you live?" or "Where do you-uns live?" or "Where do you live at?" All three of these forms are heard in the Ozark country, and they are easier to read than what the man actually said.[10]

The same Introduction makes explicit Randolph's belief that "a literal rendering" is less important with folktales than with "folksongs, rhymes, riddles, dance calls, or other material which is learned by heart." This contention is justified on the ground of "a considerable variation in the words used by the narrator"[11] when the same tale is recorded at different times from the same informant.

Given such views, which in practice result in volumes with nearly every story beginning with the same "One time . . ." introduction, it is easy to sympathize with Dorson's "collector-retoucher" gibe, and with his similar assessment of the folktale collections in particular:

> The four valuable folktale volumes of Vance Randolph [Dorson is writing before the publication of *Pissing in the Snow*, and is excluding *We Always Lie to Strangers* because the stories there are embedded in Randolph's own narrative] contain a variety of narratives, some recognizable Marchen, some floating jokes, some migratory and local legends, but all processed by the master collector-author in the same way, to emerge as fluent, idiomatic yarns, ascribed to named individuals who sound alike. Information on group knowledge of the legends is lacking.[12]

Except for *Pissing in the Snow*, which stayed unpublished until 1976, Randolph's folktale collections appeared in the 1950s, with *We Always Lie to Strangers* leading the way in 1951 and *Sticks in the Knapsack* coming last in 1958. *Who Blowed Up the Church House?* was published in 1952, *The Devil's Pretty Daughter* appeared in 1955, and *The Talking Turtle* was issued in 1957. All were reviewed widely and favorably in both academic and popular journals. Austin Fife opened his *Journal of American Folklore* notice of *We Always Lie to Strangers* with a summary assertion: "This new collection of regional tall tales is one of the best published." He went on to pay special attention to Randolph's "recognition of the frequent use and social significance of the 'group technique' in storytelling," where two or more local men, ostensibly addressing each other, will cooperate to gull an overhearing stranger.[13] The *New York Times* reviewer was no less enthusiastic—Randolph's work was "a priceless collection of tall tales" and "good, sound American folklore, too."[14]

With *We Always Lie to Strangers* and *Ozark Superstitions* Randolph made clear his mastery of the art of pleasing both academic and popular tastes. Both books provided documentation sufficient to the former—*We Always Lie to Strangers*, like *Ozark Superstitions*, came equipped with an annotated bibliography listing some 104 works dealing with Ozark "windies"—while maintaining a style and tone attractive to the general reader. In 1957, reviewing Richard M. Dorson's *Negro Folktales in Michigan*, Randolph paid tribute to another man's similar achievement. "It is not easy," he writes, "to present a book of folktales that will please the general reader and, at the same time, include the documentation required by the archivists." Dorson, he adds, "is both scholar and collector, which gives him a great advantage. Another thing is that he writes in English, avoiding the trade jargon of the schools."[15]

Randolph's own Introduction to *We Always Lie to Strangers*, in addition to the remarks about "group technique" noted by Fife, called attention to the great predominance of male storytellers in tall tale tradition. "Much of the other folk-material that I have collected in this region," he wrote, "was obtained from women. But the grotesque hyperbole of the tall tale does not appeal to the feminine sense of humor." Prominent also is the old maverick note, as the newly respectable author, even as he provides bibliographies and footnotes, reaffirms his old ties to the margins. Defending the basic honesty of tale-teller "Buck Turney," Randolph admits that he "certainly did saw off whoppers for the tourists," but adds that "I never knew him to spread slander, or lie about money, or betray the confidence of a friend." Then, having stated his case, Randolph sums up with a sharp contrastive comment: "I would take Buck Turney's word against that of any preacher I ever met." There is also, among the "intimate and remembered experience" involved in collecting the material for *We Always Lie to Strangers*, the tale "that I first heard near Hot Springs, Arkansas, from a boy who rode with the wild bunch and got his name in all the postoffices."[16] (That "Buck Turney" never existed should not militate against the substantial accuracy of Randolph's sentiments. After all, he collected stories and songs from many prominent citizens. Oakley St. John was one of Pineville's most respected men, and Dr. Young was mayor of Galena. John Turner White, who contributed an Ozark variant of Chaucer's "The Reeve's Tale" to *Who Blowed Up the Church House?* and employed Randolph to help him in the writing of other manuscripts, was a justice of the Missouri Supreme Court. But in this wide range of friendships and acquaintances clergymen are notable by their absence.)

Succeeding volumes met with much the same reception accorded the first. When *Who Blowed Up the Church House?* appeared in 1952, reprinting a number of stories previously published as articles in scholarly journals (nine were published earlier in *Hoosier Folklore*, ten in *Southern Folklore Quarterly*, and ten more in *Western Folklore*), it was hailed by annotator Herbert Halpert as the "first major collection of American-English white folktales for an adult audience." Randolph's folktale collections, like his earlier folksong volumes, included material not always understood as appropriate to a "folklore" study, but Halpert's "Comments of a Folklorist" in this, the first of three Randolph collections he annotated, provide justification for a more inclusive practice: "Probably some of the stories, such as those based on folk customs, and a few of the jests, are actually of local origin. Their inclusion in a folktale collection is amply justified by the fact that they are part of the story lore of the Ozarks. They demonstrate that the repertory of storytellers includes all yarns that interest them, not just 'folktales.' Similarly, folksingers unhesitatingly sing nineteenth century popular songs with as much enjoyment as they do the older ballads, which delight the scholar." [17]

Randolph, for his part, owned up in the Introduction to *Hot Springs and Hell* to an original preference for "the elaborate stories that the folklorists call Marchen, just as most folksong collectors begin by searching out the Child ballads." Later, though, he came "to see an equal merit in brief, humorous pieces." The support of academic opinion is then marshaled: "such folktale specialists as Stith Thompson, Herbert Halpert, and Richard M. Dorson regard these jokes as true folktales." Dorson is further cited for the view that "'shorter, swifter, modernized tales'" are especially suited to contemporary tastes. "In this regard," concludes the judicious collector, "I string along with the folklorists." [18] Back in the 1950s, however, when the inclusion of "local situations" in *The Talking Turtle* could be criticized by fellow collector Leonard Roberts, and printing of "the hillman's random anecdotal repertoire" in *Sticks in the Knapsack* could be faulted in the *New York Times Book Review* by a figure as well known as Botkin, Randolph was stringing along with his informants instead.[19] In his "Introduction" to *Who Blowed Up the Church House?* he mentions a schoolteacher who said she'd heard "dozens" of his stories as a child, but maintained they weren't "really folktales" at all: "Well, I admit that few of them are comparable to the carefully selected fairy stories she read in the college library. Many of the items in this book are scraps of local tradition and humorous anecdote, the sort of thing that German folklorists call *Sagen und Schwanke.* These are the tales that my informants liked best, and I string along with the old-timers."[20]

In general, then, the five folktale volumes issued in the 1950s met with widespread notice, mostly favorable, in both academic and popular reviews. George Korson, commenting on *The Talking Turtle* in the *Keystone Folklore Quarterly*, identified Randolph as "a collector of folklore—the best alive."[21] Jack Conroy, Randolph's old associate from the Missouri Writers' Project, praised *The Devil's Pretty Daughter* in the *Chicago Sun-Times*.[22] As always, of course, there were those who carped about the alleged obscenity of the tales. Ruth Tyler, who wrote a "Somewhere in the Ozarks" column for the monthly *Ozarks Mountaineer* and appeared in granny gown and bonnet to play her hammered dulcimer at festivals, wrote to Otto Ernest Rayburn in August, 1957, to report on *The Talking Turtle*:

> Just got V.R.'s new book from the Library and it fair stinks. *HOW* does he send such dirt thru the mail? Is he that bad off for story material? *MUST* he continue to soil the minds and taint the very souls of readers with sexy, un-natural, dirty filth—(I already knowed how to *CUSS*)—and most of those tales have been told before. Old stuff. *NO* good in the first place. His comedy is so very un-funny. I've known many characters who were dirty, low-down talkers but they *WERE* comical and amusing—*NOT* revolting. He and Tom Benton should swap notes. An infidel is always like that. An alcoholic is also a bad investment. They have twisted minds.[23]

Randolph had been dealing with similar responses to his labors since the 1920s, of course, but by 1957 he'd pretty well cowed his detractors out of the public presses. Few worlds, it would seem, are more vicious in their petty competitiveness than that of the heritage hustlers. Like all worlds, it offers limited room at the top, even if the pinnacle commands little height. After all, there can only be one Mr. Ozark at a time, and one Queen of the Hillbillies. Randolph had triumphed, of course, and by the 1950s he had little to fear from the Ruth Tylers of the world, but he had come up through the ranks of the Ozark booster press, publishing articles in Rayburn's maga-

zines, collaborating with Nancy Nance on Haldeman-Julius booklets and journalistic pieces, and collecting songs from May Kennedy
McCord, Booth Campbell, and Fred High. His own public comments
on the work of his fellow Ozark boosters were generous in the main,
and grew more generous as his own reputation grew more unassail-
able. In private, however, he could write to Church that he wouldn't
go "across the street" to hear May Kennedy McCord lecture (though
even here he adds that she is a fine singer).[24] McCord, for her part,
left on record a nasty attack on Nancy Nance, and Nance herself,
closing the circle, said privately in 1979 that Randolph's "current
vogue is primarily due to the title of his most recent book," and
added that he'd "been writing dirty books for years" with a "veneer
of academic annotations" to cover the "porno quality."[25] Under the
granny gowns and overalls, these smiling old-timers with their dul-
cimers and spinning wheels were as sharp and as savage as any
loan shark or real estate hustler. Tourist dollars are big business in
the Ozarks, and serious fighting takes place in their pursuit.

The great irony, of course, where Randolph is concerned, is that
by the time *Pissing in the Snow*, his real "dirty book," came out in
1976, his reputation was such that no real attack could be mounted.
The book was, of course, widely reviewed, sometimes with asterisks
printed in place of the first four letters of the title's first word, but
once again the general tone of both academic and popular notices
was favorable. Some would-be critics may have been awed by the
formidable apparatus that escorted the collection's appearance—
the University of Illinois Press buttressed the texts with three separate introductions, one by Randolph, one by annotator Frank Hoffman, and one by Rayna Green, who acted as Randolph's agent and
editor in arranging for the book's publication. In addition, the back
cover featured assurances from no fewer than five heavyweights in
the folklore and erotica business as to the importance, value, and
merit of the smut inside. Richard Dorson, entering the spirit of
the occasion, said the collection "fills an enormous gap," while
Francis L. Utley called it "an extremely important appendage" to
Randolph's other works. The others—Dell Hymes, Gershon Legman, to whom the book was dedicated, and Barre Toelken—testified to the volume's merits in less playful manner. Hymes was careful to distinguish *Pissing in the Snow* from "pornographic books
and movies." Readers interested in "cheap thrills" would be disappointed, he said.[26]

Small wonder that few reviewers, especially those in academic
circles, were ready to attack. The *Journal of American Folklore* car-

ried a vague nonreview by Ken Periman that managed to praise some fourteen people in the space of less than one page, and popular reviews quickly made the book Randolph's all time best seller. Avon brought out a paperback edition in 1979, and readers by the thousand, ignoring Hymes's distinction, have found many a cheap thrill in its pages ever since. The book was so successful, in fact, that Randolph, in his last years, would indulge in not entirely facetious fears that he'd end up remembered as "the man who wrote about pissing." In 1979 and 1980 he was fond of gulling visitors by telling them how famous he was getting to be, on account of *Pissing in the Snow* and the fact that people were having Vance Randolph days and special issues of magazines. "They are right now planning to put up a statue of me over on the University campus," he would say. "Seems like they want to get a big hunk of white marble and shape it up to look like a snowbank, then have me standing there beside it, hunching over a little . . ."[27]

II

There was no talk of statues in the 1950s, but a number of other honors did come Randolph's way, including a honorary Doctor of Letters degree conferred by the University of Arkansas in 1951, an Award for Meritorious Achievement from the Kansas State Teachers College at Pittsburg in 1958, and an honorary membership in the American Folklore Society in 1954 (his election was proposed by Richard Dorson and seconded by Wayland Hand). In the summer of 1958 he journeyed to Bloomington, Indiana, for the fifth Folklore Institute of America. While there he had his picture taken with fellow "elder statesmen of Folklore" (Stith Thompson, Archer Taylor, R. D. Jameson, and George Korson) and "junior interloper" Richard Dorson. On July 19 he participated in a panel discussion on "Techniques of Folklore Collecting," on July 21 he gave a lecture entitled "Collecting Ozark Tales," and on July 24 he was interviewed by Dorson on the "Great Britain and the New World" program of a six-part television series, "Folklore around the World." Randolph's presence, according to Dorson's account, "added greatly to the luster of the Institute," while Randolph's own report stressed his pleasure in meeting the "big-shots" of the discipline.[28] To Herbert Halpert, however, he confided an analysis of his position among the scholars: "They wanted me there to look at—like Geronimo at the county fairs."[29]

There were other honors in these same years that failed to materialize, apparently due in part to the lack of opportunity for other folklorists to "look at" their mysterious colleague more often. In 1948, in a move spearheaded by Herbert Halpert, Randolph was nominated for the vice-presidency of the American Folklore Society, but Halpert himself wrote to Randolph that a "surprising amount of opposition arose on the grounds that you have never attended meetings nor been active in the society."[30] (The full extent of Randolph's inactivity is clear from Halpert's previous letter, which urged the prospective vice-president to tend to the formality of joining the group he would lead; "I have your letter of August 30th," replied Randolph, "and shall hasten to invest four dollars in the American Folklore Society as you suggest."[31])

But $4 were insufficient, even in 1948, for the purchase of such high office. Randolph wrote to Halpert that his attendance at the annual meeting (in Toronto) was "out of the question," and as it turned out his two biggest boosters, Halpert and Carl Withers, were also absent.[32] The Society convened on December 28, 1948, in conjunction with the American Anthropological Association, and bestowed the office upon another, presumably more active, member. Halpert, the defeated campaign manager, was "too down in the mouth" to write Randolph until May, 1949, but the candidate himself replied in buoyant mood. "Thanks for your letter, but don't give the AFS matter another thought. Probably it's best that I should not be an officer in such a society, for I have little in common with most of the members."[33]

The candidate was in fact much more actively involved in more local folklore societies by this time, and here, in a smaller pond, he would soon be no mere vice-president but the very top pooh-bah. According to a history of its first two years published in its own newsletter, *Ozark Folklore*, the idea for an Ozark Folklore Society led John Gould Fletcher, the once well-known Imagist poet who was then artist in residence at the University of Arkansas, to meet with other interested parties "on the afternoon of April 30, 1949, in the study of Vance Randolph in Eureka Springs."[34] Fletcher was appointed president for 1949–1950, with Randolph in the vice-presidential slot. Fletcher died in 1950—he "jumped in a pond" said Randolph, who added that the poet "was a goddamn fool, but I thought he was a great man somehow"[35]—and his puzzled admirer/detractor was elected to succeed him for 1950–51.

The Arkansas Folklore Society (the name was changed in 1951) enjoyed nearly a decade of considerable vitality in the 1950s, and Randolph continued to be active in its affairs. Annual festivals were held at the University of Arkansas from 1949 through 1957, which typically combined singing and dancing by area performers with a more or less formal lecture by a distinguished visitor. J. Frank Dobie spoke on "Animal Tales of the Southwest" to the 1950 meeting, Richard Dorson took "A Fresh Look at Negro Storytelling" in 1953, and subsequent meetings were addressed by such luminaries as Mody Boatright, Herbert Halpert (in 1956, when he was president of the American Folklore Society), and W. Edson Richmond. Halpert's visit was an especially fine occasion—the two men had corresponded for more than fifteen years, and Halpert was already firmly established in Randolph's mind as "my only real friend among the folklorists." [36] For Dorson he was too sick to travel, but for Halpert, "I expect to be at the meeting, God willin' an' the creek don't rise." [37] For his part, Halpert wrote that he'd be in Eureka Springs before the meeting, "come hell or high water," and offered to take Randolph back to Fayetteville with him. [38]

The long-delayed meeting was a great success. Randolph went so far as to present Halpert with "the magnificent gift of your beautiful 'Two Patent Colt,'" and Halpert's letter of thanks so far forgot the proprieties as to propose that the two friends might address each other on a first-name basis in future letters. [39]

Randolph spent a good deal of time at various folk festivals in the 1950s. Eureka Springs, Arkansas, where Randolph had lived since 1947, had its own festival, managed from 1952 through 1956 by his old friend Otto Ernest Rayburn, and the local *Times-Echo* and other area papers frequently noted Randolph's attendance. Rayburn had arrived in Eureka Springs in 1946—"Rayburn had moved his library there from Caddo Gap [in Montgomery County, Arkansas]. He had a better Ozark library than either the University of Missouri or the University of Arkansas. That's the reason I moved there." [40] For Randolph, the attractions of Eureka Springs were also enhanced by the presence of his old friend Church. "Church had moved there not long before. He'd written earlier asking me to help him find a place, but I couldn't do no good with the real estate people. I moved into the Basin Park Hotel when I first got there, then moved to Hardy's boarding house. I wanted to live with Otto Rayburn, but they didn't have room in their house." [41] Soon Randolph had solved his housing problems by moving in with Church and his wife. Writing to Halpert in May 20, 1949, he closed with an invitation: "If you come this way, I hope you'll stop and see me. I'm a widower now [Randolph is poor mouthing again—he'd been a "widower" since 1937, of course, but Halpert did not know this], and live alone in a basement at 249 Spring Street. The house belongs to Mr. and Mrs. R. W. Church, and they've got a silly iron sign Three Pines sticking

out of the front porch. You caint miss it."[42] (The formal "Mr. and
Mrs. R. W. Church" here is of a piece with the earlier "Dr. Vernon C.
Allison" in 1926 and the "elderly couple named Gould" in 1944. One
would think his old friends were no more than landlords!)

Randolph's favorite story from the palmy folk festival days of the
1950s took place in Fayetteville, Arkansas, at the second meeting
of the Arkansas Folklore Society (then still known as the Ozark
Folklore Society). The central participants, in town for the meeting, were Randolph, the featured speaker and noted Texas author
J. Frank Dobie, and New York folksong recorder Sidney Robertson
Cowell. Here is Randolph in 1980:

> I was staying up at the old Mountain Inn, and Dobie and Mrs. Cow-
> ell came by to talk. Merlin Mitchell was there, too. He was a graduate
> student and a Texan, like Dobie. We were talking about one thing and
> another, just enjoying conversation. Pretty soon Mrs. Cowell starting
> talking about how surprised she was, when she spent some time col-
> lecting in some southern town, I think it was in Oklahoma or Texas
> somewhere, to see men walking around wearing pistols in broad
> daylight. It shocked her, she said, to think that some parts of the coun-
> try were still so primitive and backward as to permit such a barbaric
> practice in this modern day.
>
> We all listened to her carry on—she really warmed up on the sub-
> ject—about how such a thing would be inconceivable back east in
> New York where folks were civilized and sophisticated. Finally, after a
> long time, Dobie allowed as how such things as that might be surpris-
> ing to somebody from New York, but that he had grown up around
> people who toted guns and somehow it still seemed to him like a natu-
> ral thing to do.
>
> With this he up and reaches in his briefcase, right there in the hotel
> room, and pulls out a big pistol. Says he always carries it with him
> wherever he goes. "A man in my part of the country," he says, "he al-
> ways got some kind of a weapon about him."
>
> Well, poor Mrs. Cowell looked horrified, staring at Dobie and the
> gun. Here he was, a famous man, a sort of professor, come to lecture at
> a university—with a damn pistol in his briefcase!
>
> Just about then—I hadn't said anything at all about this gun busi-
> ness—I reached over under my pillow and out with my little derringer.
> Told her pretty much the same thing Dobie had said. Well that did it!
> She just gave up the whole business, didn't say anything more about
> pistols. If Mitchell had been armed too it would have been perfect.[43]

Randolph's derringer figured again in his favorite hunting story,
though one of the greatest disappointments of his life, to hear him
tell it, is the necessary anonymity surrounding his greatest feat as a

hunter. The tale appears in his tall tale collection, *We Always Lie to Strangers*, where Randolph gives the exploit to a "close friend," for reasons that are made clear in the telling:

> But a close friend of mine did kill a four-point buck with a tiny vest-pocket pistol. He was standing beside a woodland trail when the deer appeared, and on a sudden impulse he snatched out the weapon and fired. The gun was a Remington .41 derringer, with barrels only three inches long. . . . A derringer is the last gun in the world that a man would choose as a hunting arm, yet here was a running deer killed instantly at a distance of about forty yards. The shooter was aghast, for he had always been a staunch defender of the game laws. And now he had killed a deer out of season, on posted land, without any hunting license. . . . It may be that my friend is the only man in the world who ever killed a running deer with a derringer, but he is in no position to do any bragging about his marksmanship. And if he did tell the story, who would believe it? [44]

To his everlasting bemusement, Randolph the "outlaw" gained a notoriety denied to Randolph the sharpshooter. "None of them boys ever paid any mind to the game laws," he said. "But I did. I was always getting after them for shooting turkey and deer out of season. And now here I was with this dead deer on my hands, killed with a fantastic shot that I'd never repeat if I went hunting with that derringer every day for the rest of my life. They didn't let me forget it either. Went and got the deer so the meat wouldn't spoil, and hung the horns up over my door. Started calling me Deerslayer." [45]

If the folk festivals provided Randolph with opportunities like these to swap stories and visit with dignitaries from the academic world, and to meet again with fellow researchers and friends whose songs and tales had filled his books, they also joined company with his involvement in the organization of the Arkansas Folklore Society to introduce him to the woman he would marry in 1962, at the age of seventy, and live with until his death in 1980. Mary Celestia Parler was a South Carolinian who had come to the University of Arkansas in 1948. She'd done graduate work at the University of Wisconsin, taking the M.A. in 1925, and come to Arkansas as a specialist in Chaucer and English language studies. As a young student and scholar, she had published short newspaper articles and reviews (she praised James Branch Cabell's *Something About Eve* as "a book for the sophisticated reader" but worried about the upcoming marriage of one Nancy Ann Miller, of Seattle, Washington, to "the ex-Maharajah of Indore" on scientific grounds—"the findings of geneticists confirm the emotional reactions of centuries in declaring that good cannot come from the mating of widely divergent heritages"), and had contributed one article to *Dialect Notes* in 1930.[46] In the 1950s at Arkansas she would direct the university's work in folklore research, undertaking a good bit of field recording of her own and compiling a large archive of popular beliefs based on materials contributed by students in her folklore classes. She would also serve a full decade as secretary of the Arkansas Folklore Society, from 1950–60.

She also interested herself, after their meeting in Fayetteville at the "first or second" meeting of the folklore society, in Vance Randolph. "I took a shine to him as soon as I met him," she recalled in 1980. "Every woman he met fell in love with him. And he was a good looking old man. I bought a car so I could drive to Eureka Springs when I felt like it—a little second-hand Chevrolet."[47] Randolph, for his part, was impressed enough to be flirtatious and gallant. "She was the best thing that ever happened to me," he said. "Here I was, almost sixty years old, walking on the grass holding hands! It took her 'till 1962 to break down and let me marry her, but she did."[48]

Mrs. Randolph's remembrances of the courtship were somewhat different—"I begged him to marry me," she joked—but she had a clear memory for its details. Once, while he was still living in Eureka Springs, he wrote her a note saying he'd gotten a real scare when "some s.o.b. on a velocipede" nearly ran him down while he was writing "Vance + Mary" on the sidewalk. On another occasion, according to Mrs. Randolph, "he wrote me a whole letter—I was hearing from him every day then, I waited on the mail: 'Dear Mary Celestia, A woman's place is in the f___ing home. As ever, Vance.'"[49]

Randolph moved to Fayetteville in 1960, and on March 23, 1962, the seventy-two-year-old folklorist and Ozarks expert was married to his fifty-seven-year-old bride by justice of the peace Richard B. Greer. "Vance came to Fayetteville when Halperts came," Mrs. Randolph recalled. "He had a bad little 'pad' on Leverett Street—lived there a year and a half. Then we got married. I would have just moved him in. I told him, 'Vance, I've got two bedrooms, you don't have to marry me.' Frances Lemon [Church's widow, since remarried following Church's death on November 8, 1949] had fussed at him in Eureka Springs over drinking."[50]

Even before it ended in marriage, however, Randolph's new love had given him great help and encouragement. As early as 1951 Mary Parler is credited with the story "The Toadfrog," which appears in *The Devil's Pretty Daughter*, and the 1965 *Hot Springs and Hell* cites her as the source of nine jokes and anecdotes. *The Talking Turtle*, published in 1957, is dedicated to her. But the earliest sign of their substantial collaboration appeared in 1953, in the Preface to *Down in the Holler*, where Randolph first thanked his future wife for reading "the entire manuscript" and eliminating "many errors and obscurities," and then said simply that without her help "the book would not have been written."[51]

It was *Down in the Holler*, in fact, which gave Randolph his only substantial headache during a period of general success and relatively easy publication. The five folktale volumes appeared without any great problem. The voluminous Randolph/Halpert correspondence centers on deadlines (with Randolph hurrying Halpert), titles (with Halpert restraining Randolph), and introductions (with Halpert urging Randolph to give more "description of how the stuff actually operates, how people react, what they say, and so on"[52]), rather than questions of where to publish or whether the finished manuscript will be accepted. With *Down in the Holler*, however, such problems were present from the beginning.

The book was first submitted to Columbia in 1951, but they decided not to print it, writing to Randolph that the book "contains much new and valuable information about Ozark speech, but . . . this information is not interpreted or organized in a way that would make the book useful to a *scientific* student of language." The letter went on to say that the press's reader had laid particular stress on the book's failure to meet contemporary academic standards. It might, he said, "sell very well," but it would not be "used by *professional* students of language."[53]

Randolph passed the news on to his co-author Wilson on January 19, 1952, noting that the emphases were not his own and concluding with a terse, "to hell with them." He added that he would "like to offer the MS to the Oklahoma University Press, because the OUP people have done me a lot of favors, and have several times invited me to submit a MS to them."[54] Wilson, unsurprisingly, was stung— he was, after all, the "scholarly chap" whose sole function was to be sure that the book was presented in such a way as to meet whatever were passing at the moment for "professional" or "scientific" standards. He replied to Randolph immediately:

> I am not a bit surprised. When you wrote me in September that the CUP was having somebody read it—presumably somebody outside the Press—and that you thought maybe the reader might be Allen

Walker Read or Hans Kurath, I knew that neither of these boys—and I put in also R. I. McDavid—would take a book of that kind. Reasons: Kurath and McDavid hate me like hell, and Read is sore at me because he fell down on his job as president of the ADS and I moved to have a better man put in his place; because all three think that there is only one way to collect material and to treat it, and that is the *Linguistic Atlas* way. On the other hand, your method of collecting is the one I approve of. They want a book on and of folk speech stewed out of all life and taste and dry bullshit sprinkled on it. Look at the stuff they have published! Who in the hell said or pretended that you were writing a book for the *scientific* student or the *professional* student? But whatever the reader may say about the book not being useful to the scientific student, it is: it has the true facts and a damned sight of them; and they are presented fully and clearly. What does anybody want other than that—the intelligent lay reader or the *scientific* student? The term *scientific* is a favorite of the *Linguistic Atlas* boys. So is *scholarly*. I'm going to ferret out who read this book.

I think you have done a grand job of collecting and writing the book. I think that it is the best collection of dialect that has appeared in this country. The *LA* boys are just afraid for anything like your book to be published, especially since both its methods and contents at this time would prove that their methods and fecal contents are not worth over $500,000—the colossal sum they have wasted on collecting and publishing.[55]

Wilson evidently did undertake some sort of investigation. Another letter to Randolph, dated March 15, 1952, mentions a letter from Columbia. "I was so *impressed* by the typical pseudo-scholarly air of the whole damned thing that I wanted to make a copy of it; and I also wanted to check the criticisms by your MS." This letter, like Wilson's earlier riposte, is lengthy and profane. The "*LA* boys" are again clobbered—Wilson repeatedly uses the "boy" and "boys" tag in both letters—and one name is added to their number. "Bagby Atwood might be a reader; if so, your goose is cooked; and so with a number of other persons I could name."[56]

By this time Randolph had already submitted the manuscript to Oklahoma, where it was accepted. Two contracts for this manuscript have survived, one from May 15, 1952, and the other from June 30, 1952. The former lacks Randolph's signature and differs from the latter only in the matter of the advance to Randolph. By the terms of the final contract, Randolph received $650 as an advance against royalties, with Wilson to receive "the next six hundred and fifty ($650) dollars of accrued royalties," and subsequent royalties to be divided evenly between them.[57]

Wilson is, of course, the obvious fall guy in the whole story. The "scholarly chap" turned out to be a superannuated plug-horse on a track filled with a new generation of thoroughbreds not at all reluctant to hasten his pasturing. It is difficult, however, once the hard things about Wilson's shortcomings have been said, not to feel some sympathy for his position. The reader report from Columbia *was* absurdly overstated—somebody was hunting Wilson, and Randolph's work got caught in the crossfire. And as a matter of simple fact, "professional" and "scientific" students of language made considerable use of *Down in the Holler*. McDavid himself, one of the prominent "boys" of Wilson's letters, noted that the book "provides a great deal of evidence which the scholar can utilize."[58] Another Wilson *bete noire*, Bagby Atwood, in a 1963 article reprinted in hard covers in 1971, praised Randolph as one of a select group of four who "stood out for thoroughness of work," and yet another figure named by Wilson, Allen Walker Read, had long been on record with the flat assertion that "Missouri is fortunate in having had such a thorough and conscientious investigator as Randolph working in this field."[59] Randolph from his undergraduate days had seen himself as a "scientist"—from Aristotle to Watson he had judged his intellectual heritage by "scientific" standards as he understood them.

Down in the Holler was published in 1953, following *Who Blowed Up the Church House?* of 1952 and preceding *The Devil's Pretty Daughter* of 1955. By 1958, with *Sticks in the Knapsack*, the folktale collections were in print except for the bawdy materials. His folksong collections, again with the bawdy material excepted, had been out for nearly a decade, along with his book on superstitions. All told, he'd published eleven volumes since 1946, all of them transferring to durable print some portions of the collections which had filled his trunks since 1920. But there was more to do. As early as 1956, Randolph is writing to Halpert, thanking him for "eight jokebooks" recently sent, and adding that he would appreciate "any more that would be useful in the headnotes to *my* jokebook."[60]

III

Randolph's work with what became *Hot Springs and Hell* occupied him off and on for almost a decade. The great bulk of time went into Randolph's own annotations for the collection, a task for which he had no real model in Anglo-American scholarship, and his letters to Halpert from this period are sprinkled with bibliographic questions and requests connected with this job. In July, 1956, for example,

Halpert sent Randolph *The Arkansaw I Saw*, by one "Dreamy Bill," and noted that "I have also located two or three of the so-called books of humor that I intend to send you. After I have moved and unpacked my books, I can send you a copy of the typescript of that part of my thesis which discusses the history of joke books."[61]

In 1960 Randolph applied unsuccessfully for a grant from the American Council of Learned Societies in support of his annotative labors. Halpert was again called upon for a letter of recommendation—"tell 'em I am a good boy," wrote Randolph—and was provided to aid him in this task with a copy of "what I wrote on my application."

> I have a collection of some 600 folktales, anecdotes and jokes collected in the Ozark region. I wish to publish these items with full documentation and annotation, showing that most of them are British and some are very old. At the University of Arkansas I shall be able to use Professor Halpert's personal library, as well as the University Library. Halpert has rare English jestbooks and other material not easily available elsewhere. No properly annotated book of this kind has ever been published in America. Carroll G. Bowen, University of Chicago Press, wants to publish this one. It is at Mr. Bowen's suggestion that I am applying for this grant.[62]

Halpert pulled out all the stops, calling Randolph "America's greatest folklore collector" and stressing that "no British or American scholar has attempted the formidable task of annotating a large English or American collection of folk jests."[63] And if the application went the way of all but one of Randolph's other applications for grant support, the good news that came just as the application was being prepared was very likely of more use to Randolph than $2,000 from ACLS anyway. "I have just learned that you are coming to the University of Arkansas, for one semester anyhow," Randolph wrote to Halpert on June 14, 1960. "I am certainly delighted to hear it, and it will put Arkansas on the folklore map."[64]

Halpert did come, in the fall of 1960. "Halpert taught a class in Arkansas folklore with me and a seminar in the folktale," Mary Parler Randolph remembered in 1980. "He came first as a speaker for the Folklore Society—that's when Vance met him." The 1960 appointment was for one semester, "but he stayed all year. He wanted to stay, but Vance screwed that up—told me to tell the department not to offer him less than a full professorship. So they didn't offer him anything."[65] Halpert's own recollections of his year in Arkansas include detailed references to Randolph's work on *Hot Springs and Hell*:

When I was a visiting professor at the University of Arkansas in Fayetteville in 1960–1961, I saw Vance frequently. At the time he was partially crippled with arthritis and got around with difficulty. He was engrossed in annotating his Ozark jestbook, the one book he had determined to annotate entirely by himself. A couple of times a week I would carry over to his apartment a large armful of my own books, or volumes of journals from the University of Arkansas Library. He went through these systematically and was usually ready for the next batch when I returned with another load. He was making notes on nearly 500 brief stories.

Halpert goes on to describe the working method that Randolph had learned from G. Stanley Hall and H. M. Belden nearly fifty years earlier, and concludes with an assessment of *Hot Springs and Hell*. "How successful was he in annotating his jestbook by himself? The breadth of his reading is amazing. Elsewhere I have said that the comprehensive notes in his edition of *Hot Springs and Hell* make it a scholarly achievement that 'ranks with the European jestbook editions of Johannes Bolte and Albert Wesselski.'"[66]

By October, 1962, Randolph was nearly done with his work. "My jokebook is not done by any means," he told Halpert, "but I have got the bibliography and notes all typed into clean copy. I hope to get the son-of-a-bitch printed before I am called to my heavenly home on high."[67] On January 29, 1964, he wrote Halpert again with the news that the book was finished, and asked if Halpert would be willing to have the book dedicated to him. "I want to say simply 'To Herbert Halpert' or 'For Herbert Halpert.' I do not wish to say anything about what a great man you are, or about how many miles you walked barefoot through the snow to bring rare books to my pad on Leverett Street."[68]

The completed book was submitted to Columbia. On April 17, 1964, Halpert was asked for his comments by Harry Segessman, executive editorial assistant for that press, and once again went into his "Vance Randolph is America's greatest folklore collector" routine. The jestbook was "a doubly-amazing thing," a great collection with great notes. Wesselski and Bolte were mentioned again. Columbia was praised for its "notable contributions to American culture" in connection with the six titles by Randolph it had already published, and publication of the joke book was urged as "a capstone" to these earlier achievements. Halpert ended with an apology for "the length of this reply," excusing himself on the grounds that "I got excited by the uniqueness of your opportunity."[69]

But Columbia turned the manuscript down, and it was eventually sold to Kenneth S. Goldstein's Folklore Associates press in Novem-

ber, 1964. Randolph got a $500 advance, and *Hot Springs and Hell*
appeared in the fall of 1965. The dedication read "To Herbert Halpert," and Randolph's Preface called additional attention to "books
and periodicals lent me by Herbert Halpert." Otto Rayburn's "personal collection of Ozark books" was also cited as useful, as was the
aid of Mrs. Randolph. By way of apologizing for his inability to visit
"one of the major archives, such as the Schmulowitz collection
in San Francisco," Randolph called attention to his work on the
annotations.[70]

Reviewers generally failed to come to grips with the book's range.
Leonard Roberts did a brief notice for the *Journal of American Folklore* that listed it as Randolph's "seventh or eighth important book
on prose folklore," as if it were simply one more volume in the folktale series published in the previous decade. Roberts alluded to
Randolph's claim (in his Introduction) for "collector" rather than
"folklorist" status, but suggested that "by annotating these jests and
showing familiarity with some two hundred volumes of bibliography, he is now nominated to the latter title." Roberts underestimates
the size of the bibliography—312 items are listed—but his notice at
least calls positive attention to Randolph's work.[71] Jesse W. Harris,
in a *Western Folklore* review, dismisses the notes with a short quip:
"From the notes, we learn the names of the informants and the fact
that 'This tale is printed by Fred Watkins Vaughan (*Before Christ
Came to Hot Springs* [1910], p. 38).'"[72]

Surely it is more accurate, noting that *Hot Springs and Hell*
prints 460 jests and anecdotes and annotates them in much the
same fashion as Halpert and Randolph together did the stories in
the folktale volumes, to recognize in the later book a labor comparable to three or four times that devoted to the longer stories. *Sticks
in the Knapsack*, for example, prints 97 stories and thirty pages of
annotation, while *The Talking Turtle* contains 100 stories and forty
pages of notes. Randolph's 113 pages of notes for *Hot Springs and
Hell* work out to a roughly similar text-to-annotation ratio, and once
again it is Halpert, for all his obvious bias in Randolph's favor, who
comes closest to the mark in judging his friend's work. In a long
letter written just after he'd seen the finished volume, Halpert con-
gratulated his friend for a job well done even as he castigated him
for the folklorist/collector distinction:

> You owe me one night's sleep. I stayed up reading *Hot Springs and
> Hell* as critically as possible—and it's even better than I thought it
> would be. Of course I had only seen the stories and your rough notes;
> now the polished notes have your usual (as you claim Belden-inspired)
> genius for making the notes have sense and interest. . . .

Would you be kind enough to inform me of one other scholar in the United States who knows as much as you do about the people, literature and history of the Ozarks? And now that you have annotated the first collection of *Schwanke* in dem United States, the European scholars will hail you and welcome you to *Bruderschaft*, which as you know means they will drink beer with you.[73]

Hot Springs and Hell, as Leonard Roberts' *Journal of American Folklore* review suggests, continues the publication of Ozark narratives initiated in the folktale volumes of the 1950s. The earlier volumes, for their part, had included items that reviewers (including Roberts) had criticized as "random anecdotal repertoire" and "local situations," and Randolph himself had noted in the Introduction to *Who Blowed Up the Church House?* that "the sort of thing that German folklorists call *Sagen und Schwanke*" made up a significant portion of that volume's stories.[74] The jests of *Hot Springs and Hell* were collected over the same period as the more extended tales, with the 1930s again providing more items (183) and the 1920s fewer (60) than the 1940s (102) or the 1950s (113). The five annotated folktale books credit 489 stories to 133 different informants, while *Hot Springs and Hell* names 149 informants for its 460 items. (Anonymous is omitted as an informant, though his/her stories are counted, in both cases.) Missouri provided more stories (298) and more jokes (260) than any other state, with Arkansas the only other major contributor with 156 stories and 185 jokes. *Hot Springs and Hell*, completed later, includes two jests collected in the 1960s, but the general pattern is identical. *Pissing in the Snow* would stay unpublished until 1976, but Randolph's Preface is dated September 20, 1954, and no story was collected after July of that year. By October, 1955, Randolph had "abandoned" his attempts to locate a publisher for his bawdy materials, and had "deposited typewritten copies in the Library of Congress and in Dr. Kinsey's library at Indiana University."[75] It is with *Hot Springs and Hell*, then, that Randolph really brought to completion the task he'd undertaken nearly half a century before. Nearly ten years before, as the last of the Columbia folktale books were being readied for publication, he confessed that he was "losing interest in folktales, just as I did in the songs and superstitions."[76] Perhaps he kept his interest up by undertaking the annotations, by setting out to show the *Bruderschaft* that he could not only get out and collect traditional materials, but could also hole up in the library and book with the best of them.

Here, too, he would eventually prevail, and Richard Dorson himself, surveying the discipline with his patriarch's eye in 1972, would commit to print a sweeping accolade: "Folklorists who have regarded

Randolph as a collector without equal in the field can now admire him as a collector without equal in the library."[77] Even here, of course, there is the old "collector" stigmatization, and Dorson is directing specific praise not to *Hot Springs and Hell* but to *Ozark Folklore: A Bibliography.* But by 1965, with *Down in the Holler*, five folktale volumes, and *Hot Springs and Hell* in print to join the folksong volumes and the superstition book from the 1940s, Randolph had reason to feel proud of himself. He'd filled his trunks with a region's culture, with a people's voice and mind, and then he'd emptied the trunks onto pages and gotten those pages between hard covers. By 1957 he was writing to Halpert as a self-styled "gentleman of leisure": "Things are going fine with me now, as I am 65 and what with my Social Security and my army pension I can eat every day without working at all, and praise God for that. How my heart bleeds for *young* people, that don't git no pension! I don't think I shall write any more books, as there is no money in it, and nobody appreciates my stuff save a small group of folklorists. Which is OK by me and they can all kiss my ass, as I told the childern this mornin'!"[78]

PART FOUR

Mr. Ozark

It is a kind of total grandeur at the end,
With every visible thing enlarged and yet
No more than a bed, a chair and moving nuns,
The immensest theatre, the pillared porch,
The book and candle in your ambered room,

—Wallace Stevens
"To an Old Philosopher in Rome"

9

Embers

Sir, said Christian, I am a man that
am come from the City of Destruction,
and am going to the Mount Sion, and
I was told by the man that stands at
the Gate, at the head of this way that
if I called here, you would show me
excellent things, such as would be an
help to me in my journey.

—John Bunyan, *Pilgrim's Progress*

Vance Randolph died on November 1, 1980, at eighty-eight, some
fifteen years after the completion of *Hot Springs and Hell* marked
the conclusion of his immense work. *Ozark Folklore: A Bibliography* was published in 1972 by Indiana University, but like *Pissing
in the Snow* it had been finished in the 1950s, and sold to the University of Arkansas for $500 in 1959. After this for twenty years he
lived in Fayetteville, Arkansas, with his wife. He worked more slowly,
first on the annotations for *Hot Springs and Hell*, then on a supplement to the Ozark bibliography that would eventually be nearly as
large as the original volume. He did occasional reviews and articles
for local magazines and provided blurbs for books by his friends. He
received visitors and gave advice, and sometimes went riding on
weekends with old friends in Fayetteville, revisiting the places where
he'd worked so hard so many years before. Herbert Halpert's obituary notice for his friend includes a brief account of these trips:

> Most of the stories I heard Vance tell were at the informal parties his
> friends, Dean Nichols and his wife, Dorothy, had at their big sociable
> hilltop house in Fayetteville. Others came out on weekends in the fall
> and spring when the Nichols went "back-roading" in their big car.
> They usually took along Vance; the local folklorist, Mary Celestia Parler, who later became Vance's wife; and the three Halperts, including
> our ten-year-old son. Sometimes there were more people and two cars.
> We covered a great deal of beautiful country, often passing through
> small isolated communities that Vance had known years before in

his horseback-riding days. He would occasionally recall some of the interesting old-timers he had known there and tell us about his experiences.[1]

There were additional honors too, highlighted by his election as a Fellow of the American Folklore Society in 1978. He read his favorite books again each year—Sylvia Townsend Warner's *Lolly Willowes, Lavengro,* and *The Romany Rye.* He was still short of money, and even before he moved with his wife to a nursing home in 1975 their visitors were often struck by the meanness of their surroundings.

But above all there were great tracts of time, vast stretches of desolate loneliness tempered for each only by the presence of the other. Randolph, for all his wheedling and complaining via the mails when money and whiskey were his goals, found it easier to ask for favors than for company. "Come see us when you can," was his traditional last word for Ernie Deane, for Mike Luster, for Gordan McCann, for all friends who called regularly. But there is one letter, undated, written to Halpert, where the distance breaks down and the old man abandoned with his wife to fight for sanity amid senility and despair calls out for help:

Dear Herbert—

I know it is asking a great deal, what with no typists and all, but a letter from you would mean a great deal to me just now. It is an odd sort of isolation. We are well off physically, except I am 83 years old and my wife is 70. But no friends now. . . My poor wife . . . I wish I could ask Letty to write her a note. These things are [letter breaks off, without signature][2]

A wintry scene—Randolph bedfast and his wife nearly blind, their diligent lives in Ozark cabins and mountain camps narrowed to lunar light in cement block rooms and rubber food three times each day. In such a world even an interviewer is welcome, and such a world must jar even the most casual of interviewers to sympathy and allegiance. In the fall of 1976, with no notion of vocation whatever, the future biographer called, and was introduced to Mr. and Mrs. Randolph by Leo Van Scyoc, English professor at the University of Arkansas and longtime friend of both Randolphs. Polite conversation was exchanged, beer bottles were opened, and German songs sung. The biographer felt no inkling of mission, but Randolph expressed interest in his own work, said he'd be happy to read anything easily copied or lent. Other visits followed. The visitor came to know the corridors of the nursing home, grew accustomed to the sour tang of stale urine in its air, and learned where to park the aged lady who often wheeled into the Randolphs' room crying "I want my Mommy" in a voice hoarse with repetition. The first time it happened Randolph warded her off with his cane and rolled her backward out the door, and the visitor thought him impatient and rancorous. But he was defending himself. Madness and chaos hemmed him round, and with his wife, with conversation, drink, and his cane wielded like a sword, he barred them from his door.

The future biographer mostly visited with Mike Luster, his friend and student. At the beginning Luster knew more about Randolph, had a deeper interest, and throughout, until he left for graduate studies in Philadelphia, was the better interviewer. The tapes reveal the biographer as too talkative, too willing for aimless chat, too forgetful of the topics at hand. But he had his excuses. He was tardy knowing what he was about, on these visits. His major love, after all, was for the character Randolph was, the vivid stories he told. He was, finally, held most by verbal razzle, art's supremely confident, unfounded quackeries, the scams of imagination by which the citizenry is astounded, appalled, finally fed. And it was here, on this level, that Randolph first appealed. He was a man of words. Many of his stories were verbal at their core, the narrative no more than a stage for delivery of a witty line. In 1943, in a letter to Frances Church, he wrote down one of his favorite stories, one he repeated several times in the late 1970s: "Anyhow there was some Church of God people in Springfield asked me to tell a story, and I told them about the time I come out of the hotel in Marshall, Ark. one Sunday morning, and here come a little boy about 4 years old with the snappingest black eyes I ever see. And I says 'Good morning,' and he answers 'Git out of my way, you big son-of-a-bitch! I'm a-going to Sunday School!' Them people did not keer for the story."[3]

A briefer instance, no more than a remark, is found in a 1967 letter to Halpert: "A village policeman talking about the juvenile delinquents on the periphery of the university said 'Some of them boys got a little bigger than they know what to do with.'"[4]

By 1976, when Luster and the biographer dawned upon him, Randolph's last two books had appeared. The first was *Ozark Folklore: A Bibliography.* "I think it is the best thing I've ever done," he wrote to Halpert, and surely he is right to rank it with *Ozark Folksongs* and the volumes of stories and jokes at the top of his achievement.[5] Its fifteen chapters treat all aspects of Ozark folklore and folklife, including previous bibliographies. Altogether there are more than 2,500 annotated entries. Richard Dorson, in a warmly

appreciative Foreword that rises at one point to bestow the title of
"genius" upon Randolph, called the bibliography "a climax and
crowning achievement of Vance Randolph's lifelong activity in Ozark
folklore," and added that the work "transcends its regional limits" by
providing "a model and prod for comparable undertakings throughout the United States." Dorson also repaid the compliment Randolph had given his own work fifteen years earlier when he called
attention to the "entertaining digest and commentaries on the entries. Surely no bibliography was ever more readable."[6]

Dorson is right. The reader who parks *Ozark Folklore: A Bibliography* on his or her nightstand for occasional browsing will be continually rewarded with small gems of pungent criticism or under-
stated humor. As usual, Randolph seems to indulge a sharp animus
for clergymen, as when for example Milford W. Howard's 1923 *The
Bishop of the Ozarks* is treated to summary dismissal: "A dreadful
novel full of melodrama and in very heavy dialect. The author shows
no knowledge of the Ozark region." Another novel, *Heaven in the
Ozarks* (1957), is described at somewhat greater length: "Foolish
novel about the hills of southern Missouri, apparently in the 1870's
or 1880's. The dialect is poor, and the accounts of pioneer handicrafts are full of errors. The book contains many sermons, and a
good deal of bad verse." Randolph's reader appreciates especially the
sly trick of phrasing which evaluates the verse as "bad" but omits to
judge the quality of the "many sermons." Some verse is good, and
some verse is bad, says the undercurrent, but sermons are a bad
business to start with, and the more the worse.

Annotating G. M. N. Parker's 1912 work, *Footprints from the City
to the Farm in Arkansas*, Randolph calls it a "personal back-to-the-
land story," and goes on to cite several details before closing on a
humorous note: "Parker advises everybody to flee the filthy cities
and hasten to Rogers, Arkansas, where it happens he conducted a
real estate business." A more subtle comic touch is evident in his
annotation of his own 1943 Haldeman-Julius booklet, *Americans
Who Thought They Were Gods*, where he calls attention to the passages devoted to James Sharp, "an Arkansas farmer who declared
himself the father of Jesus Christ, and was widely known as Adam
God. Sharp always claimed to be immortal, but he died at Joplin,
Missouri, 8 March 1946."[7]

In annotations like these, and countless others would have served
as well, the old outlaw allegiances shine through. Randolph knew
James Sharp personally—he'd visited him near Joplin in 1935,
when the divine man was living in a tent with his wife Melissa (he

called her Eve) and making a living collecting bottles and old metal for junk dealers. Here was no mainstream hustler shriving bankers, assuring a herd of Babbitts their rapacity was pleasing to God, but instead a full-bore wildman worthy of respect. "Adam God," wrote an admiring Randolph, "is the only messiah I ever saw who was able to laugh much."[8]

Randolph's old socialist and hobo days were distant memories, however, by the time *Ozark Folklore: A Bibliography* appeared. The days in the 1930s when his scholarly labors were mostly unrecognized except by those who resented them were likewise long gone, and he could even recall them with good humor. "For a while I was public enemy number one," he told an interviewer in 1971. "I'd show up somewhere and the word would go out, 'That old S.O.B. is back.'"[9] By the 1970s the public enemy assailed in letters to the editor and chamber of commerce speeches had become a regional patriarch, laden with honors.

The honors had actually started rolling in in the 1950s, after the publication of *Ozark Folksongs* and *Ozark Superstitions*. By 1960 he had his honorary Ph.D. and was an honorary member of the American Folklore Society he'd once scraped up $4 to join for one year. Even his hackwork had stepped up in class, from Haldeman-Julius to the *New York Times Book Review*, where from 1954 to 1963 he presented his views on five studies by well-known scholars, including Richard Dorson's *American Folklore*. Randolph praised all five books but got himself in hot water anyway with his notice of LeRoi Jones's *Blues People*. In an angry letter to the editor Jones made the reasonable suggestion that "it would have been better if your reviewer, Vance Randolph, had read my book," and then, after further rancor, ended the same paragraph with reiteration: "If Mr. Randolph says he read the book he is a liar."[10]

Chastened perhaps, Randolph wrote no more reviews but limited himself to brief blurbs in praise of the work of friends and to short contributions to folklore journals and regional magazines. In the late 1970s, for example, he sent several tales to *Mid-South Folklore* and the *Ozarks Mountaineer*, and two bawdy tales appeared in *Maledicta*. Reinhold Aman, editor of *Maledicta*, was in fact one of Randolph's most aggressive and industrious supporters; his letters greatly cheered Randolph, who also enjoyed Bruce Jackson's piece in the winter, 1977, issue which celebrated by contrast with most academics the work of Randolph and Gershon Legman (and Benjamin Botkin).[11] By the 1950s, too, after a decade's absence from their pages, Randolph was again the frequent subject of newspaper feature stories, and this attention continued unabated through the 1960s and 1970s. Along with the honorary doctorate and the free membership in the American Folklore Society, the 1950s also brought Randolph his first official recognition from his old adversaries in booster circles. In 1954 he got a plaque from the surprisingly named Ozark Playgrounds Association (not a group of parents raising funds for swings and hopscotch courts but resort and tourist camp operators assembled to promote their wares) in "appreciation of the ability that has been so effectively directed in advancement of the Playgrounds of the Ozarks, The Land of a Million Smiles." [12]

One can only imagine Randolph's gratitude—no doubt he thought he'd died and gone to heaven. But even such honors as these would pale in comparison to those of the 1970s. In 1975 he was inaugurated, in the company of Thomas Hart Benton, Rose O'Neill, Harold Bell Wright, May Kennedy McCord, and Elizabeth Mahnkey, "Poet Laureate of the Ozarks," as a charter member of the Greater Ozarks Hall of Fame. In the same year there was a "Special Issue for Vance Randolph" of *Mid-South Folklore*, with a good biographical sketch by Joan Wilson Miller and articles by seven other admirers. Then, in 1976, Governor David Pryor, in an official proclamation decorated with the "great Seal of the State of Arkansas," declared June 12 as Vance Randolph Day throughout the state. [13] Finally, in 1978, the American Folklore Society got around to the one honor that really meant something to him—they elected him a Fellow of the society. The new Fellow's pleasure is apparent in his letter of gratitude to Halpert:

> Cochran tells me that I am elected a Fellow, and he says you are responsible.
> I am delighted, naturally. I realize that this honor is not ordinarily conferred on a mere collector with no degree and no university connection. I don't know how the hell you managed it, but I certainly appreciate whatever it was that you did. You are my only friend among the professionals.
> Most of our friends are newspapermen and teachers of literature and the like, with a few poets throwed in.
> Mary C. is blind now, and I am bedfast the last two years.
> This Fellow business has perked me up considerably, and Mary and I are truly grateful. If there is a ribbon goes with it I'll sew it on my pajamas. [14]

Among Halpert's many exertions in Randolph's behalf—and there would be one more, in 1981, when he would write his friend's obituary notice for the *Journal of American Folklore*—this one would cheer its beneficiary most. It was one more assurance, and one from American folklore's most august body, that his work would indeed "be setting in libraries in good company" for as long as libraries stood.

II

Now, at the end, the coy disguise of "the biographer" must be dropped, and I must say straight out that my figure may be wrong. Vance Randolph, whom I visited weekly for three years and pursued through countless books and old newspapers and letters for two more, and whom I have presented here as a spirit best understood in terms of a fundamentally romantic identification with outlaws, gypsies, socialists, and other citizens of Edge City, may after all have aspired more deeply to other archetypes. He may, for example, have wished most of all to be One of the Boys, a Man among Men. I have guessed not, but facts can be found to dress such a notion respectably. Vance Randolph lost his father early, and his stutter made his first school years painful. Cards have survived attesting his membership in the American Legion, the Society of the 353rd Infantry, and the 89th Division Society. He spoke often of his experiences at the famous House of Lords in Joplin, Missouri, and he was proud of his skill as a poker player.

So my figure may be wrong. It's a strange task, biography, and stranger when its subject is himself a region's biographer. When Michael Boyle, with Hugh Nolan the great historian of Fermanagh's Ballymenone district, died in 1974, "taking with him the last whispers of hundreds of men and women," my friend Henry Glassie, who sat by his bed as I by Randolph's, sensed a loss deeper than measure. "I am the hopeless historian," he wrote, "astronomer of a darkening universe."[15] Michael Boyle died in hospital, with his house in ruins, and in a large book rich with photographs and drawings there is a chill made by the absence of his likeness. Death takes the men we try to save by understanding, their homes crumble or are occupied by strangers, and we can only hope, not know, that we have salvaged their elusive center.

Mike Luster and I attended upon Randolph like Linnell, Calvert, and Palmer, the self-styled Ancients, upon Blake. They called his modest home the House of the Interpreter, after the figure in *Pilgrim's Progress* who aids Christian the pilgrim by showing him "that which will be profitable to thee."[16] That fit Blake, since he worked in his last years on a series of twenty-eight watercolors illustrating Bunyan's work, and it fits my portrait of Randolph since I have found in Bunyan's "Desired Countrey" a phrase and image to order Randolph's long pilgrimage in the "Delectable Mountains" of southern Missouri and northern Arkansas. It fit, too, in the fall of 1980, when I first connected Randolph and Blake by way of sharply physical association. Blake in his last days was afflicted with shivering fits, which biographers now attribute to gallstones or gall-bladder inflammation. My last visit to Randolph's bedside, the night before he died, was ended when he began to shiver so violently that he could not speak, and in my despairing love I thought of the young disciple Samuel Palmer, barely twenty, who was so awed by Blake that before "venturing to pull Blake's bell-handle, Palmer would kiss it." [17]

Samuel Palmer, Henry Glassie, Mike Luster, and myself—sharing the experience of vigil by the side of revered elders, we also share the dark obverse of that experience's inspirations, the staggering loss, the sure inadequacy of our necessarily uncertain understanding. Who is able, after all, to "tell the tale of the old man?" To attempt such a task is to attempt the protection of "a flame with dark winds hedged about," and to experience even as one's task is brought to what must stand for completion the grief of "the dark mind stumbling/through barren lands." [18]

But we do have our joys. We know, beyond doubt, that we are welcome, that our presence is a help, even a treasure. Linnell's wife delighted Blake with Scottish songs, and Michael Boyle told Glassie "this chat's better to me than me dinner." [19] Randolph often waved his dinner away for more talk with me, and while like Hugh Nolan he had too much taste for intimate effusion, he had a wife who told me straight out one late night that Mike Luster and I were tonic and joy to her husband. "He lives for your visits," she said. [20]

And we have further compensation. Our books are done. The dark winds are still hedged about, the historian not entirely hopeless. Vance Randolph set himself a task. He wrote down the stories and songs and beliefs of his neighbors, lest they be lost. He saw his neighbors as I him, and acted similarly, on a vastly larger scale. He saw a flame, something warm with life and nourished with human care, as precious and threatened. He acted, against odds, to save it. His books are on the shelves. Emma Dusenbury's songs, Lon Jordan's stories, the deeds and words of hundreds of their fellows, survive in his pages. He gave a region's voice duration, sustained its life. We have one task, call us folklorist or collector, biographer or storyteller. We are in league in time and space, athwart the dark, and our endeavor, in patience steeled to sit with ear alert to listen, partakes of the heroism of the old nekyia. We give our time, our blood, that ghosts may speak and give us direction, that the past, not wholly surrendered, may serve the present and lead to a future.

Vance Randolph lies in the National Cemetery in Fayetteville, Arkansas, a soldier among soldiers. He laughed about that often—it would be, now is, his last joke at the expense of an Army unwise enough to mess with him. His wife, who survived him less than one year, is buried in South Carolina. She laughed with me, thinking of his laughter, at the ornately printed "Full 20 Year Warranty Certificate" provided at the funeral by the Batesville Casket Company. This amazing document, which fights the dark in a silly, unimaginative way, assures Mr. Randolph and his representatives that his casket "successfully passed the vacuum test devised by Batesville," and is guaranteed to "resist the entrance of air, water or any element found in the soil in which it is interred" until the year 2000.[21]

The National Cemetery is a lovely place, where neatly tended graves circle out on the slopes of a gentle rise topped with large and gnarled evergreens. There are residential neighborhoods to the north and west, an auction barn and stockyard to the east, and to the south in the middle distance the mountains of the land Vance Randolph gifted with a lifetime's labor. This is how to end, I think, with such a man—with laughter and loveliness, with solid achievement sonorous like Stevens and Blake and low-brow loyalties scruffy like Harmonica Frank Floyd. And with gift. A human landscape lives through his labor, and he rests in that land's keeping.

PART FIVE

Sources, Notes, and Thanks

Sources and Notes

A preliminary word is necessary to explain the various sources of quotations from Randolph himself. In some instances these are straightforward, as in the passages from the Halpert/Randolph correspondence. Here I was generously provided with photocopies by Professor Halpert, and almost without exception these are dated. Citation here is an easy matter.

In other instances things are more difficult, thanks in the main to the casual beginnings of this project. In our first year of visiting Mike Luster often made tapes, and I often took notes, simply for our own pleasure, without any thought of undertaking even a bibliography, let alone anything so large as this biography. Our tapes are often dated only as to year, and in some cases even this is based on later guessing. My earliest notes, on the backs of envelopes and file folders, are likewise lacking dates. Later I acquired a notebook specifically for talking with Randolph, and the entries in this volume, taken down as Randolph spoke, are dated.

There are additional complications. Midway through my researches I was contacted by Robert and Wanda Duncan, who in the 1950s had initiated a biographical study of Randolph, and had copies of a good deal of his early correspondence. Professional obligations forced them to suspend the study, and they very generously offered me the materials they had gathered. These have been deposited in the Special Collections section of the University of Arkansas Mullins Library, and references to material from this source are identified.

Finally, I wrote a number of shorter articles about Randolph during his lifetime, and I made a habit then of allowing him to "correct" his own statements in them. These passages, then, have been once bowdlerized, but they were so treated by their author, and I have in several cases cited those articles here. These instances too are identified. In a number of cases I have relied on my memory alone for a short phrase. I am as sure as I can be that I have recorded these accurately, but again the notes will call attention to the lack of recorded or noted documentation. In short, my records of Randolph's words run the gamut from dated and undated tapes, through dated and undated notes, to copies of letters made by others some thirty years ago, to intangible memories and even unsigned typewritten pages.

CHAPTER ONE: INTRODUCTION

1. Vance Randolph. This and the remark cited in the preceding paragraph were made in the fall of 1976 or winter of 1977, and written down from memory later.

2. Robert Cochran and Michael Luster, *For Love and for Money: The Writings of Vance Randolph, An Annotated Bibliography* (Batesville: Arkansas College Folklore Archive Publications, 1979), p. 19.

3. Vance Randolph, *Ozark Magic and Folklore* (New York: Dover Publications, 1964; first published as *Ozark Superstitions*, 1947, by Columbia University Press), p. 3.

4. Margaret E. Haughawout, "Ridge Runners and Hill Billies of the Ozarks," Kansas City *Star*, Oct. 24, 1931. This review is unsigned; I owe the attribution to Gene DeGruson, librarian at Pittsburg State University, Pittsburg, Kans., authority on Emanuel Haldeman-Julius, and editor of the good regional magazine of history and the arts, the *Little Balkans Review*.

5. Letter dated July 6, 1923, postmarked Aug. 3, 1923, given to me by Vance Randolph.

6. Bosley Crowther, *The Lion's Share: The Story of an Entertainment Empire* (New York: E. P. Dutton, 1957), p. 288.

7. Jean-Paul Sartre, *Saint Genet: Actor and Martyr*, trans. Bernard Frechtman (New York: George Braziller, 1963), p. 7.

8. Peter Nemo [Vance Randolph], *Confessions of a Ghost-Writer* (Girard, Kans.: Haldeman-Julius, 1944), p. 24.

9. Harvey N. Castleman [Vance Randolph], *Sam Bass, the Train Robber: The Life of Texas' Most Popular Bandit* (Girard, Kans.: Haldeman-Julius, 1944), p. 2.

10. William Yancey Shackleford [Vance Randolph], *Belle Starr: The Bandit Queen: The Career of the Most Colorful Outlaw the Indian Territory Ever Knew* (Girard, Kans: Haldeman-Julius, 1943), p. 3.

11. Vance Randolph, May 28, 1980.

12. Vance Randolph, Tape 5, Side 2 (1978). Since Vance Randolph's death, this dedication has been used for a collection of short articles entitled *Vance Randolph in the Ozarks* (Branson, Mo.: Ozarks Mountaineer, 1981). Randolph gave it to me on a handwritten index card.

13. Vance Randolph, "Do Scientists Believe in God?" *Haldeman-Julius Monthly* 3, no. 4 (1926):476.

14. Vance Randolph to Herbert Halpert, Oct. 5, 1974. Emphasis Randolph's.

15. Mary Parler Randolph told me this anecdote, in Vance Randolph's presence, on May 6, 1980.

16. Vance Randolph, May 6, 1980.

17. W. Jackson Bate, *Samuel Johnson* (New York: Harcourt Brace Jovanovich, 1977), pp. xx-xxi.

18. An especially well-done volume in the Columbia series is Margaret Mead, *Ruth Benedict* (New York: Columbia University Press, 1974). Benedict's specifically folkloristic activities are the subject of Virginia Wolf Briscoe's article, "Ruth Benedict: Anthropological Folklorist," *Journal of American Folklore* 92 (1979):445–76. Easily the best study in this field is Robert E. Hemenway's solidly researched and gracefully written *Zora Neale Hurston: A Literary Biography* (Urbana: University of Illinois Press, 1977). George Korson's great work among Pennsylvania miners has been well documented by Angus K. Gillespie in *Folklorist of the Coal Fields: George Korson's Life and Work* (University Park, Pennsylvania State University Press, 1980). For Brewer's work see James W. Byrd, *J. Mason Brewer: Negro Folklorist* (Austin, Tex.: Steck-Vaughn Co., 1967). For Jakob and Wilhelm Grimm see Ruth Michaelis-Jena, *The Brothers Grimm* (New York: Praeger, 1970), and M. B. Peppard, *Paths through the Forest: a Biography of the Brothers Grimm* (New York: Holt, Rinehart and Winston, 1971).

Shorter studies include Peggy Martin, *Stith Thompson: His Life and His Role in Folklore Scholarship, with a Bibliography*, Folklore Monograph Series (Bloomington, Ind.: Folklore Publications Group, 1979); Alan Dundes, "Robert Lee Vance, American Folklore Surveyor of the 1890's," *Western Folklore* 23 (1964):27–34; Keith S. Chambers, "The Indefatigable Elsie Clews Parsons—Folklorist," *Western Folklore* 32 (1973):180–98; W. K. McNeil, "Lafcadio Hearn, American Folklorist," *Journal of American Folklore* 91 (1978): 947–67; Michael J. Bell, "William Wells Newell and the Foundation of American Folklore Scholarship," *Journal of the Folklore Institute* 10 (1973):7–21; Esther K. Birdsall, "Some Notes on the Role of George Lyman Kittredge in American Folklore Studies," *Journal of the Folklore Institute* 10 (1973):57–66; R. Gerald Alvey, "Phillips Barry and Anglo-American Folksong Scholarship," *Journal of the Folklore Institute* 10 (1973):67–95.

For comparable accounts of British and European scholars, see Richard M. Dorson, *The British Folklorists* (Chicago: University of Chicago Press, 1968); Dag Stromback, ed., *Leading Folklorists of the North* (Oslo: Scandinavian University Books, 1971); and Giuseppe Cocchiara, *The History of Folklore in Europe*, trans. John N. McDaniel (Philadelphia: Institute for the Study of Human Issues, 1981).

19. Herbert Halpert, Foreword to Cochran and Luster, *For Love and For Money*, p. 9.

20. Roger Abrahams, in conversation, Bloomington, Ind., 1977.

21. Luke 15:13 (King James Version).

22. Vance Randolph, remarks made in the winter of 1979 and written down from memory later. In general, banter of this type was good-natured, but Randolph did become genuinely angry with me on at least one occasion, when I brought to his attention the disparity between the contracts for his books and the accounts of advances given by him in letters to his friends. See, for example, Chapter Five, section III. I tried to learn from my mistake in this instance, and did not, for example, bring to his notice the interviews in Pineville that criticized his behavior toward Marie Wilbur.

23. Arthur S. Tolliver [Vance Randolph], *The Strange Life of George Borrow: Vagabond, Scholar, Horse-witch, Tinker, Blacksmith, Author, Linguist, Boxer, Adventurer, Jail-bird, Peddler of Bibles—There Was Never Another Like Him in the World* (Girard, Kans.: Haldeman-Julius, 1944), p. 5.

24. Tolliver [Randolph], *The Strange Life of George Borrow*, p. 10.

25. Vance Randolph. This remark, with only very slight variation, was made many times, but I reproduce it here from memory.

26. William Blake, "The Marriage of Heaven and Hell" (Plate 3), in Geoffrey Keynes, ed., *The Complete Writings of William Blake, with Variant Readings* (London: Oxford University Press, 1966), p. 149. For the plate with this phrase see David V. Erdman, annotator, *The Illuminated Blake* (Garden City, NY: Anchor Press/Doubleday, 1974), p. 100.

CHAPTER TWO: PEOPLE OF HIS OWN KIND

1. Richard M. Dorson, *American Folklore and the Historian* (Chicago: University of Chicago Press, 1971), pp. 24–25. Dorson discussed Randolph's work in other places: see "A Visit with Vance Randolph," *Journal of American Folklore* 67 (1954): 260; *Folklore and Fakelore: Essays toward a Discipline of Studies* (Cambridge, Mass.: Harvard University Press, 1976), p. 99; "Editor's Comment: Katherine Briggs, James Delargy, Vance Randolph," *Journal of the Folklore Institute* 18 (1981):91–93; "The State of Folkloristics from an American Perspective," *Journal of the Folklore Institute* 19 (1982):71–105.

2. Vance Randolph, *Wild Stories From the Ozarks* (Girard, Kans.: Haldeman-Julius, 1943), p. 3.

3. Vance Randolph, interview dated Sept. 4, 1955, Duncan papers, Special Collections, University of Arkansas Library, MS, D912, 363, File 1.

4. My information about the history of Pittsburg and Crawford County comes from a variety of sources, most importantly the special centennial issue of the *Pittsburg Morning Sun*, May 20, 1976. I was also aided by a

manuscript apparently produced in 1941 under W. P. A. auspices, *A Guide to Pittsburg, Kansas*, in the collection of the library at Pittsburg State University. For the "Tower of Babel Banquet," see the *Pittsburg Headlight*, Oct. 21, 1916. For demographic statistics see J. Neale Carman, *Foreign-Language Units of Kansas*, vol. 1: *Historical Atlas and Statistics* (Lawrence: University of Kansas Press, 1962), pp. 110–12, 224. For direction to these and other sources I am indebted again to Gene DeGruson.

5. Vance Randolph, Oct. 23, 1979, and Apr. 17, 1980. On many occasions, when Randolph would return to a topic he'd discussed earlier, I would page back in my notebook and interpolate additional materials. Characteristically I would read back to him what I'd noted before, giving him the opportunity to correct, omit, supplement, edit. When two or more dates are given for a single passage taken from my notebook, this procedure is responsible.

6. John D. Hicks, *The Populist Revolt* (Lincoln: University of Nebraska Press, 1961; first published 1931), p. 159. Hicks is himself quoting Elizabeth N. Barr, "The Populist Uprising," in *A Standard History of Kansas and Kansans*, ed. William E. Connelly (Chicago: Lewis Publishing, 1918), pp. 1115–95. There are several outstanding recent studies of the populist movement: see especially Lawrence Goodwyn, *Democratic Promise: The Populist Movement in America* (New York: Oxford University Press, 1976), and O. Gene Clanton, *Kansas Populism* (Lawrence: University of Kansas Press, 1969). For Mary Elizabeth Lease, see Dorothy Rose Blumberg, "Mary Elizabeth Lease, Populist Orator: A Profile," *Kansas History* 1 (1978):3–15.

7. James R. Green, *Grass-Roots Socialism: Radical Movements in the Southwest, 1895–1943* (Baton Rouge: Louisiana State University Press, 1978), p. 12. Green's work is superbly researched and capably written; read with Goodwyn's study of populism, it will provide the nonspecialist with a good grasp of the political movements feared and despised by John Randolph and admired and supported by his son. Randolph is mentioned (p. 337) though his name is omitted from the index.

8. Howard H. Quint, "Julius A. Wayland, Pioneer Socialist Propagandist," *Mississippi Valley Historical Review* 35 (1949): 585–606. For other treatments of Wayland's career, see Green, *Grass-Roots Socialism*, pp. 17–19, and David Paul Nord, "The *Appeal to Reason* and American Socialism, 1901–1920," *Kansas History* 1 (1978):75–89.

9. Quint, "Julius A. Wayland," p. 591, and also the same author's full-length study, *The Forging of American Socialism* (Columbia: University of South Carolina Press, 1953), pp. 175–95. For a general survey see David Shannon, *The Socialist Party of America: A History* (New York: Macmillan, 1955). Socialists and Wobblies made waves among Louisiana timber workers and Arkansas miners too; see Grady McWhiney, "Louisiana Socialists in the Early Twentieth Century: A Study of Rustic Radicalism," *Journal of Southern History* 20 (1954):315–36, and George Gregory Kiser, "The Socialist Party in Arkansas, 1900–1912" (M.A. thesis, University of Arkansas, 1980). Studies like these are important correctives to the general sur-

veys, which generally have stressed European ideological sources and east-coast events at the expense of indigenous elements and the activities of other regions.

10. Green, *Grass-Roots Socialism*, p. 128. See also pp. 126–35. For a highly partisan account of Warren's feisty career see George D. Brewer, *"The Fighting Editor," or "Warren and the Appeal"* (Girard, Kans.: George D. Brewer, 1910).

11. Vance Randolph, Oct. 5, 1980.

12. Nyle H. Miller and Joseph W. Snell, *Great Gunfighters of the Kansas Cowtowns, 1867–1886* (Lincoln: University of Nebraska Press, 1963), pp. 85–90, 129–34; William Yancey Shackleford [Vance Randolph], *Gun-Fighters of the Old West* (Girard, Kans: Haldeman-Julius, 1943), pp. 22–24.

13. Robert Cochran, "Of Guns and Memories: Conversations with Vance Randolph," unpub. article, 1980, p. 2–3. This article, read and approved by Vance Randolph, was withdrawn from scheduled publication at his death.

14. Cochran, "Guns and Memories," pp. 4–5. See also Duncan papers, File 4.

15. Duncan papers, File 4.

16. Vance Randolph, "The Pistol as a Hunting Arm," *Field and Stream*, Aug., 1928, p.84.

17. Vance Randolph, "Small Game with Big Pistols," *Field and Stream*, Nov., 1928, p. 60.

18. Arthur S. Tolliver [Vance Randolph], *The Strange Story of Lafcadio Hearn: A Brief Survey of the Life and Works of a Literary Genius Who Revelled in the Weird, Gruesome, Exotic and Unearthly* (Girard, Kans.: Haldeman-Julius, 1944), p. 21.

19. Shackleford [Randolph], *Gun-Fighters*, p. 24.

20. Vance Randolph to Ralph Church, Nov. 5, 1946, Duncan papers, File 1.

21. Vance Randolph to Frances Church, June 15, 1945, Duncan papers, File 1.

22. Randolph to Ralph Church, Nov. 5, 1946, Duncan papers, File 1.

23. Robert Cochran, "People of His Own Kind: Vance Randolph's Kansas Years," *Little Balkans Review: A Southeast Kansas Literary and Graphics Quarterly* 1, no. 2 (1980–81): 6. An early draft of this biography's identically titled second chapter, this article was read and approved by Vance Randolph before its submission, though it did not appear before his death.

24. Vance Randolph, July 9, 1980. Information about Dr. Randolph comes from a variety of sometimes contradictory sources. His son John Randolph, Vance's father, died in 1901 with Dr. Randolph still living, and his obituary in the *Pittsburg Daily Headlight* (Dec. 9, 1901) has the Randolphs coming to Kansas in 1870, and names three brothers (Thomas, "the elder brother," Adnan, and Will) and a sister (Mrs. Sarah Van Orsdel) as survivors in addition to Dr. Randolph. Census records list Dr. Randolph and one son (William) as resident in Riley County in 1875, and the 1880 federal census shows him as married to his second wife, Sarah E. Randolph, and

living with three stepsons and one stepdaughter by her previous marriage. William is still at home, at age twenty-seven, and his occupation is given as teacher. Dr. Randolph is not listed in the 1870 census.

Additional information comes from *Pioneers of the Bluestem Prairie* (Manhattan, Kans.: Riley County Genealogical Society, 1976), where Dr. Randolph's daughter Sarah is listed as marrying her cousin James Van Orsdel in 1877 in Pennsylvania. The same source names her mother, Dr. Randolph's first wife (Margaret Christy is the maiden name), and dates the move of Mr. and Mrs. Van Orsdel to Kansas at 1880. There is a problem, however, with the claim that Dr. Randolph "followed his daughter to Kansas" after the death of this wife (p. 477). Dr. Randolph, by the census records, is in Kansas by 1875, indeed he marries his second wife, the widowed Mrs. Sarah Elizabeth (Denny) Auchard, in 1876. There is also the *Headlight* obituary's claim of 1870 for Dr. Randolph's arrival in Kansas. *Pioneers of the Bluestem Prairie* also gives the date and place of Dr. Randolph's birth (Feb. 5, 1916, in Pennsylvania), his second marriage to Mrs. Auchard (Apr. 20, 1876, in Kansas), and his death (Mar. 17, 1906). He is listed as buried in the May Day cemetery (p. 217). An undated letter to Vance Randolph from his cousin Sallie R. Pyle, daughter of Thomas Christy Randolph, says that Dr. Randolph's first wife was born in Beaver County, Pa., in 1817 and died July 21, 1864, in Beaufort, S.C. I am grateful to D. Cheryl Collins and Jean C. Dallas of the Riley County Historical Society, and to Edward Swovelan of the Kansas State Historical Society, for their help with these matters.

25. "Death of John Randolph," *Pittsburg Daily Headlight*, Dec. 9, 1901.

26. *Girard Press*, Dec. 19, 1901.

27. "Home Authors," in a *A Twentieth Century History and Biographical Record of Crawford County, Kansas* (Chicago and New York: Lewis Publishing Co., 1905), pp. 89–90.

28. Felix V. Rinehart [Vance Randolph], *Confessions of a Booze-Fighter: I Took the Keeley Cure* (Girard, Kans.: Haldeman-Julius, 1943), p. 3.

29. Cochran, "People of His Own Kind," p. 6. Vance Randolph, July 5 and July 9, 1980. My information about Randolph's maternal ancestors, as for his father's family, comes from varied sources. Primary among these is Theresa Gould Randolph's obituary notice (*Pittsburg Headlight*, Feb. 9, 1938), which dates and places her birth (Jan. 26, 1868, near Dwight, Ill.). Obituary notices for Mrs. Randolph's mother, Susan (Sayre) Gould, date the family's move to Kansas at 1878. Susan Sayre was born in Lenham, Sussex County, England, in 1839, was brought to Oneida County, N.Y., as a child, and married J. Farwell Gould in Illinois in 1865 (*Pittsburg Daily Headlight*, Jan. 21, 1899; *Girard Press*, Jan. 26, 1899). Farwell Gould, according to his tombstone, was born in 1842 and died in 1930. Here, again, I am grateful to Gene DeGruson for unstinting aid.

30. Allison Hardy [Vance Randolph], *Kate Bender, the Kansas Murderess: The Horrible History of an Arch Killer* (Girard, Kans.: Haldeman-Julius, 1944), p. 8.

31. Adele Mehl Burnett, "Vance Randolph," second in series "Little Journeys to the Homes of Kansas Authors," *Kansas Teacher* 43 (1936): 43. Randolph's long-time friend and fellow writer "Nancy Clemens" suggested
Mrs. Randolph's central importance on several occasions: "I think the
woman who had the most influence on Vance and about whom he cared
most deeply was his mother" ("Nancy Clemens" to Robert Cochran, 1981).

32. Burnett, "Vance Randolph," p. 43.

33. Vance Randolph to Herbert Halpert, Oct. 5, 1974; Cochran, "People
of His Own Kind," p. 7.

34. Vance Randolph, Tape 2, Side 2 (1978); Tape 3, Side 1 (1978).

35. Cochran, "People of His Own Kind," p. 7.

36. Vance Randolph, *Ancient Philosophers* (Girard, Kans.: Haldeman-
Julius, 1924), p. 41.

37. Vance Randolph, *New Experiments in Animal Psychology* (Girard,
Kans.: Haldeman-Julius, 1925), pp. 6, 9.

38. Burnett, "Vance Randolph," p. 45.

39. William Yancey Shackleford [Vance Randolph], *Buffalo Bill Cody:
Scout and Showman* (Girard, Kans.: Haldeman-Julius, 1944), pp. 23–24.

40. Cochran, "People of His Own Kind," p. 9.

41. *Pittsburg Daily Headlight*, Oct. 3 and 4, 1900. Again, thanks to Gene
DeGruson for help in locating these accounts.

42. Rinehart [Randolph], *Confessions of a Booze-Fighter*, p. 3. Randolph's indecision concerning the spelling of Mrs. Nation's first name—
she's "Carrie" in *Confessions of a Booze-Fighter* and "Carry" in *Carry Nation of Kansas* (see note #44, below)—simply reflects Mrs. Nation's own
practice. Her early public appearances, as publisher of *Smasher's Mail*, for
example, bill her as "Carrie Nation, Your Loving Home Defender," but later,
sensing the larger scope of her mission and the potential of her name, she
began calling herself "Carry A. Nation." For a popular treatment of Mrs. Nation's career see Robert Lewis Taylor, *Vessel of Wrath: The Life and Times of
Carry Nation* (New York: New American Library, 1966). For the lady's own
testament read *The Use and Need of the Life of Carry A. Nation, Written by
Herself* (Topeka, Kans.: F. M. Steves & Sons, 1908).

43. Rinehart [Randolph], *Confessions of a Booze-Fighter*, p. 3.

44. Anton S. Booker [Vance Randolph], *Carry Nation of Kansas, Who
Fought the Liquor Traffic with a Hatchet* (Girard, Kans.: Haldeman-Julius,
1944), p. 19.

45. Cochran, "People of His Own Kind," p. 11.

46. John Randolph, "A Roll-Call," in *The Kansas Day Club: Addresses
Delivered at the Annual Banquets during the First Ten Years of the Club's
Existence, 1892–1901* (Hutchinson, Kans.: W. Y. Morgan, 1901), pp.
348, 350.

47. All these recollections of school years are from the Duncan papers,
File 1. The word "camera" does not appear in *The Five Little Peppers and
How They Grew*, but there are several "Five Little Pepper" books and Ran-
dolph may have confused another with the best-known volume.

48. Burnett, "Vance Randolph," p. 45.

49. Vance Randolph, "The Teachers College at Pittsburg," *Kansas Teacher* 42 (1935):12.

50. Randolph, "The Teachers College at Pittsburg," p. 14.

51. *The Kanza* 5 (1914), unpaginated. The photo of Randolph is on leaf 23v; the photo of Corrigenda is on 67v.

52. Cochran, "People of His Own Kind," p. 14.

53. Duncan papers, File 1. I used this material in a slightly different form suggested and approved by Randolph in my article for *The Little Balkans Review*, but editor Gene DeGruson cut out the last sentence. See "People of His Own Kind," p. 15.

54. Vance Randolph, Oct. 5, 1980.

55. Vance Randolph, Oct. 5, 1980.

56. Cochran, "People of His Own Kind," p. 15.

57. Vernon C. Allison, "On the Ozark Pronunciation of 'It,'" *American Speech* 5, (1929):205.

58. Cochran, "People of His Own Kind," p. 15.

59. Duncan papers, File 1.

60. Randolph, "The Teachers College at Pittsburg," p. 17.

61. Vance Randolph, Oct. 23, 1979.

62. Vance Randolph, Dec. 1, 1979, and June 16, 1980.

63. Vance Randolph, Feb. 18 and May 6, 1980. The recollection of Olive Schreiner is interpolated from another interview, dated only to Jan., 1980.

64. Vance Randolph, Dec. 1, 1979.

65. George Borrow, *Lavengro* (London: J. M. Dent [Everyman's Library, no. 1119], 1970; first published in 1851), p. 160.

66. Ibid., p. 61.

67. Tolliver [Randolph], *George Borrow*, p. 7. My account of Borrow's career is drawn principally from this booklet, from William I. Knapp's *The Life, Writings and Correspondence of George Borrow* (1899), which Randolph owned as a gift from Rose O'Neill and lent to me, and from Borrow's own books, cited in these notes.

68. Borrow, *Lavengro*, pp. 72–73.

69. Ibid., p. 92.

70. Ibid., p. 115.

71. Ibid., p. 119.

72. Ibid., p. 183.

73. Ibid., p. 114.

74. George Borrow, *The Romany Rye* (London: J. M. Dent [Everyman's Library, no. 1120], 1969; first published 1857), p. 366, 371.

75. Duncan papers, File 1. I suppose the letter to date from 1945, since Randolph says the "folksong book" is to be published "next July." That it was written to Church is my own conjecture—nobody else got letters from Randolph beginning, "I got your silly letter you must be drunk or else crazy. . . ."

76. Tolliver [Randolph], *George Borrow*, p. 20.

77. Borrow, *The Romany Rye*, pp. 311–12.
78. Ibid.
79. This is a composite quote, concocted with Randolph's aid in our last "formal" interview on Oct. 5, 1980, while I was working on the "People of His Own Kind" article. He looked at my draft, and was moved to make additional comments about Alec Howat. See Cochran, "People of His Own Kind," p. 18.

CHAPTER THREE: EAST AND WEST: 1914–20

1. Daniel J. Kevles, *The Physicists: The History of a Scientific Community in Modern America* (New York: Random House [Vintage], 1979; first published 1978), p. 24. For Daniel Coit Gilman and "the Hopkins idea" see also Abraham Flexner, *Daniel Coit Gilman* (New York: Harcourt, Brace, 1946).
2. Kevles, *The Physicists*, p. 24. Although Kevles's study is specifically concerned with the professionalization of American physics, his study is lucidly written and his subject carefully integrated into the more general history of American higher education. Clark University is mentioned twice (pp. 62 and 76).
3. Vance Randolph to Robert Duncan, Nov. 12, 1955, Duncan papers, File 3.
4. G. Stanley Hall, *Life and Confessions of a Psychologist* (New York: D. Appleton, 1923), pp. 265, 278, 289. My account of Hall's career is taken largely from this autobiographical account and from Lorine Pruette, *G. Stanley Hall: A Biography of a Mind* (New York: D. Appleton, 1926).
5. Hall, *Life and Confessions*, pp. 296–97.
6. Frederick Rudolph, *The American College and University: A History* (New York: Alfred Knopf, 1962), p. 352.
7. Hall, *Life and Confessions*, p. 297.
8. Sigmund Freud, "The History of the Psychoanalytic Movement," trans. and ed. A. A. Brill, in *The Basic Writings of Sigmund Freud* (New York: Random House [Modern Library], 1938), p. 950.
9. Richard Wollheim, *Sigmund Freud* (New York: The Viking Press, 1971), p. 278. For another contemporary high assessment of the Clark lectures see Janet Malcolm's superb *Psychoanalysis: The Impossible Profession* (New York: Alfred Knopf, 1981), pp. 10–22. G. Stanley Hall is mentioned on pp. 31–32. Juliet Mitchell's trenchant study *Psychoanalysis and Feminism* (New York: Random House [Vintage], 1975; first published 1974) centers on other matters, but here again the Clark lectures are noted as important (p. 296).
10. Hall, *Life and Confessions*, p. 333.
11. Philip Rieff, *Freud: The Mind of the Moralist* (Garden City, N.Y.: Doubleday, 1961), p. 415.
12. Ibid., p. 23.
13. Vance Randolph, Oct. 23, 1979. My notes indicate a second session to

amplify the remarks of the dated interview, but I neglected to date this second occasion.

14. Vance Randolph, "Some Notes of a Preliminary Study of Dreams" (M.A. Thesis, Clark University, 1915) [Clark University Library, #Univ. Case, R194], pp. 44, 28.

15. Ibid., pp. 15, 16, 39.

16. Nemo [Randolph], *Ghost-Writer*, pp. 4, 3, 6.

17. Ibid., p. 12.

18. Ibid., pp. 13, 12.

19. Ibid., pp. 14, 15, 16.

20. Vance Randolph, Tape 2, Side 2 (1978).

21. Vance Randolph, "Chronological Bibliography," unpaginated. This manuscript, given to me by Randolph, served as the starting point for Cochran and Luster, *For Love and For Money*.

22. Nemo [Randolph], *Ghost-Writer*, p. 6.

23. Vance Randolph, Tape 2, Side 1 (1978).

24. Vance Randolph, Feb. 18, 1980.

25. Elvin Hatch, *Theories of Man and Culture* (New York: Columbia University Press, 1973), p. 38. My information on Boas comes from several sources in addition to Hatch: Regna Darnell, "American Anthropology and the Development of Folklore Scholarship," *Journal of the Folklore Institute* 10 (1973):23–39; Hall, *Life and Confessions*, pp. 289, 335; and Margaret Mead, *Ruth Benedict*.

26. Darnell, "Anthropology and Folklore," p. 28.

27. Vance Randolph, Tape 1, Side 2 (1978).

28. Anonymous [Vance Randolph], "Seek . . .," *Masses* (1915), p. 14.

29. Albert Parry, *Garrets and Pretenders: A History of Bohemianism in America* (New York: Dover, 1960; first published 1933), p. 287.

30. Floyd Dell, *Love in Greenwich Village* (Freeport, New York: Books for Libraries Press, 1970; first published in 1926), pp. 25–26.

31. Parry, *Garrets and Pretenders* , p. 288.

32. Ibid.

33. Duncan papers, File 1.

34. Charles Norman, *E. E. Cummings: A Biography* (New York: E. P. Dutton, 1967), p. 113.

35. Nemo [Randolph], *Ghost-Writer*, pp. 10, 11–12.

36. Ibid., p. 11.

37. Vance Randolph, Apr. 17, 1980.

38. Vance Randolph, Tape 7, Side 1 (1978). A very similar account is given in Duncan papers, File 1, dated Sept. 4, 1955.

39. Cochran, "People of His Own Kind," p. 16.

40. Ibid. There is a brief note, dated Apr. 16, 1917, in a reading diary preserved in the Randolph papers, Box 3, Library of Congress: "Kicked out of the schoolmaster business."

41. Randolph, "Chronological Bibliography."

42. Cochran, "People of His Own Kind," p. 16.

43. Ibid., p. 17.

44. Vance Randolph, Oct. 23, 1979.
45. Vance Randolph, Tape 3, Side 1 (1978).
46. Vance Randolph, undated interview (1979).
47. Cochran, "People of His Own Kind," p. 17. My own searches failed to turn up the *Headlight* story mentioned by Randolph.
48. Vance Randolph, May 28 and June 12, 1980. For Green's account of his visit with Randolph, see Archie Green, *Only a Miner: Studies in Recorded Coal-Mining Songs* (Urbana: University of Illinois Press, 1972), pp. 142–44.
49. Vance Randolph, "Utopia in Arkansas," *Esquire* (1938), p. 148.
50. Vance Randolph, June 12, 1980. For the Debs references see David A. Shannon. *The Socialist Party* p. 116, and Ray Ginger, *The Bending Cross: A Biography of Eugene Victor Debs* (New Brunswick, N.J.: Rutgers University Press, 1949), p. 406. Randolph once owned the volume of Debs' writings and speeches published by the *Appeal to Reason* in 1908—Bruce Rogers, ed., *Debs: His Life, Writings and Speeches* (Girard, Kans.: *Appeal to Reason*, 1908). For a more recent collection see Jean Y. Tussey, ed., *Eugene V. Debs Speaks* (New York: Pathfinder Press, 1970).
51. Vance Randolph, May 28, 1980.
52. Vance Randolph, "Proverbs and Poverty," *Appeal to Reason*, September 1, 1917.
53. Vance Randolph, "The Motives of Men," *Appeal to Reason*, July 28, 1917.
54. Vance Randolph to Ralph Church, Nov. 16, 1917, Duncan papers, File 1.
55. Duncan papers, File 1.
56. Vance Randolph to Ralph Church, no date, Duncan papers, File 1.
57. Randolph gave me his dossier of correspondence in a filing folder labeled "Army Pension." The medical report comes from a letter of Sept. 14, 1934, from the Adjutant General's Office in Washington, D.C. Randolph's own letters to Church are undated; see Duncan papers, File 1.
58. R. H. Hallett, assistant director in charge of Compensation Claims Div., Bureau of War Risk Insurance, Treasury Department, to Vance Randolph, May 15, 1920.
59. Vance Randolph, undated interview (1979). There is documentary evidence in support of Randolph's memory of two examinations: a "Certificate of Discharge Because Physically Deficient" dated Aug. 14, 1917, in the "Army Pension" folder.
60. Vance Randolph to Ralph Church, no date, Duncan papers, File 1.
61. Duncan papers, File 1.
62. Randolph, *Ozark Magic and Folklore,* p. 305.
63. Randolph to Church, Nov. 16, 1917, Duncan papers, File 1.
64. Vance Randolph to Ralph Church, no date, Duncan papers, File 1.
65. Robert W. Creamer, *Babe: The Legend Comes to Life* (New York: Pocket Books, 1976), p. 147.
66. Randolph evidently told several people that he'd met Hemingway

while the latter was a cub reporter for the *Kansas City Star* in 1917–18. The story is unlikely, but not impossible. Hemingway began work in Kansas City on Oct. 18, 1917, five days after Randolph entered the Army, but when Randolph was discharged on Jan. 10, 1918, Hemingway was still working in Kansas City and would continue to do so until the end of April, when he left for service as an ambulance driver in Italy.

Randolph never volunteered any stories involving Hemingway in our interviews, and when I asked (in 1980), he said he "might have seen him around" at the *Star* offices, but "we didn't know each other." Hemingway's life is fully documented in Carlos Baker, *Ernest Hemingway: A Life Story* (New York: Charles Scribner's Sons, 1969); see esp. pp. 31–38. For more detailed treatment of Hemingway's Kansas City experiences see Charles A. Fenton, *The Apprenticeship of Ernest Hemingway* (New York: Farrar, Straus & Young, 1954), esp. Chapter II, "Kansas City," and Matthew J. Bruccoli, ed., *Ernest Hemingway, Cub Reporter* (Pittsburgh: University of Pittsburgh Press, 1970). I am grateful to Bethany Dumas for the best account I got of Randolph's "Hemingway story."

67. Randolph to Church, Nov. 16, 1917, Duncan papers, File 1.

68. *Solidarity*, Nov. 21, 1914, quoted in Joyce L. Kornbluh, ed., *Rebel Voices: An I.W.W. Anthology* (Ann Arbor: University of Michigan Press, 1964), pp. 66–67.

69. Vance Randolph to Ralph Church, no date. Duncan papers, File 1.

70. Burnett, "Vance Randolph," pp. 45–46.

71. Four letters apparently from San Francisco (and all to Ralph Church) have been preserved (in copy) in the Duncan papers, File 1. One is dated Dec. 28; the others are undated.

72. Interview dated Sept. 4, 1955, Duncan papers, File 1.

73. Vance Randolph to Ralph Church, no date, Duncan papers, File 1. I showed Randolph this letter on June 12, 1980, and he said he thought it was written in Truckee, Calif. (which certainly makes sense in terms of the letter's plan "to make Reno tonight").

74. Interview, Sept. 4, 1955. Duncan papers, File 1.

75. Burnett, "Vance Randolph," p. 45.

76. Randolph gave a typescript of this journal to Leo Van Scyoc, professor of English at the University of Arkansas, who graciously allowed me to make a copy. The typescript consists of thirty-three legal-size pages, double-spaced, with corrections in Randolph's hand. Another copy is preserved in the Duncan papers, File 1. The typescript is headed "Journal: Tallahassee to Atlanta, Dec.-Jan., 1919," which caused me several problems when I was trying to work up a time-line for Randolph's whereabouts during these years. I first wanted to know which month the 1919 went with, December or January. The journal itself was no help since its first page contained an obvious error: "Tallahassee to Live Oak," it said, "Dec. 27 (Sunday)." A check of newspapers revealed that Dec. 27 was a Saturday in 1919, a Friday in 1918, and a Monday in 1920. However, another journal date on p. 5 proved helpful: "Jacksonville to Orlando," it said, "Jan. 4 (Sunday)." If this is cor-

rect, as it was in 1920, then the Dec. 27 entry was a Saturday, and the journal covers the last days of 1919 and first three weeks of 1920. This fits well with the California letters and with the Burnett article, both of which I acquired later, and I have guessed it the correct surmise. I should note, however, that this is in direct conflict with the generally reliable (though not infallible) dates in *Ozark Folksongs*, since the headnotes to eight songs from three informants have Randolph in Pineville on Jan. 4, Fayetteville on Jan. 12, and Hot Springs on Jan. 16; see Vance Randolph *Ozark Folksongs*, (Columbia: University of Missouri Press, 1980; first published 1946–50), nos. 5A, 22, 29, 328, 573, 645, 647, 653.

77. For complete bibliographic information on all these early articles and booklets, see Cochran and Luster, *For Love and For Money*. Randolph explained that Newell R. Tripp was a friend of his, a druggist who wanted to impress his girlfriend by having his name on a book. Randolph obliged (three times) and reported in 1978 that Tripp "got great satisfaction out of it" (Tape 1, Side 1).

78. Allison Hardy [Vance Randolph], *The ABC of Geology* (New York: Vanguard Press, 1927) p. 120.

79. Vance Randolph, *The ABC of Physiology* (New York: Vanguard Press, 1927), p. iv.

80. Randolph, *Ancient Philosophers*, pp. 15, 20, 28.

81. Vance Randolph, *Modern Philosophers* (Girard, Kans.: Haldeman-Julius, 1924), pp. 14, 16.

82. Burnett, "Vance Randolph," p. 44.

83. Newell R. Tripp [Vance Randolph], *"Behaviorism" The Newest Psychology* (Girard, Kans.: Haldeman-Julius, 1925) pp. 12, 22.

84. Halpert, Foreword to Cochran and Luster, *For Love and for Money*, pp. 9–10.

85. Vance Randolph, "A List of the Butterflies of Crawford County, Kansas," *Transactions of the Kansas Academy of Science* 30 (1919–21):59.

86. Vance Randolph, "A Preliminary Study of the Life History and Habits of Dione Vanillae Linn.," *Transactions of the Kansas Academy of Science* 30 (1919–21):357–58.

87. Randolph, *Ozark Magic and Folklore*, p. 235.

CHAPTER FOUR: GETTING STARTED

1. Duncan papers, File 1.

2. Randolph, *Ozark Folksongs*, 4:388, 23.

3. Randolph, *Ozark Magic and Folklore*, p. 82.

4. Randolph, *Wild Stories*, p. 53. The deed is on file in the Office of the County Clerk, McDonald County Courthouse, Pineville, Mo., Book 73, p. 572.

5. Vance Randolph, *Who Blowed Up the Church House?, and Other Ozark Folk Tales* (New York: Columbia University Press, 1952), p. xix.

6. Duncan papers, File 1.

7. Randolph, *Wild Stories*, p. 55.

8. *Stone County News-Oracle* [Galena, Mo.], Feb. 1, 1933.

9. *Pineville Democrat*, Apr. 4, 1930.

10. *Pineville Democrat*, Jan. 7, 1921.

11. Vance Randolph, "The Pineville Mastodon," *The Ozarks Mountaineer* 25 (1977):22.

12. Ibid.

13. Ibid.

14. Ibid.

15. N. C. Nelson, review of *The Antiquity of the Deposits in Jacob's Cavern*, by Vernon C. Allison, *American Anthropologist* 30 (1928): 330.

16. Randolph, "Pineville Mastodon," p. 23.

17. Ibid.

18. Vance Randolph, Mar. 11, 1980. In his first book on Ozark folklore, *The Ozarks: An American Survival of Primitive Society* (New York: Vanguard Press, 1931), Randolph gives a similar account (pp. 10–11).

19. Vance Randolph, *The ABC of Biology* (New York: Vanguard Press, 1927), pp. 117–18. Much of the correspondence and published controversy relating to the "Mastodon" affair has been preserved in the Randolph papers, Box 5, Library of Congress.

20. An exact date for Randolph's departure for the University of Kansas is preserved in a reading diary in the Randolph papers, Box 3, Library of Congress: "Left Pineville to go to Lawrence, Kansas, Sept. 8, 1921."

21. My information about Hunter comes from my interviews with Randolph and from *Who's Who in America*, 14 (1926–27):1019, and 28 (1954–55):1314.

22. Walter S. Hunter and Vance Randolph, "Further Studies on the Reliability of the Maze with Rats and Humans," *Journal of Comparative Psychology* 4 (1924): 431, 441.

23. Walter S. Hunter, "A Reply to Professor Carr on 'The Reliability of the Maze Experiment,'" *Journal of Comparative Psychology* 6 (1926):393.

24. Duncan papers, File 1.

25. W. K. McNeil, Introduction to Randolph, *Ozark Folksongs*, p. 9.

26. "The last time I saw Frances [Church] was at Eureka [Springs, Arkansas] and she was obviously annoyed with Vance. She said he had 'this silly idea' of going back to school . . ."—"Nancy Clemens" to Robert Cochran, 1981.

27. See, for example, Margaret Larkin, *Singing Cowboy* (New York: Alfred Knopf, 1931), pp. 143, 147.

28. "College Yells Hope of Poetry—Lindsay," *University Daily Kansan*, Dec. 5, 1921.

29. Vance Randolph, typewritten diary entry dated Dec. 5, 1921. Given to me by Vance Randolph. In 1935, in an article about the University of Kansas, Randolph himself called attention to the "immortal 'Rock-Chalk Jay-

hawk' yell"; See Vance Randolph, "The University of Kansas," *Kansas Teacher* 42 (1935):16.

30. "Sandburg Delighted Audience Last Night," *University Daily Kansan*, Mar. 8, 1922.

31. Mary Parler Randolph, Nov. 11, 1980.

32. Randolph said this many times—nearly every time he spoke of his acquaintance with a well-known figure—but I quote him here from memory. For a very similar published remark, made about his "friendship" with H.L. Mencken, see Jim Lapham, "The Generation Gap Shrinks in a Collection of Folklore," *The Kansas City Star Magazine*, June 13, 1971: "I had a few beers with Mencken and you know, the older I *get* the better I *knew* him" (p. 13). There is evidence, in fact, suggesting that even this is exaggerated, that the extent of Randolph's relationship with Mencken was a brief correspondence, which included an *invitation* from Mencken for Randolph to call upon him if he found himself in Baltimore.

33. Vance Randolph, Tape 1, Side 1 (1978).

34. Carl Sandburg, *Carl Sandburg's New American Songbag* (New York: Broadcast Music, Inc., 1950), p. iv.

35. D.K. Wilgus, *Anglo-American Folksong Scholarship since 1898* (New Brunswick, N.J.: Rutgers University Press, 1959), p. 215.

36. McNeil, Introduction to Randolph, *Ozark Folksongs*, p. 13.

37. Vance Randolph, *Ozark Mountain Folks* (New York: Vanguard Press, 1932), p. 188.

38. W. H. Dunlop, rehabilitation assistant, United States Veterans Bureau, to Vance Randolph, Mar. 28, 1923, and Arthur C. Johnson, Jr., chief, Rehabilitation Division, to Dunlop, Mar. 27, 1923. Randolph gave me these letters in his "Army Pension" file.

39. Randolph, *Ozark Magic and Folklore*, p. 5. For another similar account see Tape 4, Side 1 (1978): "I carried 5 x 3 cards in my pocket always, and noted each item separately, with the name of the informant wherever I could. I kept them in a box. . . .I was always working on three or four books at once."

40. Vance Randolph, Feb. 18, 1980. These recollections are supplemented by the account in Randolph's Introduction to Vance Randolph and George P. Wilson, *Down in the Holler: A Gallery of Ozark Folk Speech* (Norman: University of Oklahoma Press, 1953), p. 6: "It was not until 1920 that I began to carry scraps of newsprint in my pocket and write down words and phrases which I heard in conversation with my neighbors. The material was later typed on cards and placed in a filing cabinet. I kept this up for thirty years, and at one time had cards enough to fill a steamer trunk."

41. "Our Contributors," *American Speech* 4 (1928):160.

42. H. L. Mencken, *The American Language: An Inquiry into the Development of English in the United States*, 4th ed. (New York: Alfred Knopf, 1936), p. 359.

43. Vance Randolph, *German Self Taught* (Girard, Kansas: Haldeman-Julius, n.d. [1926], p. 5.

44. Vance Randolph, review of *The Hobo's Hornbook*, by George Milburn, *American Speech* 6 (1931): 221. Randolph's Yiddish studies began early— his copy of I. Edwin Goldwasser and Joseph Jablonower's *Yiddish-English Lessons* (Boston: D. C. Heath, 1916) is signed and dated: "Vance Randolph . . . July 14, 1917." Thanks once more to Gene DeGruson.

45. Richard Ellmann, *Yeats: The Man and the Masks* (New York: E. P. Dutton, 1948), p. 3.

46. Vance Randolph, "A Word-List from the Ozarks," *Dialect Notes* 5 (1926):397.

47. Jay L. B. Taylor, "Snake County Talk," *Dialect Notes* 5 (1923):197.

48. Randolph, "Word List," p. 397.

49. Vance Randolph, "The Ozark Dialect in Fiction," *American Speech* 2 (1927):283.

50. Vance Randolph, "Recent Fiction and the Ozark Dialect," *American Speech* 2 (1931):427–28.

51. Thames Williamson, *The Woods Colt: A Novel of the Ozark Hills* (New York: Harcourt, Brace, 1933), p. v.

52. Randolph, *Down in the Holler*, p. 138.

53. These "Agreements," as well as the contracts for most of his books and a small number of royalty statements, were given to me by Vance Randolph.

54. Randolph, *Down in the Holler*, p. 148; Vance Randolph, *Ozark Folklore: A Bibliography* (Bloomington: Indiana University Publications [Folklore Institute Monograph Series, vol. 24], 1972), p. 407.

55. Randolph repeated this evaluation several times to both Mike Luster and myself—he knew that both of us were friends of Harington's—but I reproduce it here from memory.

56. Donald Harington, "Bawdy Ozark Tales: Vance Randolph's Collection of Local Off-Color" (review of *Pissing in the Snow and Other Ozark Folktales*), *Grapevine* 8, (1977):10.

57. Vance Randolph, "The Grammar of the Ozark Dialect," *American Speech* 3 (1927):1.

58. Allison, "Pronunciation of 'It,'" p. 205. Randolph's other friend from the "Pineville Mastodon" escapade also chastised Randolph in a sequel to his "Snake County Talk" study. See Jay L. B. Taylor, "In Defense of His People," *Missouri Magazine* 10 (1938):9–11.

59. Herbert Halpert and Violetta Halpert, "Work in Progress," *Journal of American Folklore* 62 (1949):55.

60. Randolph to Duncan, Nov. 12, 1955, Duncan papers, File 3.

61. Ibid.

62. Actually it surfaced first in "Folk Beliefs in the Ozark Mountains," published earlier in the same year in *Journal of American Folklore* 40 (1927); see esp. pp. 79, 93.

63. Randolph, "Grammar of Ozark Dialect," p. 8.

64. Vance Randolph, handwritten sheet with brief identifications of twenty-one people I asked him about in the initial stages of this project.

65. Randolph, *Down in the Holler*, pp. xii, 7.

66. Vance Randolph, "Is There an Ozark Dialect?" *American Speech* 4 (1929):203, 204.

67. Vance Randolph, "A Possible Source of Some Ozark Neologisms," *American Speech* 4 (1928):117.

68. Randolph, "Grammar of Ozark Dialect," pp. 4, 11; Randolph, *Down in the Holler*, pp. 41, 68.

69. Vance Randolph to Herbert Halpert, Jan. 21, 1951.

70. Vance Randolph to Herbert Halpert, Nov. 30, 1977.

71. Halpert, Foreword to Cochran and Luster, *For Love and For Money*, p. 13.

72. Raven I. McDavid, Jr., review of *Down in the Holler*, by Vance Randolph and George P. Wilson, *Journal of American Folklore* 67 (1954):328.

73. E. H. Criswell, "The Language of the Ozarks" (review of *Down in the Holler*, by Vance Randolph and George P. Wilson), *American Speech* 28 (1953):285, 287–288.

74. McDavid, review of *Down in the Holler*, p. 328.

75. Vance Randolph, undated interview.

76. Mary Parler Randolph, Nov. 11, 1980.

77. Randolph, *Down in the Holler*, p. viii.

78. Vance Randolph, *Pocket Dictionary: English-French, French-English* (Girard, Kans.: Haldeman-Julius, n.d. [1927]), p. 32.

79. Vance Randolph, "Old Pistols of the Ozark Mountains," *National Sportsman* 57 (1927):32.

80. Vance Randolph, "Instead of a Holster," *Outdoor Life* (1927), pp. 54, 56.

81. And this list omits one of Randolph's most unique works, the lyrics for a song, "Captain Charles Lindbergh's Great Flight," with music by Randolph's Kansas friend Carl Botefuhr. Sample verses:

#1 Oh come all you young folks and
hear the story.
Of Captain Lindbergh and the
flight he made
His name will shine forever with
the glory
Of those brave men whose fame
can never fade.

. . . .

#7 On Uncle Sammy's roll of famous
heroes,
Those gallant men who served
their country best,
Whose names will always live in
song and story—
Slim Lindberg's [sic] name is written
with the rest.

For the complete text (and my source for these two stanzas) see *The Crawford News*, June 17, 1927. The Pittsburg *Sun* (June 14, 1927) also carried a brief account, "Carl Botefuhr Writes Song about Lindbergh," which includes credit to Randolph for the lyrics.

82. [Vance Randolph] "The Songs Grandfather Sang," *Pineville Democrat*, Feb. 18, 1927.

83. Randolph, *Ozark Folklore: A Bibliography*, p. 28. Mrs. Baber contributed twenty songs to *Ozark Folksongs*, including several of the older traditional ballads Randolph prized most in his first years of collecting.

84. "The Songs Grandfather Sang," Mar. 11, 1927.

85. Ibid., Feb. 18, 1927.

86. Ibid., Feb. 25, 1927.

87. Ibid., Mar. 18, 1927.

88. For good accounts of Gordon's work see Norm Cohen, *Long Steel Rail: The Railroad in American Folksong* (Urbana: University of Illinois Press, 1981), esp. pp. 202–217, and also Green, *Only a Miner*, pp. 196–202. I am grateful to Bill McNeil for helpful guidance concerning the possible Randolph/Gordon connection.

89. "The Songs Grandfather Sang," Mar. 25, 1927.

90. Vance Randolph, "The Ozark Play-Party," *Journal of American Folklore* 42 (1929):202.

91. Randolph, "Ozark Play-Party," p. 231.

92. Vance Randolph, "The Songs Grandfather Sang," *Ozark Life* (1930), p. 12.

93. Bill C. Malone, *Country Music, U.S.A.* (Austin: University of Texas Press, 1968), pp. 350, 351.

94. Jan Harold Brunvand, *The Study of American Folklore: An Introduction* (New York: W. W. Norton, 1968), pp. 157, 170.

95. Ed Kahn, "Hillbilly Music: Source and Resource," *Journal of American Folklore* 78 (1965):260.

96. Vance Randolph, "Henry Marvin Belden (1864–1954)," *Arkansas Folklore* 5 (1954):1.

97. Vance Randolph, "The Songs Grandfather Sang," *Ozark Life* (1930), p. 33.

98. Vance Randolph, Introduction to *Hot Springs and Hell, and Other Folk Jests and Anecdotes from the Ozarks* (Hatboro, Pa.: Folklore Associates, 1965), p. xxviii.

99. Vance Randolph to Herbert Halpert, July 4, 1977.

100. Vance Randolph, "Lost in the Ozarks," *Forest and Stream* (1928), p. 341.

101. Vance Randolph, "Jumping Bass in the Ozark Country," *Forest and Stream* (1928), pp. 219, 245, 246.

102. Vance Randolph, "They Jump Right Into the Boat," *Esquire* (1939): 149.

103. Vance Randolph, Preface to "Bawdy Elements in the Ozark Speech" (typescript, dated Eureka Springs, Ark., 1954), p. i. The originals of this

and Randolph's other "bawdy" collections are in the Music Reading Room, Library of Congress (M1629, R23US, Case), housed separately from the papers in the library's Archive of Folk Culture. The 1981 reprint of "Verbal Modesty in the Ozarks" is in Miller Williams, ed., *Ozark, Ozark: A Hillside Reader* (Columbia: University of Missouri Press, 1981), pp. 33–40.

104. "W.W.," "Jewels from the Ozark Hills," *Greensboro Daily News*, May 10, 1953.

105. Randolph, Preface to "Bawdy Elements in Ozark Speech," pp. ii-iii.

106. Vance Randolph, "Miriam," *The Harp* 4 (1928): 7. It might be noted that Randolph is keeping decent company here—Alfred Kreymborg's "Manhattan Epitaphs" appears on the preceding page.

107. Vance Randolph, "A Survival of Phallic Superstition in Kansas," *Psychoanalytic Review* 15 (1928):242, 243, 245.

108. B. A. Botkin, "The Archive of American Folk Song: Retrospect and Prospect," *Library of Congress Quarterly Journal of Current Acquisitions* 2 (1945):63. For a popular treatment of Mrs. Dusenbury see Robert Cochran, "Sweet Emma," *Arkansas Times* 10 (1983):46–48.

109. Contract dated June 20, 1930, and signed by Vance Randolph and James Henle (president of Vanguard Press). Given to me by Vance Randolph.

Chapter Five: High Times

1. Dorothy Scarborough, "Where the Eighteenth Century Lives On" (review of *The Ozarks*, by Vance Randolph, *New York Times Book Review*, Dec. 27, 1931.

2. Stanley Vestal, review of *The Ozarks*, by Vance Randolph, *Saturday Review of Literature* 8 (1931):407.

3. Louise Pound, review of *The Ozarks*, by Vance Randolph, *American Speech* 7 (1932):305.

4. Robert Redfield, review of *The Ozarks*, by Vance Randolph, *American Journal of Sociology* 38 (1932):506.

5. Vance Randolph, Feb. 18, 1980, with my notes from that interview supplemented by others dated only to Mar., 1980.

6. Vance Randolph, Feb. 18, 1980, with my notes revised and supplemented by a second interview dated only to Mar., 1980.

7. Vance Randolph, Feb. 18, 1980, with, again, additions and corrections dated only to Mar., 1980. Dorson committed this jab to print, in "State of Folkloristics," p. 93 (see Chapter Two, note 1).

8. Franz Boas to Vance Randolph, Apr. 8, 1929, Randolph papers, Box 17, Library of Congress.

9. Halpert, Foreword to Cochran and Luster, *For Love and For Money*, p. 10.

10. Margaret Mead, Preface to 1973 Edition, *Coming of Age in Samoa: A Psychological Study of Primitive Youth for Western Civilization* (New York:

William Morrow, 1975; first published 1928), no page. Mead's work in Samoa has been harshly criticized on both ethnographic and theoretical grounds by Derek Freeman. See *Margaret Mead and Samoa: The Making and Unmaking of an Anthropological Myth* (Cambridge, Mass.: Harvard University Press, 1983). For a trenchant critique of Freeman's work see George E. Marcus, "One Man's Mead," *The New York Times Book Review*, Mar. 27, 1983.

11. Halpert, Foreword to Cochran and Luster, *For Love and For Money*, p. 9.

12. Mead, *Coming of Age*, p. 9.

13. Ibid., p. 11.

14. Randolph, *The Ozarks*, pp. 23, 29.

15. Mead, Preface to *Coming of Age*, no page.

16. Randolph, *The Ozarks*, p. v.

17. Mead, Preface to *Coming of Age*, no page.

18. Randolph, *The Ozarks*, p. 303.

19. Mead, *Coming of Age*, p. 9.

20. Randolph, *The Ozarks*, p. v.

21. Randolph, *The Ozarks*, pp. 89, 105.

22. Mead, *Coming of Age*, p. 93.

23. Randolph, *The Ozarks*, p. 22.

24. Otto Ernest Rayburn, "Notice," *Ozark Life: The Journal of Mid-American Folk-Lore* (1930), p. 4. For another once well-known figure espousing similar views, see Henry D. Shapiro's treatment of William Goodell Frost's career as president of Berea College and spokesman for "Appalachian America" in *Appalachia on Our Mind* (Chapel Hill: University of North Carolina Press, 1978), pp. 113–32; see also ch. 3 on the White Top Folk Festival of David E. Whishant's *All That Is Native and Fine* (Chapel Hill: University of North Carolina Press, 1983), for a devastating portrayal of the racist cultural view of John Powell. See esp. 237–47.

25. Mead, Acknowledgments to *Coming of Age*, no page.

26. Franz Boas, Foreword to Mead, *Coming of Age*, no page.

27. Carl Withers, Editor's Introduction to Clifton Johnson, *What They Say in New England* (New York: Columbia University Press, 1963; first published 1896), p. xvii.

28. Halpert, Foreword to Cochran and Luster, *For Love and For Money*, pp. 9–10.

29. Ibid., p. 10.

30. Franz Boas, Foreword to Zora Neale Hurston, *Mules and Men* (Philadelphia: J. B. Lippincott, 1935), p. 7.

31. Vance Randolph, review of *The Word on The Brazos*, by J. Mason Brewer, *New York Times Book Review*, Jan. 24, 1954.

32. Withers, Editor's Introduction, to Johnson, *What They Say*, p. xvi.

33. Randolph, Preface to *Ozark Mountain Folks*, pp. vii-viii.

34. Hemenway, *Zora Neale Hurston*, pp. 117–23.

35. Gillespie, *Folklorist of the Coal Fields*, pp. 37–38.

36. Hemenway, *Zora Neale Hurston*, p. 323. The 1950 newspaper story is discussed on p. 325 and cited on p. 350.

37. Guy Davenport, *The Geography of the Imagination* (San Francisco: North Point Press, 1981), p. 14.

38. Vance Randolph, Apr. 17, 1980.

39. See Archie Green, "Charles Louis Seeger (1886–1979)," *Journal of American Folklore* 92 (1979):393.

40. Vance Randolph, May 25, 1980. For more about Cushing, see N. B., "A Step Back in Time," *American Heritage* 27 (1976): 38–48. Thanks to John Hensley, curator of the Ralph Foster Museum, School of the Ozarks, for calling this article to my attention.

41. Vance Randolph, Feb. 18, 1980.

42. H. L. Mencken, "Famine," *Baltimore Evening Sun*, Jan. 19, 1931.

43. Randolph, *Ozark Mountain Folks*, p. vii.

44. Vance Randolph, Tape 5, Side 2 (1978).

45. Randolph, *Ozark Mountain Folks*, pp. vii-viii.

46. Randolph, *Ozark Mountain Folks*, pp. 19–20; *The Ozarks*, p. v.

47. Randolph, *Ozark Mountain Folks*, p. 142.

48. Ibid., pp. 152–158. For Mr. Hatton's version see Randolph, *Who Blowed Up?*, pp. 56–58, 196–97.

49. Randolph, *Ozark Mountain Folks*, p. 198; *Ozark Folksongs*, 1:81.

50. Randolph, *Ozark Mountain Folks*, p. 203; *Ozark Folksongs*, 1:169.

51. Randolph, *Ozark Mountain Folks*, p. 227.

52. Ibid., pp. 228–31 (Randolph does note on p. 228 that "this piece featured several unprintable stanzas"); *Ozark Folksongs*, 1:189–93.

53. Randolph, *Ozark Folksongs*, 1:132.

54. Ibid.; *The Ozarks*, p. 183.

55. Randolph, *The Ozarks*, p. 184.

56. Randolph, *Ozark Folksongs*, 1:132.

57. The foregoing analyses are at last speculative, of course, though I wouldn't have completed them had I thought them poorly grounded. It should be noted, however, especially in connection with my analysis of "Barbara Allen," that Randolph did not in every case print every variant in his collection in *Ozark Folksongs*. See Norm Cohen, Editor's Introduction to his one-volume abridgment of *Ozark Folksongs* (Urbana: University of Illinois Press, 1982), pp. xii-xiii.

58. At least John Lomax called it this even as he announced that *American Ballads and Folk Songs* (1934) would by such standards be unconventional. See Wilgus, *Folksong Scholarship*, p. 217.

59. Wilgus, *Folksong Scholarship*, pp. 182, 237, 338.

60. [William Wells Newell], "On the Field and Work of a Journal of American Folk-Lore," *Journal of American Folk-Lore* 1 (1888):3. This note retains its prominence in very recent work, especially in England, Ireland and Wales. See for example, Estyn Evans, *Irish Folk Ways* (London: Routledge & Kegan Paul, 1957), p. xv; George Ewart Evans, *Ask the Fellows Who Cut*

the Hay (London: Faber, 1965; first published 1956), p. 14; Iorwerth C. Peate, *Tradition and Folk Life: A Welsh View* (London, Faber, 1972), p. 139. It turns out, however, that folklorists have been recording and photographing "the last basket weaver and the last ballad singer" for nearly as long as fundamentalist Christians have been living in "last days." See Henry Glassie, *Passing the Time in Ballymenone: Culture and History of an Ulster Community* (Philadelphia: University of Pennsylvania Press, 1982), pp. 63, 742–43.

61. Randolph, *The Ozarks*, pp. 86, 136, 251.

62. Randolph, *Ozark Mountain Folks*, pp. 110, 278–79.

63. John C. Campbell, *The Southern Highlander and His Homeland* (New York: Russell Sage Foundation, 1921), p. 2.

64. Campbell, *Southern Highlander*, p. 124; Randolph, *The Ozarks*, p. 42.

65. Campbell, *Southern Highlander*, p. 133; Randolph, *The Ozarks*, p. 56.

66. Horace Kephart, *Our Southern Highlanders: A Narrative of Adventure in the Southern Appalachians and a Study of Life Among the Mountaineers* (New York: Macmillan, 1922; first published 1913), p. 195. A photo of "Mr. Quick" appears facing p. 184.

67. Kephart, Preface to the Revised Edition, *Southern Highlanders*, no page.

68. Randolph, *The Ozarks*, p. v.

69. Jean Thomas, *Devil's Ditties* (Chicago: W. Wilbur Hatfield, 1931). See also the same author's *Ballad Makin' in the Mountains of Kentucky* (New York: Oak, 1964; first published 1939), and numerous other productions in a similar vein. For the "mountain children" phrase see Wilgus, *Folksong Scholarship*, p. 206.

70. Thomas, *Ballad Makin'*, p. 11.

71. *Ozark Life* (1929), p. 4.

72. "More Tales of the Ozark Hill-Folk" (review of *From An Ozark Holler*, by Vance Randolph), *New York Times Book Review*, Oct. 22, 1933.

73. Vance Randolph, *From an Ozark Holler: Stories of Ozark Mountain Folk* (New York: Vanguard Press, 1933), p. 7.

74. Ibid., p. 67.

75. Ibid., p. 115.

76. *New York Times Book Review*, Oct. 22, 1933.

77. Vance Randolph, Tape 5, Side 2 (1978).

78. This contract, like the others, was given to me by Vance Randolph.

79. Vance Randolph, Tape 5, Side 2 (1978).

80. Vance Randolph, *The Camp On Wildcat Creek* (New York: Alfred Knopf, 1934).

81. Mary Parler Randolph, in Cochran and Luster, *For Love and For Money*, p. 103.

82. Contract given to me by Vance Randolph.

83. Vance Randolph to Margaret E. Haughawout, Mar. 26, 1932. This letter was brought to my attention by Gene DeGruson.

84. Randolph to Haughawout, Mar. 26, 1932.

85. Vance Randolph and Guy W. von Schriltz, *Ozark Outdoors* (New York: Vanguard Press, 1934).

86. Vance Randolph and Isabel Spradley, "Ozark Mountain Riddles," *Journal of American Folklore* 47 (1934):89.

87. The identification comes from the handwritten sheet done for me—see Chapter Four, note 64—and the testimony is from Randolph, *Ozark Folklore: A Bibliography*, p. 246.

88. Vance Randolph, "Cave Bats and a Unique Industry," *Missouri Magazine* (1934), p. 8.

89. Contracts given to me by Vance Randolph.

90. Contract in the Special Collections division, University of Arkansas Library, Fayetteville (MS.R152c, 374, Randolph).

91. Vance Randolph to Ralph Church, Apr. 23, 1934, Special Collections division, University of Arkansas Library.

92. Randolph to Church, Apr. 23, 1934. There was no "National Folklore Festival"—Randolph's reference is to the National Folk Festival. See Chapter Five, section V, 139 and note 145, below.

93. Royalty statement dated Oct. 25, 1936, given to me by Vance Randolph.

94. Percy Hutchinson, "Vance Randolph's 'Hedwig' and Other Recent Works" (review of *Hedwig*, by Vance Randolph), *New York Times Book Review*, June 23, 1935.

95. S.V. [Stanley Vestal], review of *Hedwig*, by Vance Randolph, *Saturday Review* 12 (1935):19.

96. Dust jacket of Vance Randolph and Nancy Clemens [pseud.], *The Camp-Meeting Murders* (New York: Vanguard Press, 1936).

97. Anonymous review of *Hedwig*, by Vance Randolph, *The Nation* 141 (1935):196.

98. Nemo [Randolph], *Ghost-Writer*, pp. 14, 17.

99. Given to me by Vance Randolph—see Chapter Four, note 53.

100. Duncan papers, File 1. I think this is from a 1940 letter to Church, but the identification is not clear in the Duncan copy.

101. "Ozarks Author Goes into the Backwoods for Color," *Kansas City Star*, Nov. 22, 1931. For a full-length feature story, written by Randolph's old friend in the ghost-writing business, see A. B. MacDonald, "Another Author Discovers Rich Literary Ore in Ozarks," *Kansas City Star*, May 21, 1933. MacDonald was a well-known journalist in his own right—he won a Pulitzer Prize in 1930 for news writing. MacDonald died in 1942.

102. "Wilbur-Randolph," *Pineville Democrat*, Mar. 28, 1930.

103. "Wedding Bells in Old Mexico," *Pineville Democrat*, May 25, 1907.

104. Interview dated Sept. 4, 1955, Duncan papers, File 1.

105. Randolph, *Ozark Magic and Folklore*, p. 305. The journal is in Randolph papers, Box 9, Library of Congress.

106. "Ozark Expert Lost in Ozark Cave," *Tulsa Tribune*, Aug. 7, 1932.

107. Vance Randolph, June 5, 1980.

108. Interview dated Apr. 28, 1957, Duncan papers, File 1.

109. Interview dated Sept. 4, 1955, Duncan papers, File 1.

110. Interview dated Apr. 28, 1957, Duncan papers, File 1. Randolph saved his MGM identification card and gave it to me in 1979.

111. Duncan papers, File 1.

112. Bosley Crowther, *The Lion's Share*, p. 288.

113. Dore Schary, *Heyday: An Autobiography* (Boston: Little, Brown, 1979), p. 78.

114. Crowther, *The Lion's Share*, p 288.

115. Schary, *Heyday*, p. 79.

116. Crowther, *The Lion's Share*, p. 288.

117. Joseph Blotner, *Faulkner: A Biography* (New York: Random House, 1974), p. 772.

118. Vance Randolph, Tape 3, Side 2 (1978).

119. Timothy Charles Lloyd, "Early Folk Festivals in America: An Introduction and Bibliography," *JEMF Quarterly* 14 (1978):94. See also Archie Green, "Commercial Music Graphics #32: The National Folk Festival Association," *JEMF Quarterly* 11 (1975):23–32.

120. Percival Chubb, "Folk Culture and Leisure," *Recreation* 28 (1934): 278, quoted by Lloyd, "Early Folk Festivals," pp. 94–95.

121. Felix Sper, *From Native Roots: A Panorama of Our Regional Drama* (Caldwell, Idaho: Caxton, 1948), pp. 200–201.

122. Ibid., p. 148.

123. Ibid., p. 191.

124. Ibid., pp. 35–36.

125. Paul Green, *The Lord's Will and Other Carolina Plays* (New York: Henry Holt, 1925), p. 264.

126. Thomas Wolfe to George Pierce Baker, Jan. or Feb., 1923; see Elizabeth Nowell, ed., *The Letters of Thomas Wolfe* (New York: Charles Scribner's Sons, 1956), p. 41.

127. Lloyd, "Early Folk Festivals," p. 94.

128. Bill Finger, "Bascom Lamar Lunsford: The Limits of a Folk Hero," *Southern Exposure* 2 (1974):28. Most of my information on Lunsford comes from this article. See also Loyal Jones, "The Minstrel of the Appalachians: Bascom Lamar Lunsford at 91," *JEMF Quarterly* 9 (1973):2–8. Jones also wrote a letter to the editor about Lunsford in *JEMF Quarterly* 15 (1979):1.

129. Thomas, *Ballad Makin'*, cover photograph and p. P-20 (photograph section). For additional information on Thomas see Green, *Only a Miner*, pp. 180–82.

130. For an account of McCord's career see Helen & Townsend Godsey, "May Kennedy McCord: Queen of the Hillbillies," *Ozarks Mountaineer* 25 (1977): 14–15, 26–27. Most of my information on McCord is drawn from this article.

131. Otto Ernest Rayburn, *Forty Years in the Ozarks* (Eureka Springs, Ark.: Ozark Guide Press, 1957), pp. 89–90.

132. Jerre Mangione, *The Dream and the Deal: The Federal Writers' Project, 1935–1943.* (New York: Avon [Equinox], 1972), p. 76. Randolph's account of his brush with the "colonel" comes from an interview with Mike Luster dated July, 1980.

133. The *Pittsburg Headlight*, March 22, 1934. Parts of this editorial were reprinted in the *Springfield Leader and Press*, Mar. 27, 1934.

134. "Writers Called Ignorant of the Genuine Ozarks," *Springfield Leader and Press,* Apr. 17, 1934.

135. "Mr. Randolph Taken Aback," *Springfield Leader and Press*, Apr. 17, 1934.

136. "Sees Good 'Ad' in 'Hill-Billies,'" *Springfield Leader and Press*, Apr. 18, 1934.

137. "'C.C. Always for Festival,' Leader Avers," *Springfield Leader and Press*, Apr. 20, 1934.

138. "The Laugh's on Randolph's Face," *Springfield Leader and Press*, Apr. 20, 1934.

139. The events of the National Folk Festival received extensive coverage in the *St. Louis Post-Dispatch*. See for example "Sea Chanteys and Ozark Folk Songs at Festival," May 1, 1934; "Lumberjacks at Festival Sing of Their Mighty Men," May 2, 1934; "Indians on Opening Program of National Folk Festival Today at New Municipal Auditorium," April 29, 1934. My account of the folk festival movement's sources, and of Randolph's involvement in the 1934 festival especially, is based largely upon Mike Luster's researches.

140. Lillian Freeman Wright, "America's National Folk Festival, 1934," *Journal of American Folklore* 47 (1934):263.

141. Briscoe, "Ruth Benedict," p. 466.

142. Mrs. John Bishop, "Voice of the People," *Joplin Globe*, Oct. 26, 1933.

143. Mrs. C. P. Mahnkey, "Voice of the People," *Joplin Globe*, Nov. 12, 1933.

CHAPTER SIX: HARD TIMES

1. Vance Randolph, "The Masters' Desk" (typescript, dated "1930 or 31" in pencil), pp. 5, 7. This is preserved in Randolph papers, Box 10, Library of Congress.

2. Vance Randolph to Lewis Copeland, Oct. 21, 1934.

3. Vance Randolph, in Cochran and Luster, *For Love and for Money*, p. 57.

4. Vance Randolph to James Henle, Oct. 12, 1935, Randolph papers, Box 13, Library of Congress.

5. E. Haldeman-Julius, *My First 25 Years: Instead of a Footnote, an Autobiography* (Girard, Kans.: Haldeman-Julius, 1949), pp. 12–13. A second volume, identically titled but for the substitution of *My Second 25 Years*, was also published in 1949.

6. Mark Scott, "The Little Blue Books in the War on Bigotry and Bunk,"

Kansas History 1 (1978):155. My sources for the facts of Haldeman-Julius's career include Scott's article, both volumes of Haldeman-Julius's autobiography (*My First 25 Years* and *My Second 25 Years*) and the same indefatigable author's *The First Hundred Million* (New York: Simon and Schuster, 1928).

7. George Milburn to Vance Randolph, July 14, 1930, Duncan papers, File 1.

8. Vance Randolph, in Cochran and Luster, *For Love and For Money*, p. 107.

9. Ibid., p. 58.

10. Vance Randolph to George Milburn, n.d. [note says it's written on the back of a Milburn letter to Randolph, dated Nov. 12, 1935], Duncan papers, File 1.

11. "Nancy Clemens" to Robert Cochran, n.d. [1979].

12. Burnett, "Vance Randolph," pp. 43–44.

13. The will and the record of probate are preserved in the Office of the County Clerk, McDonald County Courthouse, Pineville, Mo. See the *Will Record*, p. 489, and the *Index to Probate Court Records*, M 234.

14. Duncan papers, File 1.

15. Vance Randolph to Ralph Church, Dec. 1, 1936, Duncan papers, File 1.

16. Rinehart [Randolph], *Booze-Fighter*, p. 6.

17. Duncan papers, File 1.

18. Rinehart [Randolph], *Booze-Fighter*, p. 15.

19. Itemized bill given to me by Vance Randolph.

20. Rinehart [Randolph], *Booze-Fighter*, pp. 8, 9, 22, 23.

21. Interview dated Sept. 4, 1955, Duncan papers, File 1. I quote the remark of 1978 from memory—Randolph made it often, especially when expressing gratitude for bottled gifts.

22. "Theresa G. Randolph, Head Librarian, Dies," *Pittsburg Headlight*, Feb. 9, 1938.

23. Burnett, "Vance Randolph," p. 43.

24. *Pineville Democrat*, Jan. 7, 1921, Mar. 21, 1930.

25. Burnett, "Vance Randolph," p. 43.

26. Interview with Mr. and Mrs. Gould Randolph and Dr. Joyce Sumner (their daughter, Vance Randolph's niece), Hutchinson, Kans., Nov. 23, 1980. I visited Hutchinson shortly after Vance Randolph's death, carrying old family photos, and was treated to a fine evening of feasting and conversation and a warm bed on a cold night. Meeting such good people is one of researching's rewards, and I'm grateful to the Randolphs and the Sumners for their help and hospitality.

27. "Nancy Clemens" to Robert Cochran, n.d. [1979].

28. Randolph to Henle, Oct. 12, 1935.

29. Vance Randolph, Introduction, *An Ozark Anthology* (Caldwell, Idaho: Caxton, 1940), pp. 10–11.

30. Randolph papers, Box 8, Library of Congress.

31. " Agreement" given to me by Vance Randolph.

32. Randolph, *Ozark Folklore: A Bibliography*, p. 422.

33. Randolph, "Chronological Bibliography," n.p.—see Chapter Three, note 21.

34. WPA memorandum quoted by Mangione, *The Dream and the Deal*, p. 42.

35. Mangione, *The Dream and the Deal*, pp. 55–56.

36. Ibid., pp. 54–55.

37. Vance Randolph, Oct. 23, 1979.

38. Jack Conroy, "Musings of the Sage of Moberly," *Fool Killer: A Journal of Popular and People's Culture* 3 (1977):1.

39. Mangione, *The Dream and the Deal*, p. 76.

40. Ibid., p. 194. Mangione's treatment of Parker is so harsh that one might suspect the indulgence of personal animus were his strictures not repeated in another study, Monty Noam Penkower's *The Federal Writers' Project: A Study in Government Patronage of the Arts* (Urbana: University of Illinois Press, 1977), pp. 39, 162–63.

41. Vance Randolph to Mrs. Esther Marshall Greer, Missouri State Director, Federal Writers' Project, Jan. 16, 1937, Randolph papers, Box 8, Library of Congress.

42. Mangione, *The Dream and the Deal*, p. 198.

43. Jean Winkler to Vance Randolph, dated only "Election Day" [1936], Randolph papers, Box 8, Library of Congress.

44. Vance Randolph to Geraldine Parker, Nov. 4, 1936, Randolph papers, Box 8, Library of Congress.

45. Randolph to Greer, Jan. 16, 1937.

46. Vance Randolph to Mr. Matthew S. Murray, state administrator FWPA, May 17, 1937, Randolph papers, Box 8, Library of Congress.

47. Lewis Mumford, "Writers' Project," *New Republic* 92 (1937):306, quoted in Mangione, *The Dream and the Deal*, p. 216.

48. Gene Weltfish, Secretary, "Forty-Ninth Annual Meeting of the American Folklore Society," *Journal of American Folklore* 51 (1938):103.

49. Mangione, *The Dream and the Deal*, p. 276. Penkower, *Federal Writers' Project*, p. 149, says much the same thing: "Originally skeptical of the FWP, the American Folklore Society adopted a more positive attitude after one of its professional members became a folklore editor."

50. Penkower, *Federal Writers' Project*, p. 162.

51. Mangione, *The Dream and the Deal*, p. 199.

52. Randolph, "Utopia in Arkansas," p. 60; see Chapter Three, note 49.

53. "Randolph Makes Visit," *Commonwealth College Fortnightly* 9 (1933):1.

54. Raymond and Charlotte Koch, *Educational Commune: The Story of Commonwealth College* (New York: Schocken, 1972), p. 135. For additional information on Commonwealth College, see Sue Thrasher, "Radical Education in the Thirties," *Southern Exposure* 1 (1974):204–10; David W.

Hacker, "Dreamers and the Betrayal" (three part feature on Commonwealth), *Arkansas Gazette*, Nov. 21, Nov. 28, and Dec. 5, 1954; William Henry Cobb, "Commonwealth College: A History" (M.A. thesis, University of Arkansas, 1963). For Commonwealth's "workers' songs" movement, see R. Serge Denisoff, *Great Day Coming: Folk Music and the American Left* (Urbana: University of Illinois Press, 1971), esp. Ch. 2, "The Rural Roots of Folk Consciousness."

55. Randolph, "Utopia in Arkansas," p. 60.

56. Ibid., p. 148.

57. Ibid.

58. Vance Randolph, April 17, 1980.

59. *Stone County News-Oracle* (Galena, Mo.), Jan. 11, 1933.

60. Vance Randolph to Ralph Church, dated only "Friday," but another letter on the same letterhead is dated Oct. 11, 1936.

61. Vance Randolph to Floyd C. Shoemaker, Apr. 7, 1938. Randolph told me (in 1979 or 1980) that May Kennedy McCord read his paper at the meeting.

62. *Eureka Springs Times-Echo*, May 13, 1962. The 1945 dates come from a "patient's identification tag" given to me by Vance Randolph.

63. Dorson, "A Visit with Vance Randolph," p. 260.

64. "Nancy Clemens" to Robert Cochran, n.d. [1980].

65. Vance Randolph to Gould Randolph, July 5, 1949.

66. Vance Randolph to Gould Randolph, July 11, 1949. I am grateful to Gould Randolph for giving me copies of these and other letters.

67. Rayna Green to Alan Jabbour, Mar. 7, 1972, Library of Congress Archive of Folk Culture.

68. Patrick C. Power, Translator's Preface to Flann O'Brien [Brian O'Nolan], *The Poor Mouth* (New York: Seaver Books, 1981; first published [in Gaelic] in 1941), p. 5.

69. Duncan papers, File 1.

70. Cochran, "Guns and Memories," p. 6; see Chapter Two, note 13.

71. Vance Randolph, Introduction to *The Devil's Pretty Daughter, and Other Ozark Folk Tales* (New York: Columbia University Press, 1955), p. xv.

72. "Leonard Short and Three Other Bank Bandits Escape Oklahoma Jail after Shooting Officer," *Springfield Leader and Press*, Dec. 3, 1935.

73. "Tribute Is Paid Leonard Short," *Springfield Leader and Press*, Dec. 10, 1935.

74. Vance Randolph, Tape 4, Side 1 (1978).

75. Randolph papers, Box 10, Library of Congress.

76. Photographs and newspaper clippings given to me after Vance Randolph's death by Mary Parler Randolph.

77. James Agee, *Let Us Now Praise Famous Men* (New York: Ballantine, 1966; first published 1941), pp. 54, 147.

78. Samuel Beckett, *Watt* (New York: Grove Press, 1959; first published 1953), p. 247.

79. Duncan papers, File 1.

Chapter Seven: Songs and Superstitions

1. Will Townsend, "Vance Randolph—'Lowlander' Collecting a Legacy," *Springfield News and Leader*, Aug. 17, 1975.
2. Barbra Abernathy and Mary H. Trimble, *Rose O'Neill* (Branson, Mo.: No publisher, 1968), unpaginated.
3. Duncan papers, File 1.
4. Duncan papers, File 1.
5. Townsend, "Vance Randolph," *Springfield News and Leader*, Aug. 17, 1975.
6. Abernathy and Trimble, *Rose O'Neill*. That Rose O'Neill has been greatly victimized by her admirers—turned into a sort of human kewpie, a being of treacle and saccharine—should be clear from these citations. For other treatments in the same vein see Rowena Fay Ruggles, *The One Rose, Mother of the Immortal Kewpies: A Biography of Rose O'Neill and the Story of Her Work* (Albany, Calif.: No publisher, 1972), and Maude M. Horine, *Memories of Rose O'Neill, Creator of the Kewpie Doll* (Branson, Mo: A.C. Offset Printing Co., 1950). Horine describes herself on this booklet's cover as "of the Persimmon Patch, Branson, Missouri."
7. See Randolph, *Ozark Folksongs*, 2:360; 4:388, 17, 23.
8. Ibid., 2:261.
9. Vance Randolph to Ruth Benedict, Feb. 4, 1938. I am grateful to the Vassar College Library, and especially to Ms. Frances Goudy, special collections librarian, for providing me with copies of the Benedict/Randolph correspondence.
10. Louise Pound to Vance Randolph, Aug 6, 1927. That Pound also uses the term "pamphlet" to describe such a printing may suggest something about the size of the collection in 1927. I am indebted to the Nebraska State Historical Society, and especially to Ms. Andrea I. Paul, manuscripts curator, for providing copies of Dr. Pound's letters to Randolph.
11. Boas to Randolph, April 8, 1929. See Chapter Five, note 8.
12. Vance Randolph to Ruth Benedict, Jan. 25, 1930.
13. Ruth Benedict to Vance Randolph, Jan. 31, 1930.
14. Harold Murdock [?], director, Harvard University Press, to Vance Randolph, Jan. 28, 1931.
15. Larkin, *Singing Cowboy*, p. 143.
16. Vance Randolph to Ruth Benedict, Jan. 25, 1938; Randolph to Benedict, Feb. 4, 1938.
17. Vance Randolph to Herbert Halpert, Feb. 7, 1939.
18. Alan Lomax to Vance Randolph, Feb. 4, 1941. Some of the Lomax/Randolph correspondence has been preserved twice, in Boxes 14 and 17 of the Randolph papers, Library of Congress, and in a file of Lomax's correspondence also in the archive of American Folk Culture, Library of Congress. Each file, however, has items not in the other. I am grateful to Gerry Parsons of the archive staff for bringing the Lomax file to my attention. For helpful accounts of the archive's establishment see Botkin, "Archive of Folk Song," 16–19, and Wilgus, *Folksong Scholarship*, esp. pp. 185–88.

19. Vance Randolph to Alan Lomax, Feb. 10, 1941.

20. Alan Lomax to Vance Randolph, July 17, 1941.

21. Vance Randolph to Alan Lomax, July 20, 1941. Randolph says elsewhere that he'd been using "a portable machine which records the song on an acetate disk" since 1938; Introduction, *Ozark Folksongs*, p. 35. Norm Cohen's account of Randolph's recording methods is especially good; see Cohen, ed., *Ozark Folksongs*, pp. ix-x.

22. Vance Randolph to Dr. Harold Spivacke, Aug. 26, 1941.

23. Log preserved in Special Collections Division, University of Arkansas Library (A784.49778, R150z, 1941–43, v. 1).

24. Vance Randolph to Alan Lomax, Oct. 5, 1941.

25. Alan Lomax to Vance Randolph, Sept. 16, 1942.

26. Library of Congress Accounting Division to Vance Randolph, June 13, 1942; Vance Randolph reply, June 15, 1942.

27. Vance Randolph to B. A. Botkin, Jan. 20, 1943.

28. Ibid.

29. Vance Randolph to B. A. Botkin, Apr. 4, 1946.

30. Vance Randolph to Ralph Church [?], Mar. 16, 1945, Duncan papers, File 1.

31. Vance Randolph to Ralph Church [?], n.d., Duncan papers, File 1.

32. Vance Randolph to H. M. Belden, Nov. 15, 1945.

33. My researches into the collection and publication of *Ozark Folksongs* were greatly aided by W. K. McNeil's Introduction to the 1980 University of Missouri Press reissue, by Norm Cohen's Editor's Introduction to the 1982 University of Illinois Press abridgment, and by Rebecca M. Schroeder's review essay, "Vance Randolph and Ozark Folksongs," *Missouri Folklore Society Journal* 2 (1980):57–67.

34. Vance Randolph, "Ozark Songs," vol. 3, unpaginated. This manuscript is in the Special Collections Division, University of Arkansas Library.

35. Vance Randolph to Floyd C. Shoemaker, June 18, 1949, Randolph papers, Box 17, Library of Congress. Cohen says (Editor's Introduction, p. xii) that "Shoemaker's contributions to *Ozark Folksongs* were not of a scholarly nature, and Vance did not feel his name should have appeared on the title page." For Shoemaker's account see Floyd C. Shoemaker, *The State Historical Society of Missouri: A Semicentennial History* (Columbia: State Historical Society of Missouri, 1948), pp. 139–40, 172–75.

36. Ruth Ann Musick, review of *Ozark Folksongs*, vol. 1, by Vance Randolph, *Journal of American Folklore* 60 (1947):434; McNeil, Introduction, p. 27.

37. Archer Taylor, review of *Ozark Folksongs*, vol. 1, by Vance Randolph, *Western Folklore* 6 (1947):289, 290. One important reviewer, however, was decidedly more critical. This was Charles Seeger, whose several reviews complained mostly about the musical transcriptions. For a fine examination of Seeger's strictures, see Cohen, Editor's Introduction, pp. xv-xviii. Cohen also provides the only helpful discussion I've seen of the many problems involving copyrighted material that surfaced soon after the collection's publication; see Cohen, Editor's Introduction, pp. xviii, xxiv-xxv.

38. Louise Pound, "Absorbing Ozark Folklore through the Rind" (review of *Ozark Folksongs,* vol. 2, by Vance Randolph), *New York Herald Tribune Weekly Book Review,* August 1, 1948.

39. Louise Pound, review of *Ozark Folksongs,* vol. 1, by Vance Randolph, *New York Herald Tribune Weekly Book Review,* May 25, 1947; Taylor, review of *Ozark Folksongs,* p. 289.

40. McNeil, Introduction, p. 26.

41. Randolph, "Ozark Songs," cover sheet to each of the three volumes; see note 34 above.

42. McNeil, Introduction, p. 27; Wilgus, *Folksong Scholarship,* p. 199.

43. Halpert, Foreword, p. 12; McNeil, Introduction, pp. 9, 27, 28.

44. Vance Randolph and Frances Emberson, "The Collection of Folk Music in the Ozarks," *Journal of American Folklore* 60 (1947):115.

45. Randolph and Emberson, "Collection of Folk Music," p. 122.

46. Boas to Randolph, Apr. 8, 1929.

47. McNeil, Introduction, p. 27.

48. Randolph, *Ozark Magic and Folklore,* pp. 4–5, 7.

49. Vance Randolph, "Ozark Superstitions," *Life,* June 19, 1939, p. 182.

50. Paul G. Brewster, review of *Ozark Superstitions,* by Vance Randolph, *Journal of American Folklore* 61 (1948):402–3.

51. Wayland D. Hand, review of *Ozark Superstitions,* by Vance Randolph, *Journal of American Folklore* 67 (1954):324, 325.

52. Carl Withers, "The Folkways of the Ozarks" (review of *Ozark Superstitions,* by Vance Randolph), *New York Times Book Review,* June 15, 1947.

53. Withers, Editor's Introduction, pp. xvii-xviii; see Chapter Five, note 27.

54. Scott, "Little Blue Books," p. 166; see Chapter Six, note 6.

55. Tolliver [Randolph], *Lafcadio Hearn,* p. 20. For the *JAF* article see Chapter One, note 18.

56. Tolliver [Randolph], *George Borrow,* p. 24.

57. Randolph to Church [?], n.d.; see note 31 above.

58. Randolph to Duncan, Nov. 12, 1955; see Chapter Three, note 3.

59. See Herbert Halpert, "Story and Song: Folklore Book Notes," *Hoosier Folklore Bulletin* 4 (1945):37–39.

60. Randolph, *Ozark Folklore: A Bibliography,* pp. 19, 206. A "W. Y. Shackleford" also appears in *We Always Lie to Strangers,* credited for a tall tale about big corn, while "Anthony Gish" (another "Nancy Clemens" pseudonym) is cited twice in *Sticks in the Knapsack.* See Vance Randolph, *We Always Lie to Strangers: Tall Tales From the Ozarks* (New York: Columbia University Press, 1951), p. 78; Vance Randolph, *Sticks in the Knapsack, and Other Ozark Folk Tales* (New York: Columbia University Press, 1958), pp. 156, 158. Randolph explained—Tape 4, Side 1 (1978)—that these names protected "prominent informants who didn't want their names used." This is not entirely convincing, since Randolph often omitted informants' names when requested to do so, but I did not press him further.

61. Ramon F. Adams, *Burs under the Saddle: A Second Look at Books*

and Histories of the West (Norman: University of Oklahoma Press, 1964), pp. 109, 454, 233, 458, 459.

62. Ibid., p. 584.

63. "Ozark Booster" to Vance Randolph, July 27, 1934, Duncan papers, File 3. Having cited this letter, which Randolph often mentioned, I should record my own suspicion that it's a fake—I think Randolph wrote it himself. In support of what is basically a "hunch," subjectively based, there is one reference—a letter of 1981 from "Nancy Clemens": "He talked for some time about shooting a hole through his car and claiming that he had been fired at by someone indignant about his folklore writings."

CHAPTER EIGHT: TALES, TALK, AND LAUGHTER

1. Vance Randolph, *The Talking Turtle, and Other Ozark Folk Tales* (New York: Columbia University Press, 1957), p. xviii.

2. Randolph to Benedict, Feb. 4, 1938.

3. Randolph, *We Always Lie*, p. vii.

4. Randolph, *Who Blowed Up?* p. xvi.

5. Randolph, *Devil's Pretty Daughter*, p. xix.

6. Randolph, *Who Blowed Up?* p. xvi.

7. Randolph, *Sticks in the Knapsack*, p. xvii.

8. Randolph, *Who Blowed Up?* pp. xvii-xxiii.

9. Dorson, *Folklore and the Historian*, p. 6; see Chapter Two, note 1. For recent discussions of the art of transcription see Dennis Tedlock, "On the Translation of Style in Oral Narrative," *Journal of American Folklore* 84 (1971):114–33; Dell Hymes, "Discovering Oral Performance and Measured Verse in American Indian Narrative," *New Literary History* 8 (1976/77): 431–57; Dennis R. Preston, "'Ritin' Fowklower Daun 'Rong: Folklorists' Failures in Phonology," *Journal of American Folklore* 95 (1982): 304–26; Arnold Krupat, "An Approach to Native American Texts," *Critical Inquiry* 9 (1982):323–38.

10. Randolph, *Talking Turtle*, pp. xvi-xvii.

11. Randolph, *Talking Turtle*, xvi. For a cogent, persuasive argument to the contrary see Glassie, *Ballymenone*, chapter 2, esp. pp. 39–55, where Randolph's "considerable variation" may be nicely comprehended in terms of "freedom in the realm of discourse" (p. 47). "Discourse" is one crucial term in Glassie's portrait; the other is "truth." While only a few of Randolph's stories would qualify as "history," where the demands of "truth" are at their highest and the freedoms of "discourse" most tightly bounded, the "variation in the words" used by his Ozark informants may yet be understood as attempts "to coordinate multiple responsibilities to time, to the past event, the present situation, the future of the community" (pp. 47–48).

12. Dorson, *Folklore and the Historian*, p. 163.

13. Austin E. Fife, review of *We Always Lie to Strangers*, by Vance Randolph, *Journal of American Folklore* 65 (1952):200, 201.

14. Hoffman Birney, "'A Windy Ain't No Lie'" (review of *We Always Lie to Strangers*, by Vance Randolph), *New York Times Book Review*, May 13, 1951.

15. Vance Randolph, review of *Negro Folktales in Michigan*, by Richard M. Dorson, *Western Folklore* 16 (1957):65.

16. Randolph, *We Always Lie*, pp. 4, 5, 13.

17. Herbert Halpert, "Comments of a Folklorist," in Randolph, *Who Blowed Up?* p. 181.

18. Randolph, *Hot Springs*, p. xxvi.

19. Leonard Roberts, review of *The Talking Turtle*, by Vance Randolph, *Midwest Folklore* 7 (1957):175; B. A. Botkin, "Racy, Merry and Tall" (review of *Sticks in the Knapsack*, by Vance Randolph), *New York Times Book Review*, January 18, 1959.

20. Randolph, *Who Blowed Up?* p. xviii.

21. George Korson, review of *The Talking Turtle*, by Vance Randolph, *Keystone Folklore Quarterly* 3 (1958):51.

22. Jack Conroy, "Ozark Tales of Era That Is Vanishing" (review of *The Devil's Pretty Daughter*, by Vance Randolph), *Chicago Sun-Times*, June 26, 1955.

23. RT [Ruth Tyler] to OER [Otto Ernest Rayburn], Aug. 12, 1957. This letter was brought to my attention by Ellen Shipley.

24. Vance Randolph to Ralph Church, n.d. [1943?], Duncan papers, File 1.

25. Duncan papers, File 3. "Nancy Clemens" to Robert Cochran, n.d. [1979].

26. Richard Dorson, Dell Hymes, Barre Toelken, Gershon Legman, Francis L. Utley, dust jacket of Vance Randolph, *Pissing in the Snow, and Other Ozark Folktales* (Urbana: University of Illinois Press, 1976).

27. Robert Cochran, "Folklorist Vance Randolph: Ozark Mountain Man and Teller of Stories," *Arkansas Times* 6 (1980):48–49.

28. Richard M. Dorson, "The 1958 Folklore Institute of America," *Midwest Folklore* 9 (1959):40, 45, 44, 41. I cite the "big shots" recollection from memory. The "celebrated snapshot" described by Dorson has been printed; see E. Joan Wilson Miller, "Vance Randolph, Folklorist," *Mid-South Folklore* 3 [Special Issue for Vance Randolph] (1975):64.

29. Herbert Halpert, "Obituary: Vance Randolph (1892–1980)," *Journal of American Folklore* 94 (1981):349.

30. Herbert Halpert to Vance Randolph, Nov. 30, 1948.

31. Vance Randolph to Herbert Halpert, Sept. 4, 1948.

32. Vance Randolph to Herbert Halpert, Dec. 4, 1948.

33. Herbert Halpert to Vance Randolph, May 17, 1949; Vance Randolph to Herbert Halpert, May 20, 1949.

34. "The First Two Years: A History of the Ozark Folklore Society," *Ozark Folklore* 1 (1951):4. For additional information on this group see Robert Morris, "The First Arkansas Folklore Society," *Grapevine* 11 (1980):1, 5; Robert Cochran, "Folklore Yesterday and Today," *Grapevine* 11 (1980):1, 6;

John Gould Fletcher, "The Ozarks Folklore Society," *Arkansas Historical Quarterly* 9 (1950):115; E. L. Rudolph, "John Gould Fletcher and the Founding of the Arkansas Folklore Society," paper read at the 1981 meeting of the South Central Modern Language Association, Houston, Texas. I'm grateful to Professor Rudolph for providing a copy of this paper.

35. Vance Randolph, May 17, 1980.

36. Vance Randolph to Herbert Halpert, Oct. 30, 1974.

37. Vance Randolph to Herbert Halpert, June 4, 1956.

38. Herbert Halpert to Vance Randolph, June 18, 1956.

39. Herbert Halpert to Vance Randolph, July 5, 1956.

40. Vance Randolph, Tape 7, Side 1 (1978). For details of Rayburn's career, I have used Ethel C. Simpson, "The Ozark Quest of Otto Rayburn," *Arkansas Libraries* 39 (1982):12–19, and Ellen Shipley, "The Literary Enterprises of Otto Ernest Rayburn," *Arkansas Libraries* 39 (1982):20–23.

41. Vance Randolph, Oct. 5, 1980.

42. Randolph to Halpert, May 20, 1949.

43. Cochran, "Guns and Memories," pp. 7–8; see Chapter Two, note 13.

44. Randolph, *We Always Lie*, pp. 113–14.

45. Cochran, "Guns and Memories," pp. 5–6.

46. These articles were preserved in a scrapbook kept by Mrs. Randolph. I am grateful to Mary Nubbie, administrator at the Sunrise Manor Nursing Home in Fayetteville, Ark., for saving this scrapbook from the trash heap and giving it to me. The 1930 article is "Word-List from Wedgefield, South Carolina," *Dialect Notes* 6 (1930):79–85.

47. Mary Parler Randolph, Nov. 16, 1980.

48. Cochran, "Folklorist Vance Randolph," p. 49.

49. Mary Parler Randolph, Nov. 16, 1980.

50. Ibid.

51. Randolph and Wilson, *Down in the Holler*, pp. vii-viii. I gathered information about Mrs. Randolph from many sources. Professors Leo Van Scyoc and Lyna Lee Montgomery made her University of Arkansas academic file, with its educational and employment history, available to me. I also read the article about Mrs. Randolph's work, "Research in Folklore: To Preserve a Heritage," *Arkansas Alumnus* 12 (1958):4–7, and her own piece in the same magazine, "Collecting Folklore on Campus," *Arkansas Alumnus* 12 (1958):8–9. The *Marriage License Record (G-1)* in the Office of the County Clerk, Washington County Courthouse, Fayetteville, Ark., has the Randolph/Parler marriage license and certificate of marriage (p. 482). See also "Maggie," "Mary C.," *Grapevine* 13 (1981):1, 3.

52. Herbert Halpert to Vance Randolph, Nov. 6, 1950.

53. Quoted in Vance Randolph to George P. Wilson, Jan. 19, 1952.

54. Randolph to Wilson, Jan. 19, 1952.

55. George P. Wilson to Vance Randolph, Jan. 21, 1952.

56. George P. Wilson to Vance Randolph, Mar. 5, 1952. The Randolph/Wilson correspondence is preserved in the Randolph papers, Box 14, Library of Congress.

57. Contracts given to me by Vance Randolph. The upper right corner of the earlier contract's first page has a short note in Randolph's hand: "This ain't the contract I signed. They made a later one, with mention of $650 advance royalty to *me*."

58. McDavid, review of *Down in the Holler*, p. 328.

59. E. Bagby Atwood, "The Methods of American Dialectology," in Harold B. Allen and Gary N. Underwood, eds., *Readings in American Dialectology* (New York: Appleton, Century, Crofts, 1971), p. 8; Allen Walker Read, "Attitudes toward Missouri Speech," *Missouri Historical Review* 29 (1935): 266. Harold Wentworth's 1944 *American Dialect Dictionary* (New York: Thomas Y. Crowell) includes Randolph in a list of nine authors of "foremost studies"—see p. viii.

60. Vance Randolph to Herbert Halpert, Aug. 10, 1956.

61. Herbert Halpert to Vance Randolph, July 5, 1956.

62. Vance Randolph to Herbert Halpert, Aug. 10, 1960.

63. Herbert Halpert, draft of letter in support of Randolph's ACLS application, n.d.

64. Vance Randolph to Herbert Halpert, June 14, 1960.

65. Mary Parler Randolph, Nov. 16, 1980.

66. Halpert, "Obituary," p. 347.

67. Vance Randolph to Herbert Halpert, Oct. 20, 1962.

68. Vance Randolph to Herbert Halpert, Jan. 29, 1964.

69. Herbert Halpert to Harry Segessman, Apr. 23, 1964.

70. Randolph, *Hot Springs*, p. vii.

71. Leonard Roberts, review of *Hot Springs and Hell*, by Vance Randolph, *Journal of American Folklore* 80 (1967):304.

72. Jesse W. Harris, review of *Hot Springs and Hell*, by Vance Randolph, *Western Folklore* 26 (1967):136.

73. Herbert Halpert to Vance Randolph, Oct. 29, 1965.

74. Randolph, *Who Blowed Up?* p. xviii.

75. Vance Randolph to Herbert Halpert, Oct. 26, 1955.

76. Vance Randolph to Herbert Halpert, Dec. 15, 1956.

77. Richard Dorson, Foreword to Randolph, *Ozark Folklore: A Bibliography*, no page.

78. Vance Randolph to Herbert Halpert, Dec. 6, 1957.

Chapter Nine: Embers

1. Halpert, "Obituary," p. 349.

2. Vance Randolph to Herbert Halpert, n.d. [1974?]. "Letty" is Halpert's wife, Violetta Maloney Halpert. They were classmates at Indiana University, and married in 1945.

3. Vance Randolph to Frances Church, July 9, 1943, Duncan papers, File 1.

4. Vance Randolph to Herbert Halpert, Jan. 14, 1967.

5. Vance Randolph to Herbert Halpert, Oct. 5, 1974.

6. Dorson, Foreword, pp. vi, vii. It should be noted that *Ozark Folklore: A Bibliography* was completed with the aid of the one grant Randolph actually got. In 1954, thanks largely to the efforts of Duncan Emrich, he was awarded $1,200 from the American Philosophical Society. The correspondence relating to this grant is preserved in the Randolph papers, Box 13, Library of Congress.

7. Randolph, *Ozark Folklore: A Bibliography*, pp. 375, 373, 505, 508.

8. Vance Randolph, *Americans Who Thought They Were Gods: Colorful Messiahs and Little Christs* (Girard, Kansas: Haldeman-Julius, 1943), p. 17.

9. Lapham, "Generation Gap," p. 12; see Chapter Four, note 32.

10. Jones' letter, dated Nov. 17, 1963, is preserved in the Randolph papers, Box 14, Library of Congress.

11. See for example Vance Randolph, "Three Ozark Folktales," *Mid-South Folklore* 6 (1978):93–95; "The Magic Jack-Knife," *The Ozarks Mountaineer* 27 (Jan.-Feb., 1979):64, "Senator Johnson's Great Speech," *Maledicta* 2 (1978):299–320. For Jackson's article see Bruce Jackson, "Legman: The King of X700," *Maledicta* 1 (1977):111–24. For a wonderful portrait of Legman, see John Clellon Holmes, *Nothing More to Declare* (New York: E. P. Dutton, 1967), pp. 16–32.

12. This plaque has been preserved in the papers of Mrs. Frances N. Lemon, Ralph Church's widow. Mrs. Lemon died Feb. 26, 1982. I read these papers and copied the plaque in the law offices of Wommack, Lindsay and Associates, Fayetteville, Ark. I'm grateful to Mr. Richard L. Wommack for his courtesy and aid.

13. Copy of this proclamation given to me by Vance Randolph in 1979.

14. Vance Randolph to Herbert Halpert, Oct. 30, 1978.

15. Henry Glassie, *Irish Folk History* (Philadelphia: University of Pennsylvania Press, 1982), p. 14; Glassie, *Ballymenone*, p. 716.

16. John Bunyan, *The Pilgrim's Progress* (Baltimore: Penguin, 1970; first published 1678), p. 60.

17. Michael Davis, *William Blake: A New Kind of Man* (Berkeley: University of California Press, 1977), p. 156.

18. Beckett, *Watt*, pp. 247, 250.

19. Glassie, *Ballymenone*, p. 233.

20. Mary Parler Randolph, n.d. [1979]. I take this from memory; I won't forget it.

21. "Full 20 Year Warranty Certificate," Batesville Casket #M-50747, Nov. 3, 1980. Given to me by Mary Parler Randolph.

Acknowledgments

Thanks are a pleasure. I owe most to five people: Mike Luster, who shared this project's beginnings and helped throughout as time allowed; Gene DeGruson, who knows everything worth knowing about Pittsburg, Kansas, and E. Haldeman-Julius; Bob and Wanda Duncan, who did a lot of work in the 1950s and generously shared it with me; and John McGuigan, who read my drafts, corrected, and encouraged. At the University of Illinois Press I was encouraged, guided, and saved from many errors by Judith McCulloh and Bonnie Depp.

I got money, which bought time, from two sources. I'm especially grateful to the J. William Fulbright College of Arts and Sciences, University of Arkansas, and to Dean John C. Guilds and Associate Dean Stephen M. Day, for a research appointment in the spring semester of 1982. This gave me a large stretch of uninterrupted time at a critical juncture, and most of the final manuscript was produced during this period. The Arkansas Endowment for the Humanities also supported my work with summer grants in 1979, 1980, and 1981. I'm indebted especially to Ms. Jane Browning, executive director at AEH, for helpful guidance with my grant proposals.

Several colleagues in the English Department, University of Arkansas, shared their recollections of Vance Randolph with me. Leo Van Scyoc introduced me to Mr. and Mrs. Randolph and shared his file of Randolph memorabilia. E. Leighton Rudolph helped me with the Randolph/John Gould Fletcher relationship and with the history of the Arkansas Folklore Society. Buzz Manske helped me with the Haldeman-Julius booklets on western topics, and I learned in various ways from conversations with Dick Bennett, Margaret Bolsterli, Duncan Eaves, Claude Faulkner, John Clellon Holmes, John Locke, Lyna Lee Montgomery, Foster Park, Jim Whitehead, and Miller Williams. Ben Kimpel, who died in 1983, was my chairman and my friend. I miss him very much, and I hope this book would have pleased him.

Many people helped with the preparation of the manuscript—Karen Stauffacher, Jean Walker, Carey Madding, and Julie Deckelman in the English Department, and John Stokes and his staff (Rebecca Blake, Sara Holmes, Beverly Ludwick) in the Office of Research and Sponsored Programs.

Four students did work that aided my own. Rita Caver worked on the dates of Randolph's music collecting; Gina Lee did a term paper on George Milburn; Oteeka Miller wrote an essay on Margaret Larkin; and Susan Young gathered reviews of Randolph's books from general circulation books and magazines.

I came to admire librarians above ordinary mortals during the course of this study. My most persistent requests were directed to the University of Arkansas Library and were answered with unfailing helpfulness by Debby Cochran, Marvin Crabb, Regina French, John Harrison, Elizabeth McKee, Barbara Meyer, Larry Perry, Ellen Shipley, Ethel Simpson, and Sam Sizer. At the Library of Congress, Washington, D.C., I was helped repeatedly on my visits to the Archive of Folk Culture by Gerry Parsons and Sebastian Locurto. At the McDonald County Library, Pineville, Missouri, I owe thanks especially to librarian Zella Collie. I'm grateful also to library staff at Clark University in Worcester, Massachusetts; the University of Kansas at Lawrence; Pittsburg State University at Pittsburg, Kansas; the Kansas City Public Library in Kansas City, Missouri; the Vassar College Library in Poughkeepsie, New York, and the Galena Public Library, Galena, Missouri.

In addition to these libraries, I was aided by the Nebraska Historical Society, the Kansas State Historical Society, and the Riley County Historical Society. Where possible I have tried to recognize the specific information provided by these sources in the notes.

Many friends of Vance Randolph aided my work. My first debt here is to Mary Parler Randolph, whose recollections often stimulated Randolph's own. An extraordinary woman herself, Mrs. Randolph encouraged and assisted my interest in her husband. I learned, too, from Ed Albin, Jan Brunvand, Jim Clark, Ernie Deane, Bethany Dumas, Mrs. Blanche Elliott, Mrs. Ruth Elliott, Louis and Elsie Freund, Henry Haldeman, Herbert Halpert, Donald Harington, Mary Harrell, Mr. C. L. Householder, Gershon Legman, Mrs. Frances Lemon, Mrs. Frances Lott, Gordon McCann, Bill McNeil, Mr. and Mrs. Gould Randolph, Mr. and Mrs. Adolf Schroeder, Fern Shumate, and Virginia Tyler. Mary Nubbie, administrator at the Sunrise Manor Nursing Home in Fayetteville, Arkansas, befriended Mr. and Mrs. Randolph repeatedly and helped me accomplish my interviews. She works in the bleakest of worlds, and her care was greatly valued—Mary Parler Randolph said once she was "except for Vance the best friend I have." Richard L. Wommack permitted me to read a file of Randolph memorabilia in his law office.

Here, in a celebration of edges, the end is the center, where I give thanks to and for my own friends, in and out of the academy. Thanks from the heart to Roger Abrahams, Scott Bird, Milton and Mimi Burke, Joe and Anne-Marie Candido, Jack Clarkson, Tom and Debby Cochran, Jim and Cleda

Driftwood, Ann Dunn, Bill Ferris, Kathy Foster, Henry Glassie, Bill Harrison, Ken Kinnamon, John and Julie Long, Mike and Robin Luster, John and Nanette McGuigan, Charles and Pat Mazer, Bob and Mim Neralich, Iver Olson, John Pickerill, Bob and Lynn Pierle, Lyndon Shanley, and Frank Soos. Last, most, heart of the heart: Bob, Shannon, Masie, Suzanne.

December 10, 1983
Fayetteville, Arkansas

Index

A Note on the Author

Robert Cochran was born in Lake Forest, Illinois. He earned his B.S. and M.A. degrees at Northwestern University and his Ph.D. at the University of Toronto. He has been a member of the English Department at the University of Arkansas since 1976. He is co-author (with Mike Luster) of *For Love and For Money: Vance Randolph, an Annotated Bibliography* (1979).